Battleground

MERVILLE
THE DIVES BRIDGES

British 6th Airborne Division
Landings in Normandy D-Day 6th June 1944

Merville Battery by Major Gerald Lacoste

Battleground series:

£1.95.

Battleground Europe

MERVILLE BATTERY
&
THE DIVES BRIDGES

British 6th Airborne Division
Landings in Normandy D-Day 6th June 1944

Carl Shilleto

Pen & Sword
MILITARY

This book is dedicated to the memory of all the young men of the 6th Airborne Division who lost their lives in the Normandy Campaign.

On doit des égards aux vivants;
on ne doit aux morts que la vérité.

VOLTAIRE, 1694-1778

First published in Great Britain in 1999
Reprinted 2001, 2004
Reprinted in this revised version 2011
by
PEN AND SWORD MILITARY
an imprint of
Pen & Sword Books Ltd
47 Church Street
Barnsley
South Yorkshire
S70 2AS

Copyright © Carl Shilleto 1999, 2001, 2004, 2011

ISBN 978-1-84884-519-0

The right of Carl Shilleto to be identified as the author of this work has been asserted by him in accordance with the Copyright, Designs and Patents Act 1988.

A CIP catalogue record for this book is available from the British Library.

All rights reserved. No part of this book may be reproduced or transmitted in any form or by any means, electronic or mechanical including photocopying, recording or by any information storage and retrieval system, without permission from the Publisher in writing.

Typeset in Palatino

Printed and bound in England by
CPI UK

Pen & Sword Books Ltd incorporates the imprints of Pen & Sword Aviation, Pen & Sword Maritime, Pen & Sword Military, Wharncliffe Local History, Pen & Sword Select, Pen & Sword Military Classics and Leo Cooper.

For a complete list of Pen & Sword titles please contact
PEN & SWORD BOOKS LIMITED
47 Church Street, Barnsley, South Yorkshire, S70 2AS, England
E-mail: enquiries@pen-and-sword.co.uk
Website: www.pen-and-sword.co.uk

CONTENTS

CLARENCE HOUSE

This book is dedicated to the men of the 6th Airborne Division who gave their lives in Normandy during the battle for the liberation of France. On 6th June 1944 the role of the Division in the initial assault onto the Normandy coast was to seize, intact, the bridges over the River Orne and Canal de Caen ('Pegasus Bridge') East of Benouville and to establish a bridgehead east of the river to secure these crossings. Additional tasks were to silence the guns of a coastal defence battery south east of Merville and to destroy certain bridges over the rivers Dives and Divette.

These objectives were achieved with great courage and determination. In the early hours of the morning a coup de main party landed in the dark in gliders and captured the bridges, whilst before dawn the Merville Battery had been silenced. The securing of this east flank was vitally important, as it was eventually the hinge on which the entire Allied armies would pivot as they broke out of the bridgehead to sweep on to Paris, Brussels, Antwerp and the Rhine.

Today the Airborne Assault Normandy Trust works to preserve both the memory of those who died in the battle and also the history of the Campaign. As Colonel-in-Chief of the Parachute Regiment, I salute those who took part in the 6th Airborne Division Campaign.

ACKNOWLEDGEMENTS

His Royal Highness The Prince of Wales.

Much has been written about the D-Day landings of the British 6th Airborne Division over the years. This work, originally titled *Pegasus Bridge & Merville Battery*, was the first to be commissioned that extensively guided the battlefield visitor to the exact locations and tells the story, in depth, using the words of so many veterans. Now, the work has been extensively revised and updated and divided into two works; the second titled *Pegasus Bridge & Horsa Bridge*. For this opportunity I would first like to thank the Chief Executive, Charles Hewitt, Editorial Manager, Brigadier Henry Wilson and Series Design Manager, Roni Wilkinson, also Jonathan Wilkinson and Jonathan Wright, of Pen & Sword Books Ltd.

My gratitude also to: The Airborne Assault Normandy Trust who have provided me with so much information in the course of my research. My most sincere thanks to the Patron of the Trust, His Royal Highness The Prince of Wales KG KT GCB OM, for his endorsement of my work; also to Lieutenant General Sir Michael Gray KCB OBE DL FI MGT F Inst D, Lieutenant Colonel Joe Poraj-Wilczynski, Major Jack Watson MC and Major Mike McRitchie MC for their support, invaluable assistance and advice with proofs.

I would also like to extend my thanks to the following: all the staff and workers, past and present, at the *Musée de la Batterie de Merville* including: Military Historian, Curator and fellow battlefield guide Tony Lea for sharing his knowledge of the Parachute Regiment and for providing the use of the museum, and his own, extensive archives; Archivist and battlefield guide Mike Woodcock; Monsieur Michael More, Pascaline Dagorn, Stéphanie, Céline, Nathalie, Elisa and Morgane who have always made my visits there most welcoming.

Thanks also to the Curator of the *Musée Mémorial Pegasus* Mark Worthington, Director Beatrice Boissee, Assistant Curator Nicolas Dumont and Martin Janssen, Saudrine Gabrol, Pascal

Crespin, Rolande Vimond and Halima Fringaut.

The staff at the Commonwealth War Graves Commission (CWGC) for their tireless work in tending and preserving the war cemeteries in Normandy and for answering all of my numerous enquiries, in particular Barry Murphy, Roy Hemington, Christine Woodhouse, Chris Hawes Nigel Haines and Peter Francis; Peter Hart at The Imperial War Museum for the use of their sound archives; Eddie Hannath MBE of the Normandy Veterans Association; Beverley H. Davies at The Royal British Legion; and staff at the Public Records Office (now National Archives) in Kew, the Airborne Forces Museum in Aldershot, and the French Tourist Office in London and Caen.

I would also like to acknowledge the overwhelming hospitality and friendship I have received from many of the local people in Normandy who have always made my many visits there all the more worthwhile and enjoyable. Thanks to Delphine Bautmans, Pascaline Dagorn, Patrick Elie, Corinne Hamon (née Lecourt), Marc Jacquinot, Christian Keller, Patrig Lagadu, Lionel Laplaise, Daniela Lemerre, Gérard Maillard, Patrick Moutafis, William Moutafis and Alan Soreau. Thanks also to the many expatriates who also make my visits all the more welcoming, particularly to fellow battlefield guide and historian Stuart Robertson and his wife Jenny for their hospitality, friendship and company in the many hours shared walking the battlefields.

For my appeals I would like to thank the staff at Channel 4's Service Pals Teletext Service, Editor John Elliot and Chris Kinsville-Heynes from *Soldier* Magazine, Colonel K. Coates Editor of *The Pegasus Journal*, Robert Beaumont of *The Yorkshire Evening Press* (now *The Press*) and Mike Laycock, also thanks to the secretaries of several regimental associations and Ken Wintle for the use of his extensive appeal database.

As always, the most interesting and rewarding part of this type of research is gained through interviews and correspondence with the veterans themselves. To hear their first-hand accounts of the events, and on occasion escort them around the Normandy battlefield; often concluding with a visit to the War Cemetery at Ranville so that they may pay their respects to their fallen comrades, has been, and always will be, a great privilege. Overwhelmed by the response to my appeals, I must apologise to those whose anecdotes I have not been able to use because of the inevitable editorial restrictions.

Thanks to the many veterans and their families who have kindly loaned valuable documents or photographs. A few I would like to mention, who have helped specifically with this work, are: R. Daeche, R. Deller, Peggy and Mary Eckert and family of Cyril and Stan Eckert, Denis Edwards, Major Ellis Dean MBE MC, Ted George, Major John Howard DSO, David 'Dai' King, Bill McConnell, H. Pegg, Edward Pool MC, Brigadier G. Proudman CBE MC, family of John Rollingson, James Sanders, family of Peter Sanderson, Maurice Segal, Ray Shuck and family, Norman Stocker, Ernie Stringer, Richard Todd, Major N. Ward, Major Jack Watson MC, Harry White and family of George White, Charlie Willbourne and Major Anthony Windrum,

Thanks also to Don Mason, who passed away before the completion of my manuscript for the first edition of my book *Pegasus Bridge & Merville Battery* back in 1999, and I offer my condolences to his family. Sadly, many other veterans, some who became very close friends, mentioned in this acknowledgement have also passed away in the time leading up to this extensively revised and updated new edition; and the accompanying work *Pegasus Bridge & Horsa Bridge*. While their company and presence is sorely missed, their memory lives on as strong as ever. I hope this work helps to preserve some of that memory for posterity.

Others who have assisted or provided valuable information are Rev. Neil Allison, David Ashe, Neil Barber, Ted Barwick, Tom Buttress, Captain R. Clark, Lt Cdr W. N. Entwisle RN, Lt Cdr John Lavery RN, Cheryl Hamilton, Paul Harlow, Helen Hartley, Mark Hickman, Al Jones, Michiels Kris, William J. Lewis Platt, Major Will Mackinlay SCOTS DG, Paul McTiernan, Capt G. M. Timms, Angus Newbould, Doug Oxspring, Keith Petvin-Scudamore, Paul Reed, Victoria Raynor, Carl Rymen, Paul van Rynen, Chris Summerville.

Thanks to Dave Popplewell for sharing his extensive knowledge on German and British vehicles, weapons and unit formations, and for his generous assistance in proof reading and checking of statistics. Thanks to Lance McCoubrey for help with maps and sketches and to the late Lieutenant Colonel Sir James Stormonth Darling CBE MC TD for his advice. Also to my late dear friend military historian, author and former Associate Professor, Charles Whiting; for sharing his unquestionable knowledge of the Second World War and his literary skills.

Thanks also to other friends who have been supportive of my work.

Special thanks, and love, go to my family: to my daughters Michaela and Hannah for their interest and curiosity in their father's work. They have both made wonderful travelling companions around the battlefields over the years. Thanks also to them for putting up with a dad whose head seems forever submerged in papers, books or behind a camera lens. Last, but by no means least, to my 'other half', Irena, for her patience, interest, help and hours of tireless proof reading during my research and writing; and without whose constant support and help, I would not be able to complete any of the many projects I undertake.

Any errors in the text are mine alone, and if anyone can provide any further information or photographs about any individuals, veterans or places relating to the 6th Airborne Division in Normandy, please forward any details to fallenheroes@btinternet.com. Please add '6 Ab Div' as the subject title.

To everyone I hope my work justifies all our efforts.

Spring 1944, German coastal troops prepare for the Allied invasion.

INTRODUCTION

It was during the course of my research in Normandy that I became aware of the dedicated efforts of a number of people who have all volunteered their time to uphold the aims set out by a trust that was initially proposed by the Commander of the 6th Airborne Division, General Sir Richard Gale. Supported by General Sir Anthony Farrar-Hockley, then Colonel Commandant The Parachute Regiment, the Airborne Assault Normandy Trust was founded to preserve the history of the 6th Airborne Division's assault into Normandy with the following aims:

* To provide a memorial, in France, of the airborne assault into Normandy in 1944.
* To honour the many who gave their lives in achieving success.
* To preserve the memory of the vital part played by the French people of the region as well as that of the assault force.
* To continue into the future the happy relationships of wartime years between the people of Normandy and the liberating forces.
* To preserve and accurately relate the history of the 6th Airborne Division and other Allied forces who operated in the area in the first few days after 6 June, 1944.

There are two main projects that the Airborne Assault Normandy Trust has helped to finance over the years:

The first has been the preservation of *Musée de la Batterie de Merville* (The Merville Battery Museum). Opened in 1982, to date, extensive work has been carried out and it has been transformed into the wonderful museum that you can see today. It is hoped that one day the whole site will eventually be restored to its original condition complete with rearmament and the opening up of the underground chambers and tunnels.

The second, in conjunction with the *Comité du Débarquement*, is the *Musée Mémorial Pegasus* (Pegasus Memorial Museum). Opened on 4 June, 2000, by HRH The Prince of Wales, the memorial park is dedicated to all those who served in Normandy with the British 6th Airborne Division. The centrepiece of the memorial garden is the original, and now restored, Pegasus Bridge. The bridge was relocated, having been rescued from a nearby field where it had been left to rust, after it was replaced in 1994 from its position over the Caen Canal.

11

Like all registered charities though, despite the tireless efforts of its members, the Trust is reliant upon public donations and in need of more funding if it is able to maintain its aims and turn future project ideas into a reality. If you wish to ensure that this part of our history is to be remembered by future generations, then the Airborne Assault Normandy Trust would be most grateful of any donation, however small, to help them achieve their aims. All donations should be forwarded to: The Airborne Assault Normandy Trust, Regimental Headquarters, The Parachute Regiment, Browning Barracks, Aldershot. Hampshire, GU11 2BU. All donations, made payable to the Trust, will be gratefully acknowledged.

Whatever the contribution, it is a small price to pay for the freedom that we have gained through the sacrifice of so many young men who will never return from the battlefields of France.

Carl Shilleto
RANVILLE, FRANCE

German defenders in a cliff top position practice with balls of TNT intended to be rolled down on any Allied invaders.

ADVICE FOR VISITORS

Your visit, to the 6th Airborne Division area of operations, will cover ground in the north-eastern part of Calvados, which is the smallest of Normandy's five departments. The scene today is one of a picturesque countryside, with half-timbered houses and sprawling farmland, reminiscent of what it must have been like before the invasion and inevitable destruction that came in 1944. The towns and villages have long since been rebuilt and have grown in size to accommodate the ever-increasing population. New roads now make travelling across the area more comfortable and quicker than anything that was experienced by the troops during the Second World War and the lunar landscape of carpet-bombed countryside has once again returned to smooth, lush, green grazing land or to golden fields of corn. Still clearly visible in places though, are the high hedgerows and small fields that make up the infamous *bocage*.

A visit during the winter months will allow you to see the area in the Dives valley partially flooded, although the floods are never as extensive as they were back in June, 1944. I recommend that the best time to visit the area is during the summer when the climate is more agreeable, places of interest are open and you are seeing the environment in climatic conditions similar to that experienced by the troops during the campaign itself. Normandy is very much like the British climate with unpredictable rainstorms. The only exception is that in summer it is likely to get very warm; therefore sun cream, sunglasses and a bottle of water are all sensible additions to your travelling pack. Also include a small first-aid kit and a comfortable rucksack to carry everything in. Sturdy shoes or walking boots are essential and good waterproofs should also be taken as rain storms can be torrential.

For British Nationals, in case of any accident or illness that may require medical attention, you should take your European Health Insurance Card (EHIC) This is available online via the National Health Service (www.nhsdirect.nhs.uk – type EHIC into the search bar), by telephone 0845 606 2030, or by post (application form available at your local post office). This will cover medical treatment in France. Also ensure that your tetanus jab is up to date and it is advisable to take out medical insurance while travelling abroad.

Emergency numbers in France are: 112 for any emergency service, 17 for the Police, 15 for an Ambulance and 18 for the Fire Brigade. The Operator is 13 and Directory Enquiries is 12. When telephoning the UK dial 0044 then the UK area code minus the first 0, and then the number you require. Finally, do not forget that a valid ten year British passport is still required for British Nationals to enter the country.

A camera, plenty of film or memory cards, and a notebook and pencil (ink smudges when wet) are the best way to record your visit, but don't burden yourself with unnecessary equipment. A tripod is not really essential (unless you are going to be taking photographs in low-light or of yourself) and the average compact digital zoom camera will more than meet your needs. For the more avid photographer, I find an SLR and 10-20mm, 18-70mm and 70-300mm lenses are an ideal choice. Remember not to shoot into direct sunlight and a good tip if taking pictures of headstones or memorials is to crouch down to the same level and, when the light is bright; take your picture from an oblique angle so that the inscription is more defined by the shadow.

Unlike the static trench warfare of the First World War, where the fighting was carried out on the same battlefield for several years, the Second World War saw the arrival of modern warfare; here technology played as greater part in the battle, as did the men who had to fight it. However, despite the weapons of mass destruction, the task of securing an area and expanding the bridgehead was still left to the men on the ground, the infantry. Unlike their forefathers though, these men would find themselves making advances over ground in days rather than months and years. Consequently, you are unlikely to find anything in the way of old munitions lying about today on or beside the well-trodden tourist tracks. Nevertheless, there are still many munitions left over from the battles, buried beneath the ground or in woods and pathways off the beaten track. There are also other grim discoveries still being found today.

On 8 May 2009, the bodies of five German soldiers, still wearing their metal identity tags, were found in a shallow unmarked grave near Bavent. The bodies were later reinterred at the German cemetery at la Cambe. On 14 February 2010, some 20,000 of Caen's 110,000 inhabitants had to be evacuated when a 1,000lb (453kg) Allied bomb was found during building work at Caen University. A bomb disposal squad safely disarmed the bomb during the day. So if you do find something unusual, do not touch!

What also remains today are the extensive fortifications that once formed part of Hitler's Atlantic Wall. Positioned all around the Norman countryside these concrete monoliths remain as formidable and awesome as they were over half a century ago. Normandy also has what is probably the greatest concentration of war memorials, than any other battlefield in the world. Over 200 are connected with the 6th Airborne Division alone.

Maps and Satellite Navigation

The most detailed maps of this area are IGN SÉRIE BLEUE (Series Blue). You will need two: the 1612OT 1:25000 CAEN map and the 1612E 1:25000 DIVES-SUR-MER/CABOURG map. The IGN SÉRIE VERTE (Series Green) 1:100 000 No. 6 map is also useful if you wish to explore the rest of the Normandy landing beaches or American airborne sector. Maps may be ordered via most good bookshops or online (www.ign.fr).

To assist those who have satellite navigation equipment there is, in the appendices of this work, a list of the satellite navigation coordinates of all the places of interest and locations of many of the memorials and exhibits mentioned in the text. For the armchair tourist and traveller alike, I can highly recommend using these coordinates to reference places on www.earth.google.com. The resources available on this site, along with the aerial photography, are particularly valuable to the reader as it will allow them to understand the distances involved and appreciate the terrain of the area much more easily.

Travel and Accommodation

Travelling to this part of France is probably best done by using one of the ferry companies: Brittany Ferries (www.brittanyferries.com) sailing from Portsmouth to Caen (approx. 6hr day crossing and 7hrs at night), Portsmouth to Cherbourg (high-speed 3hr crossing); LD Lines (www.ldlines.co.uk) sailing from Portsmouth to Le Havre (approx. 5hrs day crossing and 8hrs at night); P&O Ferries (www.poferries.com) from Dover to Calais (approx. 1hr 30mins crossing). The latter will involve a 3 to 4hr drive from Calais to Caen but can work out to be a cost-effective way of travelling, even with the added cost of the toll roads, called the *Péage*. From Calais you take the A16 to Boulogne and Abbeville, the A28 towards Rouen, then the A29 towards Le Havre and finally the A13 to Caen.

If driving, comprehensive insurance is advisable. If it is your own vehicle you must carry the original vehicle registration document (V5), if it is not your vehicle you must have a letter from the registered owner giving you permission to drive. A full valid driving licence and current motor insurance certificate is also required and an international distinguishing sign (GB) should be displayed on the rear of the vehicle (unless your vehicle displays Euro-plates). You should also carry spare bulbs as it is illegal to drive with faulty lights. A high visibility reflective jacket in the passenger compartment, in case you need to exit the vehicle after a breakdown, and a warning triangle to be used in conjunction with the vehicles hazard warning, are also compulsory. Headlight beams should also be adjusted for right-hand driving using headlight convertors.

The minimum age for driving a car is eighteen years. You should not drink alcohol and drive. Seat belts are compulsory for all occupants and children under ten years of age are not permitted to travel in the front of the vehicle. As a general guideline, speed limits (unless otherwise indicated) are: 130kmh (80mph), or 110kmh (68mph) when wet, on motorways (autoroutes); 110kmh (68mph), or 100kmh (62mph) when wet, on dual carriageways; 90kmh (55mph), or 80kmh (49mph) when wet on open roads; and 50kmh (31mph) in built-up areas. The lower limit applies if the driver has held his driving license for less than two years. Fines are on the spot and if caught speeding at 25kmh (15mph) above the speed limit you may also have your driving licence confiscated immediately.

Driving is on the right-hand side in France. While driving, take particular care at junctions. The rule of giving right of way to traffic coming from the right can still apply (*Priorité à Droite*). A yellow diamond sign indicates you have priority. On a roundabout you generally give priority to traffic coming from the left. One word of warning, if a driver flashes his headlights in France it generally indicates that he has priority and that you should give way. This is contrary to the standard practice (but not the law) in the UK.

Further up-to-date advice can be obtained from the Foreign and Commonwealth Office (www.fco.gov.uk).

16

Some of the tours in this book do use some single track roads, so take care when driving, parking and walking. When travelling please be courteous to the local people and show respect when looking about near their property or land. Please do not trespass.

Another cost-effective way of travelling to, or around, Normandy is to use one of the many battlefield tour coach travel companies. With experienced guides to enhance your tour of the area these can provide an invaluable insight into Normandy landings. Leger Holidays, offer many tours, some conducted by authors who write for the **Battleground Europe Series**. A brochure can be obtained by calling 0845 408 07 69 or by visiting their website (www.leger.co.uk).

For more personal tours, in smaller groups, these can be arranged on a daily basis. These tours can also include visits to areas not open to the general public. For more details contact Stuart Robertson at www.normandybattletours.com.

There are plenty of hotels to choose from in this area of Normandy, though remember that these are always busy around each anniversary. I have often used the Hôtel Restaurant Kyriad Caen-sud (www.kyriad-caen-sud-ifs.fr), 698, route de Falaise, 14123 IFS Caen. Tel: 0033 (0)2.31.78.38.38. that is situated on junction (*sortie*) No. 13 of the Caen Southern ring road (*péripherique Sud*) from where you can join the A13 (*Autoroute de Normandie*) which leads to the D515 and D514 to Bénouville.

Accommodation can also be found on the official website of the French Tourist Office (www.francetourism.com) and French Government Tourist Office (wwww.franceguide.com). Local tourist information can also be found at the following regional and county tourist boards and tourist offices (*Office de Tourisme or Syndicat d'Initiative*): Normandy Tourist Board (www.normandie-tourisme.fr), Calvados Tourist Board (www.calvados-tourisme.com), Cabourg Tourist Office (www.cabourg.net), and at Caen Tourist Office (www.tourisme.caen.fr).

To make the best use of this guide it would be of benefit to read it before you travel. This will help you become familiar with the operation and objectives given to the 6th Airborne Division as well as highlighting the significance of the local features and the area in general. While on your tour this guide will provide a ready reference and direction to the villages, memorials and cemeteries as well as a description of the battles.

Since much of the story is told in the words of the veterans themselves it will also vividly recreate the emotional turmoil of excitement, uncertainty, comradeship and horrors that face men in times of war. Above all, it is my intention that this guide will allow you to better understand the reason why the sacrifices made by these young men so many years ago should never be forgotten; along with the hope that, while that memory remains fresh, another generation of mothers, fathers, daughters and sons need never again experience the indiscriminate killing, and waste, of total war.

Admirals of the *Kriegsmarine*, including *Gross-Admiral* Dönitz (second from left), are shown over *Battery Lindemann*, (four coastal guns between Calais and Wissant) by the commander, K K Schneider (saluting).

GLOSSARY

The following abbreviations cover not only abbreviations that may be found in this publication, but also abbreviations that are used on the many memorials, plaques, headstones and museum information boards in this area of Normandy. Some of these abbreviations are non-standard; others have been compiled with the use of the following documents and publications: 6th Airborne Division War Diaries. The War Office, FSPB, Pam No. 2 (1940). The War Office, TM 30-410 Handbook on the British Army (1943). The War Office, Vocabulary of German Military Terms and Abbreviations (1943). Lee, Defence Terminology, Brassey's UK (1991) and The Oxford Dictionary of Abbreviations (1992).

A

AA	..	..	..	Anti-Aircraft
AAC	..	..	..	Army Air Corps
AA & QMG	..	..	..	Assistant Adjutant and Quartermaster General
AARR	..	..	..	Armoured Airborne Reconnaissance Regiment
Ab (or A/b)	..	..	..	Airborne
ack-ack	..	..	..	Anti-Aircraft fire
ADC	..	..	..	Aide de Camp
Adj	..	..	..	Adjutant
Adm	..	..	..	Administration
ADMS	..	..	..	Assistant Director of Medical Services
ADS	..	..	..	Advance Dressing Station
Adv	..	..	..	Advance
AFC	..	..	..	Air Force Cross
Airldg	..	..	..	Airlanding
Airfd	..	..	..	Airfield
AKC	..	..	..	Associate of King's College, London
Amb	..	..	..	Ambulance
Amn	..	..	..	Ammunition
Armd	..	..	..	Armoured
Artillerie	..	..	..	German for Artillery
Arty	..	..	..	Artillery
ASN	..	..	..	Airborne Support Net
Att	..	..	..	Attached
A Tk	..	..	..	Anti-tank

B

Bangalore Torpedo	..	..	Piping filled with explosive, used to blow gaps in barbed wire
Bataillon	..	..	.. German for Battalion
Bde	..	..	.. Brigade
BM	..	..	.. Brigade Major
BFMC	..	..	.. *Battalion de Fusiliers Marins Commando* (French Commandos)
Bn	..	..	.. Battalion
BOWO	..	..	.. Brigade Ordnance Warrant Officer
BRASCO	..	..	.. Brigade Royal Army Service Corps Officer
Br	..	..	.. Bridge
Bren	..	..	.. .303in British Light Machine-Gun capable of firing 500 rounds per minute
Brig	..	..	.. Brigadier

BST	..	..	..	British Summer Time
Bty	..	..	..	Battery

C

Capt	..	..	..	Captain
Cas	..	..	..	Casualty
CB (Award)	..	..	..	Companion of the (Order of the) Bath
CB (War Diary)	..	..	..	Counter Battery
CCS	..	..	..	Casualty Clearing Station
Cdn	..	..	..	Canadian
Cdo	..	..	..	Commando
CF	..	..	..	Chaplain of the Forces
C in C	..	..	..	Commander-in-Chief
cm	..	..	..	centimetre (Metric measurement of length = 10mm or 0.3973in)
CO	..	..	..	Commanding Officer
Col	..	..	..	Colonel
Comd	..	..	..	Commander
Comn	..	..	..	Communication
Comp	..	..	..	Composite
Coup de Main	..	..	..	A sudden blow or attack
Coy	..	..	..	Company
Cpl	..	..	..	Corporal
CRA	..	..	..	Commander Royal Artillery
CRASC	..	..	..	Commander Royal Army Service Corps
CRE	..	..	..	Commander Royal Engineers
CREME	..	..	..	Commander Royal Electrical Mechanical Engineers
CSM	..	..	..	Company Sergeant Major
CSMI	..	..	..	Company Sergeant Major Instructor
CSMPTI	..	..	..	Company Sergeant Major Physical Training Instructor
CWGC	..	..	..	Commonwealth War Graves Commission
cwt	..	..	..	hundredweight (Imperial measurement of weight = 112lbs or 50.8023kg)

D

DAA & QMG	..	..	..	Deputy Assistant Adjutant and Quartermaster General
DCM	..	..	..	Distinguished Conduct Medal
Def	..	..	..	Defence
det	..	..	..	Detachment
Devons	..	..	..	The Devonshire Regiment
Div	..	..	..	Division
DSO	..	..	..	Distinguished Service Order
DZ	..	..	..	Drop Zone

E

E	..	..	..	Engineer
ENSA	..	..	..	Entertainment National Service Association
Estd	..	..	..	Established
EUREKA	..	..	..	A radar beacon used by the pathfinders to mark the DZ/LZ

F

Fallschirmjaeger	..	..	German for Paratrooper
Fd	..	..	Field
FDL	..	..	Forward Defended Locality
Feldwebel	..	..	German Army rank of Sergeant
Festung Europa	..	..	Fortress Europe, aka Atlantic Wall
Flak	..	..	German for Anti-Aircraft fire
Fm	..	..	Farm
FO	..	..	Flying Officer
FOB	..	..	Forward Observer Bombardment
FOO	..	..	Forward Observation Officer
FOS	..	..	Forward Observation Section
FS or F/S	..	..	Flight Sergeant
ft	..	..	foot (feet) (Imperial measurement of length = 12ins or 0.3048m)
FUP	..	..	Forming Up Point
Fwd	..	..	Fwd

G

Generalfeldmarschall	..	..	German Army rank of Field Marshal
Generalleutnant	..	..	German Army rank of Lieutenant General
Generalmajor	..	..	German Army rank of Major General
Generaloberst	..	..	German Army rank of General
Gammon Grenade	..	..	No 82 Grenade, consisted of a bag and igniter, into which a variable amount of plastic explosives could be packed. An ideal weapon for mouse holing or disabling tracks of armoured vehicles.
Gnr	..	..	Gunner, Royal Artillery's equivalent rank of Private
GOC	..	..	General Officer Commanding
GOLD	..	..	Codename for one of the five designated landing beaches in Normandy
Gefreiter	..	..	German Army rank of Lance Corporal
GSO	..	..	General Staff Officer (graded 1-3)

H

Hauptfeldwebel	..	..	German Army rank of Company Sergeant Major
Hauptmann	..	..	German Army rank of Captain
HE	..	..	High Explosives
Hitlerjugend	..	..	Hitler Youth – name for 12 SS Panzer Division
HQ	..	..	Headquarters
Hvy	..	..	Heavy

I

I (also Int)	..	..	Intelligence
IA	..	..	Inter-Allied
In(s)	..	..	inch(es) (Imperial measurement of length = 25.4mm)
Ind	..	..	Independent
Infanterie	..	..	German for Infantry
Int (also I)	..	..	Intelligence
IO	..	..	Intelligence Officer

J

Junc	..	..	..	Junction
JUNO	..	..	..	Codename for one of the five designated landing beaches in Normandy

K

kg	..	..	..	kilogram(s) (Metric measurement of weight = 2.2046lbs)
km	..	..	..	kilometre(s) (Metric measurement of length = 1000m or 0.6214miles)
kmh	..	..	..	kilometre per hour (Metric measurement of speed = 0.6214mph)
KOSB	..	..	..	The King's Own Scottish Borderers
KStJ	..	..	..	Knight of St John
KwK	..	..	..	*Kampfwagenkanone*, German tank gun, sometimes used as a static anti-tank gun on the Atlantic Wall

L

LAD	..	..	..	Light Aid Detachment
Lb(s)				pound(s) (Imperial measurement of weight = 0.4536kg)
L Bdr	..	..	..	Lance Bombardier
L Cpl	..	..	..	Lance Corporal
L Sgt	..	..	..	Lance Sergeant
Leutnant	..	..	..	German Army rank of 2nd Lieutenant
Lieut	..	..	..	Lieutenant
LMG	..	..	..	Light Machine-Gun
Lt	..	..	..	Light or Lieutenant
Lt Col	..	..	..	Lieutenant Colonel
Lt Col Arty	..	..	..	*Luitenant Kolonel Artillerie* (Dutch rank of Lt Col)
Lt Gen	..	..	..	Lieutenant General
LZ	..	..	..	Landing Zone

M

m	..	..	..	metre(s) (Metric measurement of length = 100cm or 3.2808ft)
Major	..	..	..	German Army rank of Major
Maj Gen	..	..	..	Major General
MALLARD	..	..	..	Codename for glider landings at LZ N & W at 2100 hrs on the evening of 6 June 1944
Mauser	..	..	..	German 7.92mm Rifle
MC	..	..	..	Military Cross
M/C	..	..	..	Motorcycle
MDS	..	..	..	Main Dressing Station
ME	..	..	..	Messerschmitt, German aircraft manufacturer
Med	..	..	..	Medium
MG	..	..	..	Machine-Gun
MID	..	..	..	Mentioned in Despatches
MIKE	..	..	..	Codename for one of four sections of JUNO Beach
miles	..	..	..	mile(s) (Imperial measurement of length = 1760yds or 1.6093km)
Mk	..	..	..	Mark
mm	..	..	..	millimetre (Metric measurement of length = 0.0394in)

MM	..	..	..	Military Medal
MMG	..	..	..	Medium Machine-Gun
Min	..	..	..	minutes
MO	..	..	..	Medical Officer
mouse-holing	..	..	..	Term used for making an internal passage between two buildings.
mph	..	..	..	miles per hour (Imperial measurement of speed = 1.6093kmh)

N

NAAFI	..	..	..	Navy, Army and Airforce Institutes
NAN	..	..	..	Codename for one of the four sections of JUNO Beach
NCO	..	..	..	Non-Commissioned Officer
NEPTUNE	..	..	..	Codename for assault phase of OVERLORD

O

OB	..	..	..	*Oberbefehlshaber* (Commander-in-Chief)
OBOE	..	..	..	RAF radar precision bombing system
Oberleutnant	..	..	..	German Army rank of Lieutenant
Obergefreiter	..	..	..	German Army Rank of Corporal
Obershütze	..	..	..	German Army rank of Private (also *Schütze*)
Oberstleutnant	..	..	..	German Army Rank of Lieutenant Colonel
OC	..	..	..	Officer Commanding
Offr	..	..	..	Officer
O Group	..	..	..	Orders Group
Op	..	..	..	Operation
OP	..	..	..	Observation Post
Ops	..	..	..	Operations (Staff Branch)
OR	..	..	..	Other Ranks
Ord Fd Park	..	..	..	Ordnance Field Park
OT	..	..	..	*Organisation Todt*, German construction organisation
OVERLORD	..	..	..	Codename for the invasion of Normandy
Oxf Bucks	..	..	..	The Oxfordshire and Buckinghamshire (52nd Foot) Light Infantry

P

PaK	..	..	..	*Panzerabwehrkanone*, German mobile or static anti-tank gun
Panzer	..	..	..	German for Armour
Panzerfaust	..	..	..	German hand-held anti-tank weapon
Para	..	..	..	Parachute Battalion (ie 7 Para, 9 Para etc)
Para Bde	..	..	..	Parachute Brigade
pdr	..	..	..	Pounder, as in the British 25pdr field gun
Ph	..	..	..	Phase
PIAT	..	..	..	Projector Infantry Anti-Tank (British hand-held anti-tank weapon)
Pl	..	..	..	Platoon
P/O	..	..	..	Pilot Officer
Posn	..	..	..	Position
POW (also PW)	..	..	..	Prisoner of War
Pk	..	..	..	Park
PRA	..	..	..	Parachute Regimental Association
Pro Coy	..	..	..	Provost Company
Pt	..	..	..	Point

23

Pte	..	..	..	Private, the lowest rank in the British Army
PW (or POW)	..	..	..	Prisoner of War
Pz	..	..	..	*Panzer*
Pz Gren	..	..	..	*Panzergrenadier*, German infantry of a Panzer Division

Q

QLB	..	..	..	Quad Long Bofors
QM	..	..	..	Quartermaster
QUEEN	..	..	..	Codename for one of the four sections of SWORD Beach

R

RA	..	..	..	Royal Artillery
RAC	..	..	..	Royal Armoured Corps
RAMC	..	..	..	Royal Army Medical Corps
RAP	..	..	..	Regimental Aid Post
RASC	..	..	..	Royal Army Service Corps
Rd	..	..	..	Road
RE	..	..	..	Royal Engineers
Recce	..	..	..	Reconnaissance or Reconnoitre
Ref	..	..	..	Reference
Regt	..	..	..	Regiment
REME	..	..	..	Royal Electrical Mechanical Engineers
Rep	..	..	..	Representative
Rfts	..	..	..	Reinforcements
RHQ	..	..	..	Regimental Headquarters
Rly	..	..	..	Railway
RM	..	..	..	Royal Marine
RMO	..	..	..	Regimental Medical Officer
ROGER	..	..	..	Codename for one of the four sections of SWORD Beach
Rommel's Asparagus		..		Name given to the anti-airborne defence poles set up in open fields
RSM	..	..	..	Regimental Sergeant Major
RUR	..	..	..	The Royal Ulster Rifles
RV	..	..	..	Rendezvous, the point at which troops would group together before moving to their Objective

S

SAS	..	..	..	Special Air Service
Schmeisser	..	..	..	German 9mm sub-machine-gun
Schütze	..	..	..	German Army rank of Private (also *Obershütze*)
Sec	..	..	..	Section
Sgt	..	..	..	Sergeant
Sigmn	..	..	..	Signalman
Sigs	..	..	..	Signals
SL	..	..	..	Start Line
SNAFU	..	..	..	American acronym for Situation Normal All F****d Up
SOE	..	..	..	Special Operations Executive
Spandau	..	..	..	German 7.92mm MG34 or MG42 machine-gun
SP	..	..	..	Self-Propelled (gun)
Spr	..	..	..	Sapper, Royal Engineer's equivalent rank of Private
Sq	..	..	..	Square

Sqn	..	..	..	Squadron
SS	..	..	..	Special Service
ss	..	..	..	Steam Ship
SS (German)	..	..	..	*Schutzstaffel* (Waffen-SS) armed defence echelon, German elite troops
SSM	..	..	..	Staff Sergeant Major
S Sgt	..	..	..	Staff Sergeant
Stabsfeldwebel	..	..	..	German Army rank of Staff Sergeant
Sta	..	..	..	Station
Sten	..	..	..	British 9mm sub-machine-gun
Stick	..	..	..	One aircraft load of parachute troops, to be dropped in one run over one dropzone
Str	..	..	..	Strength
SWORD	..	..	..	Codename for one of the five designated landing beaches in Normandy

T

TAF	..	..	..	Tactical Air Force
TD	..	..	..	Territorial (Army Efficiency) Decoration
Tks	..	..	..	Tanks
THOMAS	..	..	..	Codename for the green light location devices fitted to parachute containers
ton(s)	..	..	..	ton(s) (Imperial measurement of weight = 20cwt or 1.0160 tonnes)
tonnes	..	..	..	tonne(s) (Metric measurement of weight = 1000kg or 0.9842 UK tons)
TONGA	..	..	..	Codename for the first three waves of glider landings at LZ X, Y, K, V & N prior to seaborne landings
Tp	..	..	..	Troop

U

unkn	..	..	..	unknown
Unterfeldwebel	..	..	..	German Army rank of Sergeant
Unteroffizier	..	..	..	German Army rank of Sergeant (as above)

W

Warwick	..	..	..	The Royal Warwickshire Regiment
W/C	..	..	..	Wing Commander
Wehrmacht	..	..	..	German Armed Forces
Wkshop	..	..	..	Workshop
WO or W/O	..	..	..	Warrant Officer
WO	..	..	..	War Office
W Y	..	..	..	Worcestershire Yeomanry

Y

yds	..	..	..	yards (Imperial measurement of length = 3ft or 0.9144m)
Yeo	..	..	..	Yeomanry

Misc

2ic (or 2i/c)	..	..	..	Second in Command

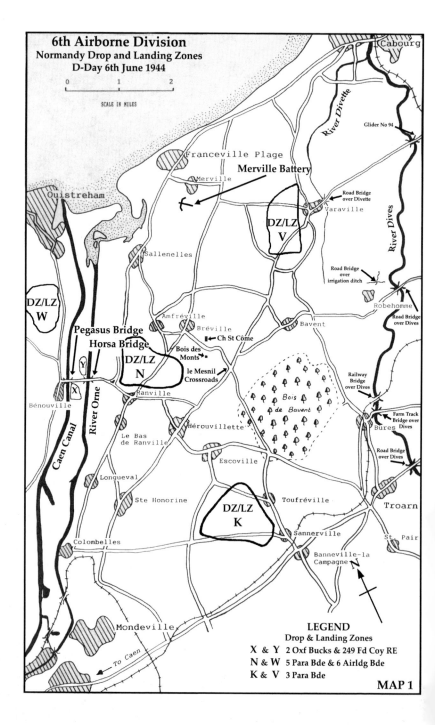

6th Airborne Division
Normandy Drop and Landing Zones
D-Day 6th June 1944

SCALE IN MILES

0   1   2

Cabourg

River Divette

Glider No 94

Franceville Plage

Merville

Merville Battery

Road Bridge over Divette

Varaville

River Dives

Ouistreham

DZ/LZ V

Sallenelles

Road Bridge over irrigation ditch

Robehomme

Road Bridge over Dives

DZ/LZ W

Amfréville

Bréville

Bavent

Pegasus Bridge
Horsa Bridge

Ch St Côme

DZ/LZ N

Bois des Monts

le Mesnil Crossroads

Railway Bridge over Dives

River Orne

Ranville

Bois de Bavent

Farm Track Bridge over Dives

Bénouville

Bures

Caen Canal

Hérouvillette

Road Bridge over Dives

Le Bas de Ranville

Longueval

Escoville

Ste Honorine

DZ/LZ K

Toufréville

Troarn

St. Pair

Colombelles

Sannerville

Banneville-la Campagne

N

Mondeville

To Caen

LEGEND
Drop & Landing Zones
X & Y 2 Oxf Bucks & 249 Fd Coy RE
N & W 5 Para Bde & 6 Airldg Bde
K & V 3 Para Bde

MAP 1

CHAPTER ONE

PLANNING THE INVASION

THE ALLIED PLAN

Operation OVERLORD involved the initial landing of six divisions – three American, two British and one Canadian – on five beaches over a 50-mile (80.46km) stretch of Normandy coastline between Quinéville on the east coast of the Côtentin Peninsular and Ouistreham at the mouth of the River Orne. It had been decided that the best time to land on the beaches was just after first light in the morning, just below mid tide, and on a flooding tide, as this gave the advantage that most of the beach defences would be seen and could therefore be destroyed or avoided. Low tide would have created too large an area of open ground for the troops to cross, up to six hundred yards (549m) in places, making the beaches a killing field. High tide would leave the beach defences of mines and obstacles undetectable and also leave too small an area for the troops to disembark and organise themselves.

Due to the distance involved, and the run of the tide, the First (US) Army were due to land first on UTAH and OMAHA Beaches at 0630hrs. These would be followed by the Second (British) Army at GOLD and SWORD Beaches at 0725hrs, and JUNO Beach at 0750hrs.

Pre-invasion exercises at a Training Centre of Combined Operation Command. RAF Mustangs come in low over landing craft in a simulated attack.

In order to protect the outer flanks of the seaborne invasion and help disable the German Atlantic Wall from the rear, an additional assault of three airborne divisions, two American and one British, would precede the beach assault at just after midnight on the night of the 5/6 June, 1944. On the right flank

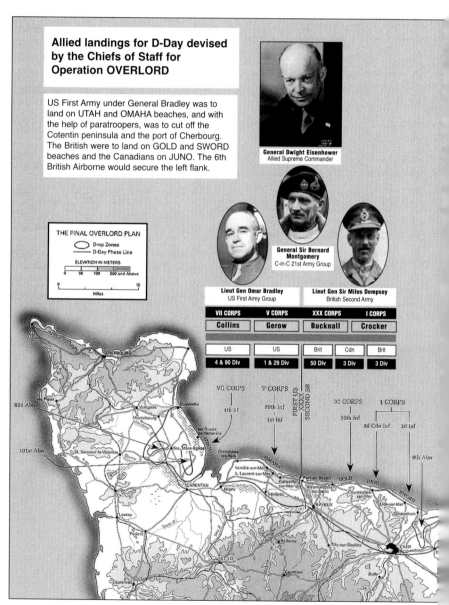

Allied landings for D-Day devised by the Chiefs of Staff for Operation OVERLORD

US First Army under General Bradley was to land on UTAH and OMAHA beaches, and with the help of paratroopers, was to cut off the Cotentin peninsula and the port of Cherbourg. The British were to land on GOLD and SWORD beaches and the Canadians on JUNO. The 6th British Airborne would secure the left flank.

General Dwight Eisenhower
Allied Supreme Commander

General Sir Bernard Montgomery
C-in-C 21st Army Group

Lieut Gen Omar Bradley
US First Army Group

Lieut Gen Sir Miles Dempsey
British Second Army

THE FINAL OVERLORD PLAN
Drop Zones
D-Day Phase Line
ELEVATION IN METERS
0   50   100   200 and Above
0   15
Miles

VII CORPS	V CORPS	XXX CORPS	I CORPS
Collins	Gerow	Bucknall	Crocker

US	US	Brit	Cdn	Brit
4 & 90 Div	1 & 29 Div	50 Div	3 Div	3 Div

28

15,000 troops of the 82nd (All American) and 101st (Screaming Eagles) US Airborne Divisions would land on the Côtentin Peninsula and, on the left flank, approximately 12,000 troops of the British 6th Airborne Division would come to ground and secure an area around and between the Caen Canal and River Dives (see Map 1).

After the firm establishment of a bridgehead on the beaches and a link-up of the British and Canadian armies with the 6th Airborne Division, General Montgomery planned to use the threat of a breakout in the 6th Airborne Division sector to draw and contain enemy reserves on the eastern flank.

> *My plan was to make the break out on the western flank, using for this task the American Armies under General Bradley, and to pivot the whole front on Caen. The American break out thrust was to be delivered southwards down to the Loire and then to be developed eastwards in a wide sweep up to the Seine about Paris. This movement was designed to cut off all the enemy forces south of the Seine, over which river the bridges were to be destroyed by air action.*[1]

GENERAL MONTGOMERY, COMMANDER, 21ST ARMY GROUP

Within the first forty-eight hours of the invasion General Eisenhower, the Supreme Commander of the Allied Expeditionary Force, planned to land, by sea, 176,475 men along with 20,111 vehicles (these included 1,500 tanks, 5,000 tracked vehicles, 3,000 guns and 10,611 assorted vehicles from jeeps to bulldozers). In total, by D-Day,* thirty-seven divisions (twenty-three infantry, ten armoured and four airborne) were to be available in Britain to carry out the mission of invading north west Europe. The use of 5,000 ships and 4,000 additional landing craft and air cover supplied by 171 fighter squadrons[2] ensured that D-Day was set to be the greatest combined operation ever attempted.

Subsequent books in this *Battleground Europe* series cover, in detail, the beach and American airborne landings in Normandy. This book *Merville Battery & The Dives Bridges*, and the accompanying book in this series, *Pegasus Bridge & Horsa Bridge*

---

* The term D-Day is actually standard army nomenclature to signify the day a military operation begins. The letter D does not represent anything other than to emphasise the word Day. The first recorded use was in 1918 in Field Order No. 8, First Army, Allied Expeditionary Force. Such an expression allows the build-up and operation phases to be measured in days (i.e. D-1, D+1, etc.). Similarly, H-Hour is used to represent the actual time on D-Day that an operation begins. However, because of the scale of the Normandy landings the term D-Day has now passed into common usage to represent the events of 6 June 1944 and Operation OVERLORD (see The Oxford English Dictionary).

will concentrate on the objectives and operations of the British 6th Airborne Division; looking in detail at the events that surrounded their landings on the left flank of the invasion force on 6 June 1944.

FORMATION OF THE 6th AIRBORNE DIVISION

Orders were issued by the War Office on 23 April 1943 for the formation of the 6th Airborne Division.[3] On 7 May 1943, Major General Richard Gale, the appointed commander, arrived at Syrencot House near Durrington, on Salisbury Plain in Wiltshire and formed the divisional headquarters (HQ). Meanwhile 6 Airlanding Brigade (6 Airldg Bde) HQ was formed at Amesbury. It was around this time that the decision was made that the 1st Airborne Division sign – Bellerophon mounted astride the winged horse Pegasus, the first recorded airborne warrior – should be adopted as the airborne forces sign. This now famous emblem was also supported by a divisional motto that Major General Richard Gale placed in one of the first copies of Divisional Routine Orders – GO TO IT.

> *This motto will be adopted by the 6th Airborne Division and as such should be remembered by all ranks in action against the enemy, in training, and during the day to day routine duties.*
>
> *In this wise and from these beginnings was the 6th Airborne Division born.*

MAJOR GENERAL RICHARD GALE, GOC 6TH AIRBORNE DIVISION

Major General Richard Gale

Although the 6th Airborne Division was in fact Britain's second airborne division, the number six was chosen in order to mislead enemy intelligence. From May to 22 September the division grew in size to its full strength; then on 23 December 1943, the division was ordered to complete its training and mobilize in preparation for operational duty by 1 February 1944. In less than nine months after its initial formation the 6th Airborne Division was assembled and ready for active service. Considering that some 12,000 men were involved, it was a remarkable achievement. Sixteen days later Lieutenant General Frederick 'Boy' Browning, commander of I Airborne Corps, briefed Major General Gale on the role his division would play in the Normandy invasion.

In less than nine months after its initial formation the 6th Airborne Division was ready for active service.
***Right* : British paratroopers during a practise jump.**

Lieutenant General F. 'Boy' Browning.

So it came about that on the 24th February, the 6th Airborne Division was definitely placed under command of the I British Corps for Operation OVERLORD. For planning, a small party consisting of myself, Bobby Bray, my GSO 1, Lacoste, my GSO 2, Intelligence, one GSO 3, Shamus Hickie my CRA and Frank Lowman my CRE with the chief clerk went up to I Corps Headquarters in Ashley Gardens, London.

It was here that I received my orders and

*here that we worked out our outline plan. A plan which, save for
very minor modifications, we never altered.*[5]

MAJOR GENERAL RICHARD GALE, GOC 6TH AIRBORNE DIVISION

OBJECTIVES OF THE 6th AIRBORNE DIVISION
The 6th Airborne Division had three primary tasks[6] as part of
their role in covering the eastern flank of the invasion:

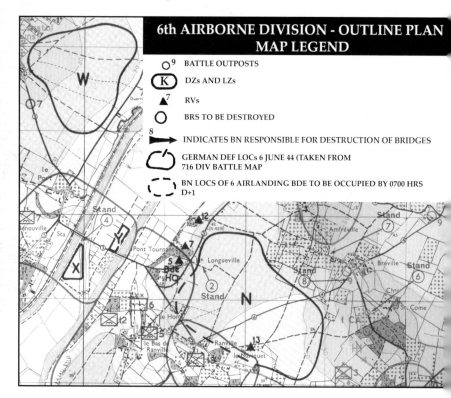

**6th AIRBORNE DIVISION - OUTLINE PLAN
MAP LEGEND**

O⁹	BATTLE OUTPOSTS
(K)	DZs AND LZs
▲⁷	RVs
O	BRS TO BE DESTROYED
⤵⁸	INDICATES BN RESPONSIBLE FOR DESTRUCTION OF BRIDGES
	GERMAN DEF LOCs 6 JUNE 44 (TAKEN FROM 716 DIV BATTLE MAP
	BN LOCS OF 6 AIRLANDING BDE TO BE OCCUPIED BY 0700 HRS D+1

TASK ONE (see Map 1, p.26)
The bridges over the Caen Canal (Bénouville Bridge) and the
River Orne (Ranville Bridge) were to be captured intact in order
to allow the rapid deployment of reinforcements from SWORD
Beach. This would then greatly help the defence of the
bridgehead, which by then would have already been established
by the rest of the 6th Airborne Division, so that it could be
maintained and exploited. This operation was to be carried out
in a *coup de main* glider operation by one reinforced company

32

(six platoons) from B and D Company (Coy) of 2nd Battalion Oxfordshire and Buckinghamshire Light Infantry (2 Oxf Bucks) of 5 Parachute Brigade (5 Para Bde).

Under the command of Major John Howard the infantry were accompanied by thirty engineers from No. 2 Platoon of 249 Field Company Royal Engineers (Fd Coy RE). All were due to land at Landing Zone (LZ) X & Y at approximately 0020hrs in six gliders.

Simultaneously, three advance parties of pathfinders from the 22nd (Independent) Parachute Company [22 (Ind) Para Coy]would drop at Landing Zone/Drop Zone (LZ/DZ) N, V & K and mark the LZ/DZs for the main body of 3 Parachute Brigade (3 Para Bde) at DZ V & K and 5 Para Bde at DZ N at 0050hrs.

5 Para Bde, commanded by Brigadier Nigel Poett, would then reinforce the *coup de main* party and secure and hold the area around the bridge at Bénouville (today known as Pegasus Bridge) and at Ranville (today known as Horsa Bridge) until relieved by a battalion from 8 Infantry Brigade (8 Inf Bde) of the British 3rd Infantry Division who would be landing on SWORD Beach at 0730 hrs.

Brigadier Nigel Poett.

TASK TWO (see Map 2, p.79)
The destruction of the coastal gun emplacement known as the Merville Battery had to be achieved, as it was believed that each of the four casemates would contain 150mm (5.91in) calibre howitzers. Such weapons potentially had a range of over 20,000 yards (18,288m), some 11.36 miles (18.29km) and would wreak havoc among the assault craft as they approached the landing beaches. As heavy bombing could not guarantee the destruction of the battery guns, it was ultimately decided that the only way of neutralizing this position was by the use of another *coup de main* operation by the airborne forces.

This operation would involve the landing of three gliders within the German battery perimeter and between the casemates, while the main assault force launched its attack through the perimeter mined and barbed wire defences. This assault was assigned to the 9th Parachute Battalion (9 Para), under the command of Lieutenant Colonel Terence Otway. With 9 Para were a troop of engineers from 591 Parachute Squadron Royal Engineers (591 Para Sqn RE), to help clear the minefields around the battery and destroy the guns in the casemates.

The main assault force of 9 Para were to drop with the rest of 3 Para Bde, less HQ and the 8th Parachute Battalion (8 Para), at DZ/LZ V.

TASK THREE (see Map 1, p.26)
The destruction of four bridges over the River Dives (one near Robehomme, two in Bures-sur-Dives and one near Troarn); one bridge over the River Divette at Varaville and a culvert (small bridge) across an irrigation ditch near Robehomme. This was necessary to delay the advance of enemy reinforcements from the east into the area of operations for 6th Airborne Division.

These tasks would be carried out by the 3rd Parachute Squadron, Royal Engineers (3 Para Sqn RE), under the command of Major Adams 'Tim' Roseveare.

The 1st Canadian Parachute Battalion (1 Cdn Para), under the command of Lieutenant Colonel George Bradbrooke, and No. 3 Troop of 3 Para Sqn RE, were to land at DZ/LZ V. One company and a platoon of 1 Cdn Para were assigned the task of protecting No. 3 Troop 3 Para Sqn RE, while they destroyed the bridge at Varaville and the bridge and culvert near Robehomme.

Meanwhile, Lieutenant Colonel Alastair Pearson's 8 Para were to land some 5 miles (8.05km) south-west at DZ/LZ K. One platoon of paratroopers from 8 Para were then to cover sappers from No. 2 Troop 3 Para Sqn RE, while they destroyed the bridges at Bures-sur-Dives. Meanwhile another platoon from 8 Para were to provide protection for No. 1 Troop 3 Para Sqn RE, as they destroyed the bridge near Troarn.

SECONDARY TASKS
Secondary tasks to be carried out, without prejudice to the three main tasks, were to secure the area between the River Orne and River Dives north of the road (now the D226) that runs, west to east, from Colombelles, through DZ/LZ K, into Sannerville and then on to Troarn (now N175), and to delay any enemy reserves from moving into this area.[7]

REINFORCEMENTS

The first reinforcements would arrive at LZ N at 0320hrs, followed, in the second *coup de main* operation of the night, by a detachment from 9 Para at 0430hrs who were due to land in three Horsa gliders, inside the 400 square yard (366sq m) area of the Merville Battery. This operation was timed to coincide with the main assault on the position by the rest of the 9 Para. It was then planned that No. 4 Commando (4 Cdo), of Lord Lovat's No. 1 Special Service Brigade (1 SS Bde), would land on SWORD Beach at La Bréche at 0820hrs. Also attached to 4 Cdo were No. 1 and No. 8 French Troop of *1er Bataillon de Fusiliers Marins Commando* (*1 BFMC*). This unit having recently been transferred, on 1 May 1944, from No. 10 (Inter Allied) Commando [10 (IA) Cdo].

RAF reconnaissance photograph taken in March, 1944. Bénouville (Pegasus) Bridge, over the Caen Canal, is in the foreground to the left. Ranville (Horsa) Bridge over the River Orne in the lower right. In the distance at the top is Ouistreham and part of SWORD Beach.

The objective for 4 Cdo was to destroy the coastal defence battery, on the site of the former casino at Riva-Bella in Ouistreham, thereby aiding the landing at 0840hrs of the remaining units of 1 SS Bde and 3rd Infantry Division. Lord Lovat would then lead his men over the 6.5miles (10.46km) of enemy held territory and form the link-up between the airborne and seaborne troops[8] at approximately H+4 hrs at the captured bridges. They would then move on and patrol an area between Amfréville, the *Château St Côme* and Bavent. The leading elements of the 3rd Infantry Division were expected to reach Bénouville by H+5 hours.[9]

At 2100hrs, on the evening of D-Day, 6 Airldg Bde would make up the final and largest reinforcement by air at LZ/DZ N & W.

The remaining units of the 6th Airborne Division, due to a shortage of suitable planes, gliders and pilots were to arrive by sea between D-Day+1 and D-Day+7. These would include elements of: 2nd Airlanding Light Anti-Aircraft Battery, Royal Artillery (2 Airldg Lt AA Bty RA); 3rd Airlanding Anti-Tank Battery Royal Artillery (3 Airldg A Tk Bty RA), less one troop; 12th Battalion the Devonshire Regiment (12 Devons) less one company; 53rd (Worcestershire Yeomanry) Airlanding Light Regiment [53 (WY) Airldg Lt Regt RA], less the 211th battery; 195th Airlanding Field Ambulance (195 Airldg Fd Amb), less two sections; and other divisional troops.[10] In total some 3,253 troops and 530 vehicles would be landed on QUEEN and ROGER sectors of SWORD Beach, west of Ouistreham and NAN and MIKE sectors of JUNO Beach at Courseulles-sur-Mer.[11]

The task of delivering all the airborne troops to their designated DZs and LZs was given to the squadrons of No. 38 and No. 46 Group, Royal Air Force (RAF).

No. 38 Group RAF had fleets of: Halifaxes of No. 298 & No. 644 Squadrons (Sqns) flying out of Tarrant Rushton; Albemarles of No. 296 & No. 297 Sqns from Brize Norton and No. 295 and No. 570 Sqns from Harwell; Stirlings of No. 196 and No. 299 Sqns from Keevil and No. 190 and No. 620 Sqns from Fairford.

No. 46 Group RAF had fleets of: Dakotas of No. 512 and No. 575 from Broadwell, No. 48 and No. 271 Sqns from Down Ampney and No. 233 Sqn from Blakehill Farm.[12]

The RAF would also tow the Horsa and Hamilcar gliders of No. 1 and No. 2 Wing of the Glider Pilot Regiment. Operation TONGA would be the codename for the night operations on the

5/6 June and Operation MALLARD would be the codename for the resupply mission on the evening of the 6 June.

GROUPING
Each parachute brigade had under its command the following units:

3 Para Brigade (DZ/LZ V & K)	5 Para Brigade (DZ/LZ N)
Det 22 (Ind) Para Coy	Det 22 (Ind) Para Coy
1 Cdn Para	7 Para
8 Para	12 Para
9 Para	13 Para
4 Airldg A Tk Bty RA (one sec)	3 Airldg A Tk Bty RA (one tp)
3 Para Sqn RE	4 Airldg A Tk Bty RA (less one sec)
591 Para Sqn RE (one tp)	D Coy 2 Oxf Bucks
FOO, 53 (WY) Airldg Lt Regt RA	591 Para Sqn RE (less one tp)
FOB attd 3 Para Bde	FOO 53 (WY) Airldg L Regt RA
224 Para Fd Amb	FOB attd 5 Para Bde
	225 Para Fd Amb
	286 Fd Pk Coy RE (one sec)
	RASC (elements)
	FOB 3 Div

(for complete Order of Battle see Appendix C)

The two parachute brigades also had the use of two cruisers and two destroyers off the coast of Normandy: HMS *Arethusa*, equipped with 6in (152.4mm) guns, and a destroyer for 3 Para Bde; HMS *Mauritius*, equipped with 4.7in (119.38mm) guns, and a destroyer for 5 Para Bde. Four further destroyers were also available for 1 SS Bde. These naval guns could be called upon for artillery support.

The cruiser, HMS *Arethusa*, one of the warships assigned to provide covering fire for the parachute brigades.

A mixed team would make up artillery support for each of the brigades. Army Forward Observer Officers (FOOs) would direct ground artillery fire and army officers trained in naval gunnery procedures, aided by Royal Navy wireless operators, would form Forward Observers Bombardment (FOBs). These teams, dropped with the paratroopers, would use radio contact to control the ships' fire[13] and other ground artillery support. Four FOOs and three FOBs were allotted to both 3 Para Bde and 5 Para Bde. A further eight FOOs were allotted to 6 Airldg Bde.

6th Airlanding Brigade (DZ/LZ N & W)
2 Oxf Bucks (less six pl)
1 RUR
A Coy 12 Devons
6 AARR
211 Airldg Lt Bty RA
249 Fd Coy RE
195 Airldg Fd Amb (two sec)

Landing by sea on D+1
12 Devons (less A coy)
53 (WY) Airldg Lt Regt RA (less one bty)
3 Airldg A Tk Bty RA (less one tp)
2 Airldg Lt AA Bty RA
195 Airldg Fd Amb (less two sec)
210 Airldg L Bty RA

SUMMARY OF ORDER FOR AIRBORNE LANDINGS
For the two airborne operations, Operation TONGA and Operation MALLARD the parachute drops and glider landings were divided into four waves using 266 paratrooper carrying aircraft and 352 gliders with tugs. Please note: the nominal roll for the Glider Pilot Regiment indicates that there were 352 gliders involved in operations. Records for the 6th Airborne Division account for only 344 gliders. Therefore, eight Horsa gliders, from the total believed to have been involved in the third and fourth wave of operations, are not accounted for in the following summary.

Operation TONGA

First Wave

Time	DZ/LZ	Units	Aircraft
0020hrs	X & Y	D & B coy 2 Oxf Bucks	6 Horsas + tugs
	N	Pathfinders	2 Albemarles
	N	Adv Party 5 Para Bde HQ	1 Albemarle
	N	Adv Party 7 Para	1 Albemarle
	N	Adv Party 13 Para	3 Albemarles
	V	Pathfinders	2 Albemarles
	V	Adv Party 3 Para Bde	2 Albemarles
	V	C Coy 1 Cdn Para	12 Albemarles
	K	Pathfinders	2 Albemarles
	K	Adv Party 8 Para	2 Albemarles

Second Wave

Time	DZ/LZ	Units	Aircraft
0045hrs	V	HQ 3 Para Bde	2 Horsas +tugs
	V	9 Para	2 Horsas + tugs
	V	591 Para Sqn RE	1 Horsa + tug
	V	1 Cdn Para	1 Horsa + tug
	V	224 Para Fd Amb	3 Horsas + tugs
	V	Det 4 Airldg A Tk Bty RA	2 Horsas + tugs
	K	8 Para, 3 Para Sqn RE, RAMC & RASC	6 Horsas + tugs
0050hrs	N	5 Para Bde	83 Stirlings + 27 Dakotas, 19 Albemarles & 2 unkn. para aircraft

Time	DZ/LZ	Units	Aircraft
0117hrs	N	Adv party HQ 6 Ab Div	2 Stirlings
	V	HQ 3 Para Bde	7 Dakotas
	V	3 Para Bde (less 8 Para)	56 Dakotas
	V	3 Para Sqn RE	3 Dakotas
	V	224 Para Fd Amb	3 Dakotas
	K	8 Para	31 Dakotas
	K	3 Para Sqn RE	6 Dakotas

Top: **Albemarle.**
Above: **Stirling.**
Right: **C-47 Skytrain (Dakota DC3)**

Third Wave

The nominal role for the Glider Pilot Regiment lists 216 gliders destined for LZ N and 110 gliders for LZ W. However, 6th Airborne Division records indicate that only 202 gliders were destined for LZ N, but that 116 gliders were destined for LZ W. This discrepancy in official records therefore does not allow the actual number of gliders destined for each of these two LZs, in the third and fourth wave, to be accurately determined.

Time	DZ/LZ	Units	Aircraft
0320hrs	N	HQ 6 Ab Div, RE & FOOs	44 Horsas + tugs
	N	4 Airldg A Tk Bty RA	20 Horsas + 4 Hamilcars + tugs
0430hrs	Merville	Det from 9 Para	3 Horsas + Albemarle tugs

Operation MALLARD

Fourth Wave

Time	DZ/LZ	Units	Aircraft
2051hrs	N	HQ 6 Airldg Bde	15 Horsas + tugs
2123hrs	N	1 RUR	70 Horsas + tugs
	N	6 Ab Div Armd Recce Regt	19 Horsas + tugs & 26 Hamilcars + Halifax tugs
	N	3 Airldg Anti-Tank Bty RA	4 Hamilcars + Halifax tugs
	W	2 Oxf Bucks (less D Coy)	65 Horsas + tugs
	W	195 Airldg Fd Amb	6 Horsas + tugs
	W	716 Ab Lt Comp Coy RASC	10 Horsas + tugs
	W	211 Airldg Bty RA	27 Horsas + tugs
	W	A Coy 12 Devons	8 Horsas + tugs

Before we consider the most obvious danger that faced the men of 6th Airborne Division – the strength of the German defences in Normandy – it is important to bear in mind a few of the other

40

hazards that faced the airborne troops as they went into battle. For gliderborne troops this took the form of the aircraft itself. The Horsa Airspeed AS I glider was a plywood and fabric construction which offered very little protection from anti-aircraft or machine-gun fire. The glider was fitted with a removable undercarriage which would sometimes become detached if landing on uneven ground (which was often the case), leaving the glider to land on its central skid.

As the floor of the aircraft could well disintegrate on landing, the passengers, up to thirty fully equipped troops, would wear a lap belt and brace themselves by linking arms or putting their arms around each others' shoulders and then lifting their feet up off the floor in anticipation of the landing. This, at around 90mph (145kmh), proved to be a nerve-wracking experience for all concerned.

The glider pilots themselves were even more exposed and, in the event of hitting any ground obstacles such as 'Rommel's Asparagus', trees, a ditch or indeed another crashed glider, the perspex and wooden nose of the aircraft offered almost no protection on impact.

The Horsa was also used for transporting pieces of equipment

A light tank exiting a Hamilcar glider during a training exercise. Thirty-four Hamilcars were used on D-Day.

such as Jeeps, motorcycles and 6-pounder (2.25in/57mm) anti-tank guns; from which there was always a danger of the cargo breaking loose under the impact of a rough landing.

The Hamilcar, could carry a payload up to 17,500lbs (7,938kg), some 7.8 tons (7.9 tonnes), the equivalent of its own weight. It was used to transport larger pieces of artillery and armoured vehicles such as the Tetrarch tank employed by 6th Airborne Armoured Reconnaissance Regiment (6 AARR).

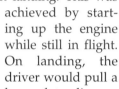

The tank crews would stay inside the tank for added safety during the flight, which also enabled them to make a quick exit on landing. This was

achieved by starting up the engine while still in flight. On landing, the driver would pull a lanyard to disconnect the lashings that held the tank in place. As he drove forward a trip would automatically release the nose of the glider and allow him to drive straight out and into battle, all within fifteen seconds of landing. Naturally, this complicated procedure held built-in potential danger.

Life for the paratroopers was no less dangerous. Exiting their aircraft at an altitude of between 500ft (152m) and 700ft (213m), laden with in excess of 60lbs (27kg) of equipment, they would be on the ground within 25 seconds. In this time they had to

British glider pilots, once on the ground, fought alongside the airborne infantry. They had the added responsibility of safely delivering their comrades unharmed and equipment undamaged and ready for action.

Workhorse of the British airborne forces – the Horsa glider.

check that their parachutes had opened, go through their anti-collision drill, attempt to get their bearings by locating a landmark and then, in the dark and hoping that they would not become snagged in a tree, building or 'Rommel's Asparagus', make a safe landing!

For those carrying a kitbag or weapon valise there was the added difficulty of releasing this bulky item. The kitbag was designed to carry up to 80lbs (36kg) in weight (although this was often exceeded) and was suspended by a 20ft (6m) rope from the parachute harness. The kitbag was initially attached to the paratrooper's right leg. Upon exiting the aircraft, the paratrooper would have to release the kitbag and steadily lower it to the end of its suspension line. If the kitbag was released too quickly the weight of his equipment would cause the rope line to snap and the kitbag would be lost. If the release pins were not freed correctly it would remain attached to the paratrooper's leg and result, almost certainly, in a broken limb upon landing.[14]

Finally, adding to the potential problems of all the aforementioned, the paratroopers and gliderborne troops would also come under fire from German anti-aircraft guns and machine-guns while they descended.

Manhandling a Jeep aboard via the nose of a Horsa. Approximately 350 Horsas were used on D-Day by 6th Airborne Division.

Glider-towing crews and glider pilots receive their final briefing.

45

CHAPTER TWO

THE GERMAN DEFENCES IN NORMANDY

THE ATLANTIC WALL

Festung Europa, Hitler's Fortress Europe, more commonly known as the Atlantic Wall, was a system of fortifications under the command of *OB West*, *Generalfeldmarschall* von Rundstedt, which was built by the *Organisation Todt* (*OT*) and stretched some 1,700 miles (2,736km) from the Spanish border to the Netherlands. It proved its worth in the failed raid on Dieppe by the Allies in August of 1942. The Nazi Propaganda Minister, Joseph Goebbels, used the statistics gathered from that bloody fiasco as a warning to the Allies of how impregnable the German fortifications were. From an assault force of over 6,000 British and Canadian troops, Anglo-Canadian casualties amounted to 3,613.[1] Records

Our Atlantic Wall defences are unbreakable. No one can pass them. If they try, results will be like Dieppe.
Joseph Goebbels

for German casualties, by comparison, show fewer than 600 from all their three services.[2] Nevertheless, until *Generalfeldmarschall* Erwin Rommel, was appointed Inspector General of the Atlantic Wall on 21 November 1943, the coastal defences were, in most places, little more than a propaganda myth.

With manpower constantly being drained to resupply exhausted divisions on the Eastern Front, von Rundstedt believed that the Allies could not be prevented from landing and that they possessed a strategic flexibility that could not be countered by a static defence system. He therefore concentrated most of his defences around the Pas de Calais, Cherbourg, Brest and the mouths of the River Somme and River Seine with the intention of denying the Allies the use of any of the major ports. Without a port it was hoped that the invading army would be denied the opportunity to resupply quickly and it was von Rundstedt's plan then to use his mobile reserves to drive the Allies back into the sea before a sizeable bridgehead could be established.[3]

> **The enemy must be annihilated before he reaches our battlefield. We must stop him in the water. destroying all his equipment while it is still afloat.**
> *Generalfeldmarshall* Erwin Rommel

Rommel disagreed with von Rundstedt and believed that the invasion force must be defeated on the beaches. He appealed to Hitler for command of the Seventh and Fifteenth Armies who defended the coast from north-east France, at the mouth of the River Loire, on to Belgium and through into Holland. At this stage, in January 1944, much of the coastline of Calvados in Normandy was relatively unfortified.

Although he retained his position as *OB West*, von Rundstedt's command was divided into two army groups with Rommel taking command of Army Group B. Immediately

> **Just as the defending force has gathered valuable experience from Dieppe, so has the assaulting force. He will not do it like this a second time.**
> *Generalfeldmarshall* von Rundstedt

Rommel inspecting beach obstacles.

Rommel began to modify von Rundstedt's plan and Army Group B records show that more than 500,000 foreshore obstacles and 4,000,000 land mines were laid by the end of May 1944. Also, the construction of pillboxes, reinforcement of shelters for anti-tank positions and many other obstacles were in place by June 1944. This would also include (and these would have most effect on the airborne forces) the appearance of anti-glider poles that became known as 'Rommel's Asparagus'. These thick wooden poles, some tipped with explosive shells and trip wires, were placed in many open areas of land within 7 miles (11.27km) of the coastline. At the same time, all low-lying land was flooded and the intermediate areas between were planted with mines.

'Rommel's Asparagus' – anti glider poles.

In June 1944 von Rundstedt had sixty divisions under his command, forty-three of which came under Rommel's Army Group B, with eighteen divisions (fifteen infantry

Generalleutnant Reichert, 711 Infanterie Division.

Generalleutnant Richter, 716 Infanterie Division.

Generalleutnant Kraiss, 352 Infanterie Division.

and three armoured) situated between the River Seine and the River Loire. Eisenhower, by comparison, had thirty-seven divisions in Britain, but, due to the logistics involved, all of these could not be brought into action until seven weeks after D-Day.[4]

Three German infantry divisions, the *711*, *716* and *352*, and two armoured divisions, *12 SS Panzer* and *21 Panzer*, were all in the vicinity or within reach of the area where the 6th Airborne Division was due to land on the night of the 5/6 June 1944.

711 Infanterie Division was best situated to counter the attack by the 6th Airborne Division. It had an estimated strength of 13,000 troops, twenty anti-tank guns, sixty pieces of field and medium artillery and a French, Renault 35, tank squadron.

SS-Brigadeführer Fri' Witt. 12 SS Panzer Division Hitlerjugend

716 Infanterie Division was considered a low category division and was situated mainly west of the River Orne with its complement of eight infantry battalions which included two Russian battalions each of a thousand men. It also had artillery support in the form of twenty-four gun-howitzers, twelve medium howitzers and one anti-tank company.

352 Infanterie Division was deployed around Port-en-Bessin and intelligence reports suggested that this was a counter-attack division which, if deployed, could be in the Caen area within eight hours.

12 SS Panzer Division (*Hitlerjugend*) was believed to be up to its full strength of 21,000 men. The number of Panther tanks it had was undetermined. It was assumed that its operational role was north of Lisieux or

Generalleutnant Edg Feuchtinger 21 Panz Division.

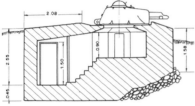

Troops put through their paces by
an NCO.

Plan for a bunker with a Renault
turret from a French tank.

Generalfeldmarschall Erwin Rommel
examines the building work.

Soldiers of the *Ost Bataillon* attached to *711 Infanterie Division* defending the area between the River Orne and the Seine. These were recruited from among Russian prisoners of war. They would be in the best position to counter-attack the 6th Airborne Division.

Sleeve badge for the Russian Army of Liberation that formed units from Russian and Georgian prisoners of war.

east of the River Seine. However, in the event of an attack it was expected that it would be ready to operate south-east of 6th Airborne Division's drop and landing zones within twelve hours of the landings.

The *21 Panzer Division* was also believed to be up to full strength – 21,000 men – and had been stationed in Rennes until May when it was unexpectedly transferred to Caen. On the night of the 5/6 June 1944, the Division was actually on anti-invasion manoeuvres in the Caen area.

In reaction to the invasion the Allies expected that the

German forces would, after determining the strength of the landings and assuming they failed in an initial counter-attack, choose a line on the high ground east of the flooded valley of the River Dives and hold the invading forces there. Once the threat of the invasion had clearly declared itself west of the River Orne and there was no sign of an attack east of the River Dives or on the River Seine estuary, it was assumed that part of the *711 Infanterie Division* would move across to take up the high ground east of the River Dives, even though this would weaken the estuary defences on the River Seine. The reaction of the *716 Infanterie Division*, effectively in the middle of the invasion, was expected to be completely disrupted.

Panzer MkIVs of *21 Panzer Division* in Normandy.

THE DECISION TO GO – D-DAY -1

The planned date for the invasion had been 5 June 1944, but low clouds, high winds and the bad conditions forecast by the meteorologists forced Eisenhower to postpone the invasion on the morning of 4 June. The weather front prevailed throughout the next day as predicted and Eisenhower feared the worst, for if the attack did not take place on 6 or 7 June there would be a wait of at least fourteen, possibly twenty-eight, days before the combination of moon, tide and time of sunrise would allow another attempt. Suspending the movement of over 2,000,000 men for this length of time without losing morale and letting the secret out seemed an impossible task. Also, if the invasion was to be rescheduled Rommel would be given even more time to prepare his growing defences. At 0330hrs on 5 June 1944, Eisenhower received some unexpected news.

> *Our little camp was shaking and shuddering under a wind of almost hurricane proportions and the accompanying rain seemed to be travelling in horizontal streaks. The mile long trip to the naval headquarters was anything but a cheerful one, since it seemed impossible that in such conditions there was any reason for even discussing the situation.*
>
> *When the conference started the first report was given by Group Captain Stagg and the meteorological staff... Their astonishing declaration was that by the following morning a period of relatively good weather, heretofore completely unexpected, would ensue, lasting probably thirty-six hours...*
>
> *The consequences of delay justified great risk and I quickly announced the decision to go ahead with the attack on June 6. The time was then 4.15 am, June 5.*[5]
>
> GENERAL DWIGHT 'IKE' EISENHOWER, SUPREME COMMANDER, ALLIED EXPEDITIONARY FORCE

As soon as the order had been given the wheels of the well-oiled Allied war machine were set in motion. The greatest combined assault force in the history of warfare was moving relentlessly towards its target on the French coastline of Normandy. At this point the potential outcome of the invasion was taken away from the politicians, chiefs of staff and planners, and transferred to those soldiers, sailors and airmen who would have to endure the sharp end of war. In less than twenty-one hours the first

Rommel at les Petites Dalles. His defences were still incomplete but he was determined to repel the assault force on the beaches.

British and Canadian paratroopers and gliderborne troops, of the 6th Airborne Division, would be fighting, and dying, on Normandy soil in the opening engagements for the battle for Normandy.

Counting out invasion money prior to its distribution to the airborne soldiers.

The invasion fleet heads across the Channel to the Normandy coast.

Glider pilots receive their final instructions.
Lorries carry 6th Airborne Division paratroopers to waiting Albemarles.

Paratroopers boarding an aircraft during a training exercise.

CHAPTER THREE

MERVILLE BATTERY DEFENCES AND DROP

THE DEFENCES

To get to the Merville Battery take the D514 from Pegasus Bridge to Merville-Franceville-Plage and follow the signs for the *Musée de la Batterie de Merville*. Leave your car in the car park in front of the main entrance. Enter the grounds of the battery (a small admission fee is payable) and make your way along the footpath until you are opposite the second casemate at Point A (Map 2 p.79). For more information on memorials and exhibits in this area refer to Ch. 5, D (p.103).

Intelligence reports made on 8 May 1944, with the aid of RAF aerial reconnaissance photographs, suggested that the size of the casemates at the Merville Battery indicated that each of the four gun emplacements would contain a medium-calibre gun or howitzer of 150mm (5.91ins). If this was the case then the range of these weapons could be over 20,000 yards (18,288m), some 11.36 miles (18.29km), with the capability of firing a 96lb (43.5kg) shell every fifteen to twenty seconds. After considering that SWORD Beach, where the 3rd Infantry Division were going to land on D-Day, was only 3 miles (4.83km) away and the potential devastation that these weapons could cause to the landing forces, it was decided that they had to be destroyed at all cost.

The casemates themselves were set out in an arc facing the landing beaches and were protected by 6ft 6ins (1.98m) thick reinforced concrete walls and roofs. In addition, they were covered and camouflaged by up to 13ft (3.96m) earth banks, while the entrance to each of the casemates was protected by a steel door.

Around the north and north-west side of the battery there was an anti-tank ditch some 250 yards (228m) in length and up to 15ft (4.57m) wide and 10ft (3.05m) deep. This started at a point approximately 60 yards (55m) to the front of No. 1 casemate and extended across the front of the remaining three casemates. The battery was surrounded by two belts of barbed wire of which the inner belt was up to 15ft (4.57m) thick and wide by 5ft (1.52m) high. The area between the two belts of barbed wire had an average depth of 100 yards (91m) and contained a minefield that

MERVILLE BTY. (155776/
(VIEW LOOKING

CASEMATES COMPLETE

RAF reconnaissance photograph taken on 31 March 1944, while the battery was still under construction

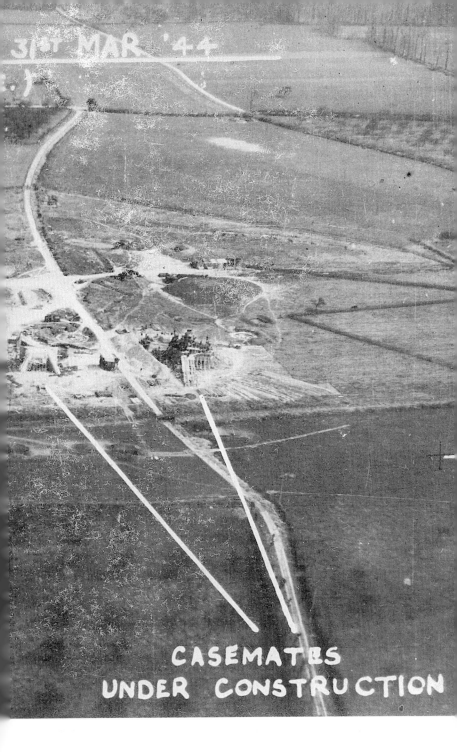

31st MAR '44

CASEMATES
UNDER CONSTRUCTION

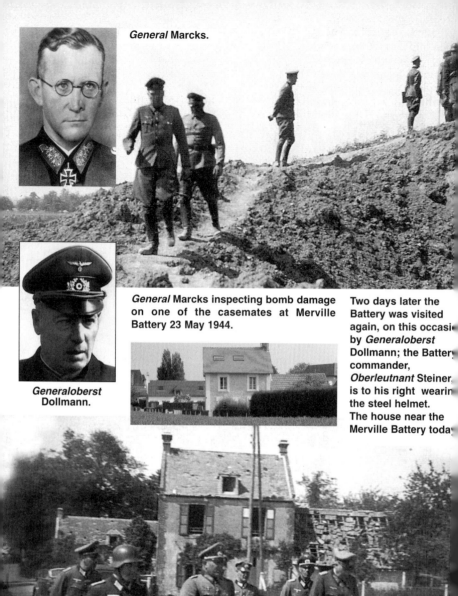

General Marcks.

Generaloberst Dollmann.

General Marcks inspecting bomb damage on one of the casemates at Merville Battery 23 May 1944.

Two days later the Battery was visited again, on this occasio̶ by *Generaloberst* Dollmann; the Batter̶ commander, *Oberleutnant* Steiner̶ is to his right wearin̶ the steel helmet. The house near the Merville Battery toda̶ varied between 18 yards (16m) and 25 yards (23m) in depth.

The strength of the garrison was estimated at 180 to 200 men all ranks. 100 to 120 of these would have been used to man the guns, communication posts and defences while at action stations, leaving the remainder to defend the ammunition, vehicles and horse lines outside the perimeter of the battery.

The area was defended by a number of machine-gun posts; five camouflaged emplacements in the hedgerows and fifteen additional weapon pits, each capable of containing another machine-gun post. Three light anti-aircraft positions were identified, each of which could house a 20mm (0.79in) anti-aircraft gun, in the event of a ground attack. These could also be used as anti-tank weapons.[1]

THE PLAN

Because of the formidable defences protecting the Merville Battery the plan for attacking this objective had to be more complex and involve a larger and better equipped force than the 181 man strong *coup de main* party that attacked Pegasus Bridge. And so it was that the task of destroying this coastal gun emplacement went to twenty-nine year old Lieutenant Colonel Terence Otway and 650 men of 9 Para, 3 Para Bde.

The plan involved an initial advance party, which included the reconnaissance (aka Trowbridge*) party plus a rendezvous (RV) party, totalling ten men. These would land twenty minutes before the main body of 9 Para, on DZ/LZ V (Map 1). Landing at 0020 hrs, they would be landing at the same time as the pathfinders of 22 (Ind) Para Coy.

The three companies of 1 Cdn Para were each assigned different tasks. C Coy, under the command of Major Hugh Murray MacLeod, dropped first, approximately 30 minutes before the rest of the battalion. They were assigned the job of securing the DZ/LZs and destroying a nearby German HQ and strongpoint. They were then, with one section of No. 3 Troop of 3 Para Sqn RE under their command, to destroy the bridge at Varaville over the River Divette. They were also tasked with destroying a German signal exchange nearby, and neutralising enemy positions in the area around the village.

* 'Trowbridge' also referred as 'Troubridge' in some publications, is used in the war diary of 9 Para to describe their reconnaissance party. It is rumoured that it is derived from the name of a Captain (or Admiral) Trowbridge (Troubridge) who served with Lord Nelson (some also say at the Battle of Trafalgar) and that he was sent to reconnoitre the French Fleet. However, there seems to be no historical evidence to support this theory and therefore appears to be a legend.

B Coy, under Major Clayton Fuller, also had one section of 3 Troop from 3 Para Sqn RE under their command. They were assigned the task of destroying the bridge over the River Dives some 0.7 miles (1.12km) south-east of Robehomme and then holding the high ground feature at Robehomme.

Meanwhile, A Coy, under Major Don Wilkins, was to provide protection to the left flank of 9 Para as they stormed the battery. They would then cover 9 Para as they advanced to the high ground near Amfréville. Finally, they would take up their own positions around the crossroads at le Mesnil with 1 Cdn Bn HQ.[2]

As the advance party made their way to their respective objectives, 100 Lancaster Bombers from RAF Bomber Command would drop, using the OBOE[†] electronic navigation system, their load of 4,000lb (1814kg) bombs onto the battery. Commencing at 0030hrs this would soften up, if not destroy, the German defences.

The advance party, which was split up into two sections, would then perform their designated tasks. The battery reconnaissance party, or Trowbridge party, was assigned the task of infiltrating the battery perimeter by cutting their way through the barbed wire and making a path through the minefield, then reporting if there was still any activity in the battery after the bombing raid. This party consisted of Major George Smith, NCOs Company Sergeant Major 'Dusty' Miller and Company Sergeant Major 'Bill' Harrold.

The second section of the advance party was the RV party consisting of Major Allen Parry, his batman, Private George Adsett, an NCO from each of the four companies: Sergeants Easlea, Knight, Lukins and Pinkus and Private Mason from the Intelligence Section. Their task was to locate the RV, which was described as a bushy topped tree on the bank of a ditch near an orchard, and set up an Aldis lamp to indicate its position to the rest of the battalion when they arrived. The officers were also given a mouthpiece that imitated the sound of quacking ducks to help any stragglers to locate the RV.

A second Trowbridge party, under Lieutenant Dennis Slade, with Company Sergeant Major Frank Stoddart and Regimental Sergeant Major 'Bill' Cunningham, would determine if a second battery situated nearby, which had shown up on the aerial reconnaissance photographs, was indeed a dummy battery as

† OBOE, so called because the signal pulses transmitted from ground stations in the UK sounded like the musical instrument.

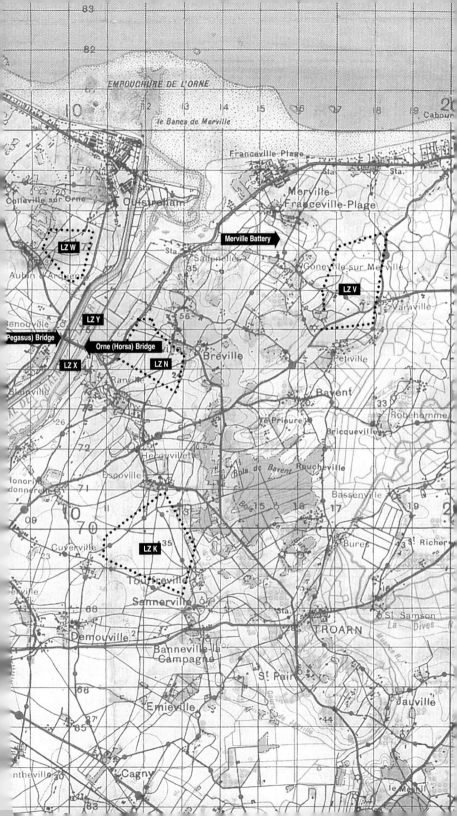

Stabsfeldwebel Johannes 'Hans' Büskotte, *Major* Karl Werner-Hof and *Hauptmann* Schimpf from the Merville Battery.

suspected. They would arrive with the main body of 9 Para that would drop on DZ/LZ V at 0050 hrs. This drop also included the landing of five gliders carrying the heavy equipment such as the jeeps and trailers, anti-tank guns, explosives for destroying the guns and additional Bangalore torpedoes. In addition, a section from 224 Para Fd Amb RAMC would arrive and a troop of sappers, from 591 Para Sqn RE, under the command of Captain 'Tony' Jackson, would be brought in with their Polish mine-detectors and mine clearance equipment. Once on the ground everyone was instructed to make direct for the RV. Everyone was expected to be assembled and ready for moving off the RV by 0235hrs. It was estimated that the battalion would arrive at the Firm Base at just after 0400hrs.

The taping party, consisting of B Coy, led by, the 2ic of B Coy, Lieutenant The Hon Paul Greenway, and a troop of 591 Para Sqn RE, under Captain 'Tony' Jackson, would proceed towards the battery in order to make gaps in the barbed wire defences and clear several lanes through the perimeter minefield using their mine-detectors and mine clearance equipment. These lanes would then be marked with tapes and coloured lights. The breaching party would follow the taping party and use Bangalore torpedoes to clear more of the barbed wire entanglements on the inner security fence. The detonation of the Bangalore torpedoes would then be used to signify the start of the main assault.

As the main assault started, a diversionary attack was to be created by the small house at the entrance of the battery. For this task German-speaking paratroopers were to be used, to distract the Germans' attention away from the main assault group of C and part of A Coy.

At the same time, at 0430hrs, there would be the arrival of a *coup de main* force, in three gliders, carrying the remainder of A Coy as well as the sappers from 591 Para Sqn RE. Commanding this force was Captain Robert Gordon-Brown, and thus came to be known as the G-B Force. They would land between the casemates after receiving a Morse code signal and upon seeing the area illuminated by 3ins (76.2mm) mortar flares. On landing the troops, who were armed with Sten guns and flame-throwers, would attack each of the four casemates. The gliders also carried explosives, known as General Wade charges, which would be used to disable the battery guns. To help distinguish themselves from the enemy the glider assault force had painted skull and crossbones on their tunics in luminescent paint.

The main assault force also had, as support: a medium machine-gun platoon, who were to provide protection on the assault companies' flanks along with sniping parties; an anti-tank troop, who were to fire at the steel doors of the casemates as the attack began; and a mortar platoon, whose primary task throughout the battle was to illuminate the battery while the gliders landed.

As an extra measure, to ensure that the Merville Battery was put out of action, 9 Para also had a FOB party to direct the fire of the battleship HMS *Arethusa*. It was believed by Otway's men that in the event of no signal being received from 9 Para confirming that the battery guns had been destroyed, whether by wireless or by yellow flare signal, then HMS *Arethusa* was under orders to open fire on the battery after 0530hrs.

Extra troops with the force, to carry out their own essential field work, were made up of a detachment from the 6th Airborne Division Signals (6 AB Div Sigs), a section from 224 Para Fd Amb RAMC and two jeeps and trailers from 716 Ab Lt Comp Coy RASC.

Upon completion of their tasks 9 Para were then to move to a Calvary (see Ch. 6, A1) which was their second RV point, and proceed with their next objective which was to seize and hold the high ground around Amfréville at le Plain south of Hameau Oger (operational orders and maps issued to the airborne troops mistakenly refer to these places as 'le Plein' and 'Hauger' – as do the war diaries and many histories that have perpetuated the error) until relieved by the commandos of 1 SS Bde. Lieutenant Colonel Otway was also tasked with setting up road blocks on the routes leading up to the high ground from the direction of Merville and Franceville-Plage (now Merville-Franceville-Plage) and to attack the German naval radar station and HQ at Sallenelles[3] (see Ch. 5, A4).

A Company, 9 Para. Major Allen Parry is seated centre with Pte Corteil and his Paradog 'Glen' seated in front.

THE DROP

The first men of 9 Para dropped on DZ V (Map 1) were the advance party of ten men who dropped with the pathfinders. But not everyone landed on the DZ. Major Parry found himself alone when the bombing raid on the Merville Battery began at 0030hrs. Unfortunately the bombers overshot their mark and the majority of bombs landed in and around the village of Gonneville-sur-Merville (now Gonneville-en-Auge). Others landed as far away as 2 miles (3.22km) from DZ V.

Major Allen Parry, Officer Commanding A Coy 9 Para.

I made off in the direction of the RV, had just reached a ditch when the [bombs] descended all around me. I felt certain that I couldn't be missed. Bombs were dropping on my right and left for some ten minutes. When they ceased to fall I breathed a sigh of relief. In contrast to this noise the next I heard was a rustling in the hedge. I lay very still for a few moments and breathed yet another sigh of relief when I heard whispered PUNCH†† to which I replied, enthusiastically, JUDY. At long last I was no longer alone and joined up with two Canadians who were as lost as I was. They seemed to think that I should be able to direct them to their RV... By this time, 0100hrs, I was getting a little agitated at the passing of time and still I hadn't made the RV. I collected about a dozen chaps and eventually saw a red light... I hastily erected my Aldis lamp, took stock of my position and set about organizing the RV. Sgt Easlea was there, waving his torch; also Major Charlton, 2ic, and the Adjutant Captain 'Hal' Hudson, but precious few others.

MAJOR ALLEN PARRY, OFFICER COMMANDING,
A COY 9 PARA

The main drop over DZ V was widely dispersed due to a number of factors, despite one of the EUREKA transmitters and holophane lights being set up on the DZ by the men of 22 (Ind) Para Coy. There were high winds, intermittent

†† A number of different passwords were used to identify British and Canadian Troops on D-Day. In each case a matching name had to be given in reply to validate the password. Hence *PUNCH* would need the reply of *JUDY*, *FISH* reply *CHIPS*, *V* reply *VICTORY*, etc.

67

Men of the 22 (Ind) Para Coy prepare to board Albemarle V1740 on the night 5 June 1944.

Eyes on the red light – waiting for the green.

moonlight, ack-ack casualties and some pilots had taken evasive action, when they entered the flak pockets, as they crossed the French coastline. To add to these problems smoke and dust from the bombing raid on the Merville Battery was also blown across the DZ. Subsequently the paratroopers were dispersed over an area of some 50sq miles (80.46 km^2). Many landed in the flooded marshland of the Dives valley, with some subsequently drowning due to the weight of their equipment.

> *Our Dakota was hit in the port engine. The pilot went round for another try. The shrapnel was rattling on the aircraft and everybody was more than eager to get out. We got the green light. I went out and it was suddenly quiet, tracers were all over the sky, some went through my chute. I heard somebody on my right scream as he got hit. I cleared a five bar gate and then nearly drowned. I had fallen into 8ft (2.4m) of water. I had to climb up the rigging lines to get out. I found a chap walking around in circles, he was dazed, he came out of it. At first we didn't know the place we were in. It turned out we were east of the battery not far from the Dives.*
>
> CORPORAL ROBERT FERGUSON, MEDICAL ORDERLY, C COY 9 PARA

The searchlight beams, moving ceaselessly back and forth across the sky, were blocked only by some cloud. The large areas of concentrated ack-ack fire seemed to cover the sky. Wave after wave of Dakotas continued to cross the French coastline and into the maelstrom. The men on board the aircraft waited, all hooked up and ready to jump, for the light in the aircraft cabin to turn from red to green.

> *I don't remember who was in the same stick, but I do remember the dog handler and 'Glen' the dog and I had to help him put the dog out of the door... I think everyone was a bit afraid as we hadn't been in action before. We kept our spirits up by singing... All the stick jumped wide and I landed in water and the cord on my kitbag snapped so I lost my gear. On landing, I found I was alone and very wet and anyone who said he wasn't afraid in some way is not telling the truth. I was more afraid of what the CSM would have to say.*
>
> PRIVATE 'JIM' BATY, A COY 9 PARA

For many of the heavily laden paratroopers it was also a struggle to move in the confines of the aircraft fuselage, and this was not helped by the constant buffeting the planes received from flak.

Subsequently this delayed the time it took for each man in the stick to clear the plane, causing the landings to be dispersed over a greater distance than expected.

I was eighteen in the stick and due to the flak throwing the aircraft all over the place I was quite a while trying to get out; then the despatcher pushed me out of the door. My equipment consisted of 2in (50.8mm) mortar, six 2in (50.8mm) bombs, 150 rounds of .303 (7.69mm), rifle, and two grenades. My small pack was strapped to my valise on my leg holding my 2in (50.8mm) mortar and rifle. Through being pushed out of the door I did a somersault and the valise broke from my leg and disappeared. I corrected my descent and got ready for landing which turned out to be not on dry land, but in water. The shock I got really scared me, I am a non-swimmer. There was I, in about 3ft to 4ft (0.91m-1.22m) of water with my 'chute over me. I drank quite a lot of water before I managed to stand up.

PRIVATE JOE HUGHES, MORTAR PLATOON, C COY 9 PARA

Not everyone landed in water, though; some had good landings on or near the DZ and were able to make for the RV quite quickly or help others who had not had such a good landing. Apart from the water and 'Rommel's Asparagus' there were also other hazards in the Norman countryside for the paratroopers.

My actual drop into Normandy was very good. I landed in a cornfield, but one of the other lads was not as lucky as myself; he was caught up on an electricity pylon twenty feet (6.1m) from the ground, with his canopy tangled around the cables. Myself and several others managed to get him down using the fireman's method, only we used an old chute. He released his harness and fell into the chute.'

PRIVATE ROBERT 'BOB' J. ABEL, B COY 9 PARA

THE RENDEZVOUS

Lieutenant Colonel Otway had also missed the DZ, coming down with Lance Corporal Wilson, his batman, near the buildings of a farm. Unfortunately, German troops were billeted in the farmhouse and were disturbed when Wilson had landed on top of, and then fell through, the roof of a greenhouse. The Germans fired at the two

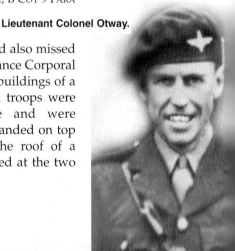

Lieutenant Colonel Otway.

paratroopers but Wilson caused a diversion by throwing a brick through the farmhouse window. The two men, once clear, then made their way to the RV.

At the RV I soon discovered that the battalion was not much over company strength and that B Coy was at about platoon strength. Specifically I remember that B Coy had dropped about twelve bundles each containing ten lightweight Bangalore torpedoes to cut the wire defences. Only one of these bundles had been found and brought to the RV. Apart from this serious loss of breaching material this threatened the well rehearsed plan of assault, because the firing of the Bangalore torpedoes was more or less the signal for the assault company to surge through the gaps.

MAJOR HAROLD BESTLEY, OFFICER COMMANDING, B COY 9 PARA

At 0235hrs, the time when the whole battalion was supposed to be at the RV and ready for setting off, only 110 men had arrived. None of the gliders had turned up and therefore the heavy equipment: jeeps, trailers, anti-tank guns, 3in (76.2mm) mortars, and additional Bangalore torpedoes, were all missing. The engineers, from 591 Para Sqn RE, with their mine clearance equipment and tapes, had not turned up and neither had any of the section from 224 Para Fd Amb RAMC. In the next fifteen minutes only a few more stragglers turned up.

The road leading from Gonneville-en-Auge (formally Gonneville-sur-Merville) crossroads to the Firm Base and on to the Merville Battery.

We had heard a few whispering voices in a copse, so we lay still, trying to find out what language they were talking when all of a sudden a bloody great corporal with a Sten gun nearly on my temple whispered 'Halt'. God, what a fright, I thought it was Hitler himself. I managed to get the password out and then everything was OK. I could see more or less that there was a single line of men in the copse. How far the line stretched I do not know. I was sent one way and my friend the other. On getting to where I was sent, I found my medical officer Captain Watts and only four other medics instead of about thirty. So about 80 per cent of our medical supplies were lost.

CORPORAL 'DOUG' TOTTLE, MEDICAL ORDERLY, A COY 9 PARA

About forty extra men had shown up by 0250hrs, and Lieutenant Colonel Otway was still left with a seriously depleted force, a force that was equipped with only one medium Vickers machine-gun, a few Bren guns and one container of ten Bangalore torpedoes. The rest of their equipment was all standard issue, such as Sten guns, rifles, 36M grenades, 82 (Gammon) grenades and fighting knifes.

With time passing Otway, was forced to make the most difficult decision of his career; to attack the battery against a force that was well entrenched behind formidable defences, and risk the complete annihilation of his men or leave the battery and join the fighting elsewhere. He considered the effect the battery would have on the beach landing forces, in less than five hours time, if it remained operational, and weighed this against the quality and determination of his men. Otway quickly made his decision;

It was a question of move off, or give up. In The Parachute Regiment giving up is not an option.

LIEUTENANT COLONEL TERENCE OTWAY, COMMANDER 9 PARA

Now that the decision had been made Otway reorganised his men and set off on the one hour march towards the battery. As they marched he modified his attack plan in his head. In the meantime Major George Smith, Company Sergeant Major 'Dusty' Miller and Company Sergeant Major 'Bill'

CSM 'Dusty' Miller.

CSM 'Bill' Harrold.

Harrold were busy clearing two roughly marked lanes through the minefield. In addition the men in the second Trowbridge party, under Lieutenant Dennis Slade, were carrying out their task.

I was quickly at the RV... And we left to investigate a second [battery] site which appeared on the aerial photos and establish if it was a dummy. This was established and we returned to join the battery assault.

LIEUTENANT DENNIS SLADE, ASSISTANT ADJUTANT 9 PARA

If you wish to see the point from which 9 Para began the second leg of their approach to the Merville Battery after leaving the RV, the area for the firm base and assault start line, you will need to leave the battery via the entrance/exit (retain your ticket for re-entry later). Walk (due north) along the entrance/exit road of the battery and turn right (due east) at the T junction. Continue for 475 yards (434m) to a crossroads in *Hameau de Descanneville* and turn right (due south, south-west). Walk along the side of the D233 for a further 635 yards (581m) and take the next left (due east, east-south) down the lane and stop after 620 yards (567m) at Point B (Map 2, p.79). This is the crossroads where Lieutenant Colonel Otway met up with his reconnaissance party. On the corner is a memorial (see Ch. 5, E2). Walk back along the track you've just come down and 200 yards (183m) on your left was the orchard (now just a field) where the third glider landed about 20 yards (18m) from the lane. 60 yards (54m) farther along the lane is the area where Lieutenant Colonel Otway established his Firm Base.

By 0250 hrs the assault force now consisted of approximately 150 men and Otway led the men to the crossroads on the north-east corner of Gonneville-sur-Merville (now Gonneville-en-Auge) where Major Smith reported the findings of the first Trowbridge party. They had established that the battery was still active and the Germans were alert but unaware of any immediate threat to their position. They were also able to confirm the layout and strength of the battery defences. Otway adjusted his attack plan after considering Major Smith's report. He also had to consider how the ground force could carry out the destruction of the guns themselves. Since no mortar flares had been found, the area around the battery could not be illuminated for the gliders. Therefore he could not rely upon the gliderborne supplies, of flame-throwers and high explosives, arriving and landing in the

73

battery as planned. All that remained to destroy the guns was the limited explosive power of the No. 82 Gammon Grenade and his men's own ingenuity.

On arriving at the RV we were split up into three groups of about platoon size, each group to do the job of what the company would have done. If I remember correctly our gun was No 4. Another problem of putting it out of action was made rather difficult because of the shortage of sappers. There was CSM Jack Harries, another man and myself. We decided to elevate the gun, damaged the elevating gear and placed a Gammon bomb on the breach block with a short fuse.

SERGEANT FRED DORKINS, A COY 9 PARA

CHAPTER FOUR

MERVILLE BATTERY ASSAULT

THE ATTACK

Continue to walk back onto the D223, turn right and stop on the corner of the track leading back into the battery at Point C (Map 2, p.79). Please note there is no access into battery grounds from this lane. It was along this road that the assault force gathered. As you continue along the D223 past the narrow lane, the area to your left was a small wooded area back in 1944. Today it is just an open field. It was through these woods that Otway and his men, heading north-west, approached the battery perimeter fencing and waited for the order to attack. The whole area though was then also covered with bomb craters from the Allied bombing raids.

Lieutenant Colonel Otway had already given the order to Major Allen Parry to lead the assault since the CO of C Coy, Major Ian Dyer, had not turned up. Otway then led the men up the lane, past the Firm Base, and towards the battery perimeter itself at 0400hrs. There they waited for the gliders to approach. Unknown to him at the time, they were already experiencing their own difficulties. One of the gliders had to turn back after it was found to be overladen with men and equipment. The glider pilot, Staff Sergeant Arnold Baldwin, had attempted to correct the glider's flight as they left the airfield at Brize Norton. However, the strain was too much for the tow rope and it snapped whilst in flight.

> *I felt physically sick. Although we had only been training for this job for about three weeks, all the previous month's training had led me to believe that the end of this flight would mean France and at first I couldn't accept the fact that we were off tow still over England. I eased back on the stick very gently and had a look around. There, to my amazement and great relief, I saw a runway's lights just off our starboard wing... The passengers already knew that their big night was a flop, as their officer had been standing in the doorway when the rope broke, and they were a very disconsolate unit as they disembarked.*
> STAFF SERGEANT ARNOLD BALDWIN, GLIDER PILOT REGIMENT

Staff Sergeant Arnold Baldwin.

The two pilots found themselves having to land at Odiham and the troops were taken, by truck, back to Brize Norton and put aboard another glider for the evening landings. The second glider, piloted by Staff Sergeant S. Bone, also had some problems, but this time they were encountered after they had crossed the French coastline.

Private Gordon Newton.

We came under heavy fire, mainly small arms and flak. It was heavy and very accurate, but fortunately no one was hit, probably because we were not fully laden with troops. We tried not to think of all the high explosives under the seats! We decided to open the doors front and aft for easy exit when we landed. I was sitting opposite a door and, fearing that I may fall out particularly if the aircraft banked, I moved from port to starboard positions. As I moved over the flame-thrower on my back was hit but damaged the air supply and not the fuel tank.

PRIVATE GORDON NEWTON, A COY 9 PARA

As the glider and tug approached the battery there was no sign of the flares, or signals from the EUREKA beacons, that were supposed to guide them in. They circled the area at between 5,000ft and 6,000ft (1,524m and 1,828m), under constant fire from the ground until the tug pilot gave the glider pilots the option of casting off then or being towed back to England, Captain Gordon-Brown told the pilots to cast off.

As they descended the pilots realized that they had mistaken a village for the battery in the darkness. The pilot pulled the glider up and turned away from the village, and aimed to put the glider down in a nearby flooded field. The tailpiece was torn off the glider as it skimmed across the water, but finally came to a standstill in about 3ft (0.91m) of water, allowing the crew and passengers to get out of the glider without too much difficulty. However, some of the men very soon found themselves out of their depth when they stepped into an irrigation ditch, which was hidden by the flood water. Twenty year old Private Gordon Newton, with the 117lb (53kg) flame-thrower on his back, had to be pulled out by his comrades. Fortunately the Germans had not noticed their arrival and the group finally made their way to dry land. But since they had landed several miles from their objective they subsequently missed the assault on the battery.

Major Allen Parry, having been given the task of leading the assault groups, also had the task of destroying the guns in the casemates. He had been given two officers some NCOs and about fifty other ranks which he then split into four sections,

To assault casemate No. 1 he assigned one group led by Lieutenant Alan Jefferson and for casemate No. 2 he assigned a group led by Lieutenant Michael 'Mike' Dowling. With no more officers left he appointed Company Sergeant Major Barney Ross to lead a group in the attack on casemate No. 3 and Colour Sergeant Harold Long to attack casemate No. 4.

Each *ad hoc* party had been assigned its specific task and had made their way through the Firm Base towards the start line near the battery perimeter fencing. Major Parry let each group know that a blow on his whistle would sound the order for the Bangalore torpedoes to be detonated.

> *We started to approach the battery. I will always remember the moon coming out from behind the big dark clouds and the lonely bellow of the cows... occasionally having to wait a few minutes now and again while the forward patrol did some prowling. My first glimpse of the defences came just before dawn, a barbed wire area with a notice on it* 'Achtung Minen!' *I knew then we weren't far from the battle we had been specially trained for. I was well prepared in myself to do my part.*
>
> PRIVATE WALTER JOHNSON, C COY 9 PARA

The third glider, piloted by Staff Sergeant 'Dickie' Kerr, had also had a rough time from enemy ground fire, but was on a direct heading for the battery. On the approach the glider was hit several times and four of the men inside were wounded. Lieutenant Hugh Pond and the rest of the men braced themselves for the landing. This time they were on course.

The casemates came into sight. Travelling at over 90mph (145kmh) flak hit the aircraft again, this time on its tail. Swerving from the impact, the glider's heading shifted from between the casemates and towards the field just beyond the battery. Just before the glider was about to touch down the pilot caught sight of a large skull and crossbones sign and he immediately pulled back on his control stick to avoid the minefield. The glider became airborne again. It passed only feet above the heads of the assault force as they waited for the order to attack. The arrester parachute was deployed and the glider crashed into a bomb cratered orchard near the Firm Base.

> *On crossing the French coast, ack-ack and small arms fire, while gliding in, hit [us]. Then the corporal sitting opposite to me, and showing half his arm, next held my hand and said, 'Tug I've been hit.' It was machine-gun fire, he had been hit from the wrist up to the elbow. The corporal's name I can't remember, but I believe he lost that left arm. We crashed outside the battery, the glider broke up, and I fell into a bomb crater.*
>
> PRIVATE JAMES TUGWELL, A COY 9 PARA

But their troubles were not yet over, as the sound of a German patrol was soon heard approaching along the lane near the glider. It would seem that these were German reinforcements heading towards the battery. Lieutenant Pond immediately dispersed his men on either side of the lane and opened fire on the patrol. The Germans scattered and began returning fire. By this time the assault on the battery had already started.

Since they had no sappers or mine-detectors to clear the minefield, or tapes to mark the lanes, the first Trowbridge party had cleared, as best they could, four lanes through the minefield. This they managed to do by using their bare hands and marking the safe areas by digging up the ground with the heel of their boots.[1] Once this had been accomplished the path was clear for the few Bangalores that had been recovered to be put through the inner barbed wire fence ready for detonation to clear two gaps in the barbed wire. Private 'Bob' Abel was in one group assigned to clear the left hand gap.

> *My actual task, with nine other lads in the section, was to breach the wire around the battery with Bangalores. When the command for the attack was given, Jerry was already opening up with machine-guns, but we just ran through the perimeter wire which was already down and just followed the path through the minefield. I remember seeing bomb craters everywhere, but we didn't stop until we reached the concertina wire. When we reached the wire we pushed our Bangalores under the wire.*
>
> PRIVATE ROBERT 'BOB' J. ABEL, B COY 9 PARA

Clearing the right hand gap was Sergeant Len Daniels, men were also assigned the job of holding back the barbed wire once it had been cut by the explosion. Lieutenant Colonel Otway witnessed the glider miss the battery. Nevertheless, at 0430hrs,

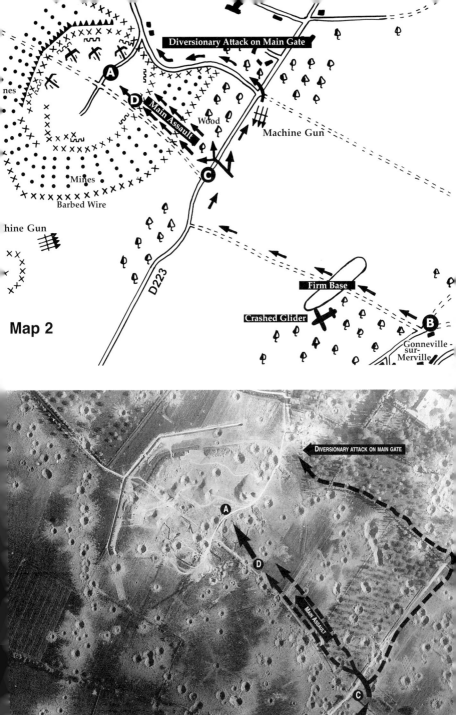

Diversionary Attack on Main Gate

A

D

Main Assault

Wood

Machine Gun

nes

Mines

Barbed Wire

hine Gun

C

D223

Firm Base

Crashed Glider

B

Gonneville-
sur-
Merville

Map 2

DIVERSIONARY ATTACK ON MAIN GATE

A

D

Main Assault

C

he gave the order to attack. Major Parry blew his whistle signalling that the Bangalore torpedoes were to be detonated.

Our Second in Command, Captain Greenway, set the fuse. Having blown the wire, the assault parties went through to attack the casemates. Our section stayed outside in a defensive position until after the attack.

PRIVATE ROBERT 'BOB' J. ABEL, B COY 9 PARA

The deafening explosion created two 20ft (6m) gaps in the barbed wire. Otway immediately gave the order to attack.

Immediately his words were 'Get in. Get in.'... In the next ten minutes, or maybe more, I seemed to be deafened by the noise of the battle and confusion which was now going on, as I found myself running and looking for cover, seeing Germans running here and there. In all this I seemed to have run into a mortar bomb and I'm afraid that's as far as I got, plus a couple of bullets of which one passed through my arm, which stopped my advance.

Captain The Hon Paul Greenway.

PRIVATE WALTER JOHNSON, C COY 9 PARA

With only one medium Vickers machine-gun left after the drop Sergeant 'Sammy' McGeever, Corporal Jim McGuinness and Private Fenson had been assigned the task of covering the left flank of the assault.

We were at the rear of the battery as we came into the open field, Jerry opened up with his machine-gun, a good job he used tracers, he missed us by about three feet, everyone including myself jumped into a bomb crater. But when McGeever called to get the bloody gun into action, Fenson ran out, mounted the tripod, I put the gun on, he loaded and McGeever gave the range, then the order to fire. We heard no more from the machine-gun. By then the battalion were advancing on the battery. We stayed until they came out.

CORPORAL JIM MCGUINNESS, MACHINE-GUN PL 9 PARA

In addition the breaching and assaulting parties also had supporting fire provided by Bren gunners and snipers. These men had been moved up with the main assault force and had taken up positions by the battery perimeter wire.

80

As we moved forward it was obvious that various machine-gun positions had been prepared around the area and this caused some initial trouble but some Bren fire soon silenced them. The assault groups were moving in to my right, firing as they went, but the wire, bomb craters and minefield made slow going. I moved to the entrance of the gun emplacement but there was plenty of activity inside with bodies milling around.... Germans were running out of the exit and being picked off as they went. Another party of B Coy was now moving into the area to mop up the rest of the garrison, whilst noise could be heard from the main gate area where our diversion party was keeping the enemy busy. Explosions from the four gun emplacements signified that the guns were receiving treatment mainly by the use of the Gammon bombs.

COMPANY SERGEANT MAJOR JACK HARRIES, A COY 9 PARA

The assault force charged through the perimeter fence and across the bomb cratered fields. As they crossed the minefield, not all were able to see the crudely marked lanes. Inevitably some were crippled or killed as they stood on mines. Along with the deafening sounds of machine-guns and the exploding mines the night sky was also now lit by the flares fired by the German sentries. In addition the Germans soon began shelling the perimeter of the battery.

At the time of the attack *Stabsfeldwebel* Büskotte was in the command post. After hearing the attack he immediately contacted *Oberleutnant* Raimund Steiner, the Merville Battery

Stabsfeldwebel Büskotte in the grounds of Château de Merville.

Oberleutnant **Raimund Steiner, Commander of the Merville Battery.**

Commander, who was in the observation bunker nearly 1.5 miles (2.41km) away on the beach. After Steiner had received the telephone call he contacted another battery at Cabourg and asked them to lay down shellfire on the perimeter of the Merville Battery.[2]

Walk back to and through the entrance of the Merville Battery, stop at Point D (Map 2, p.79) just to the left of the concrete platform on which now stands the British 5.5in (139.7mm) medium gun. From here you have the same view that Lieutenant Colonel Otway had as he commanded the assault on the battery.

Lieutenant Colonel Otway in the meantime had taken up a position just inside the battery to the right of one of the gaps blown in the barbed wire fencing. From here he was able to observe the battle as it unfolded. However, this was a dangerous position he was nearly hit by at least two bullets. One having passed through his smock and another hitting his water bottle.[3]

> *My three skeleton platoons had been quickly reorganized into one breaching platoon and went through the well practised routine, opening a gap for C Coy to assault. Soon after this Terence Otway ordered me to sort out a machine-gun half left of the axis of the assault. The rest of my company being committed to the gap they had blown, I set off with my batman in the direction indicated. I had not gone more than 50 to 100yds [46m-91m] when a bullet clipped a nerve behind my left knee incapacitating me.*
> MAJOR HAROLD BESTLEY, OFFICER COMMANDING B COY 9 PARA

82

As his men were entering the casemates they overpowered the defenders in hand to hand fighting. Otway decided to send in his reserve force to deal with the rest of the German machine-guns that were killing his men. During the chaos of the battle it was impossible to discern what was happening or who was winning. Bodies lay scattered around the battlefield as the men charged into the casemates. It was important to keep up the momentum once the attack had started, so the men were under orders not to stop and help anyone who was hit during the attack. These men were to be left for the six medical orderlies to deal with.

> *I being a medical went in a few minutes after the attack. My God what a terrible sight. I thought I could stand anything like dead men, arms and legs blown off, men crying for their mums. I couldn't. It made me feel sick and I am sure I was. I then helped and did what I could with the aid of the other medics.*
> CORPORAL 'DOUG' TOTTLE, MEDICAL ORDERLY, A COY 9 PARA

Once inside the casemates the men were surprised to find 100mm (3.94in) Czech howitzers instead of the 150mm (5.91in) calibre weapons they had expected. Nevertheless, they set about

Czech howitzer of the type the attackers found in the gun emplacements at the Merville Battery – 100mm calibre weapons instead of the 150mm guns they had expected.

making the guns inoperable, using their Gammon grenades. The explosives were placed, the fuses set and they all exited the casemate to avoid the blasts of the explosions. They then returned through the thick acrid smoke to check that the guns were damaged beyond repair should the Germans reoccupy the battery later. By now the fight had gone out of the Germans in the garrison and those that were still alive surrendered.

Lieutenant Colonel Otway surveyed the battlefield to ensure that their mission had been accomplished. As he did so the medics were treating the wounded that littered the battlefield and beginning to make arrangements to move them out.

> *I glanced at the huge guns of the battery itself and saw the lads marching out the German prisoners who had, after some hand to hand fighting, surrendered. At that moment I heard cries from within the minefield. It was from Captain Hudson, the adjutant. Scared stiff, I ran through the minefield and did what I could for him. He was very badly wounded and I was unable to move him on my own. I looked up and the prisoners were being marched along the mine free lane, I called out for some help and the corporal in charge ordered two of the Germans over to help me. They refused to walk through the minefield. This was soon sorted out by a few bursts of fire at their heels. With their help I managed to get Captain Hudson and a lot more of the lads out of the battery area.*
>
> CORPORAL 'DOUG' TOTTLE, MEDICAL ORDERLY, A COY 9 PARA

The walking wounded made their way out mostly unassisted. One of them, Major Parry, decided to go and check on the damage to the other guns before he left. As he moved off Lieutenant Dennis Slade, himself wounded, reported that all the guns had been spiked. He also reminded Parry that HMS *Arethusa* needed to be contacted with the success signal otherwise the 6in (152.4mm) guns of the battleship would open up on the battery. Since no naval signallers had arrived at the battery there was only a carrier pigeon and some smoke flares.

The carrier pigeon was carried under the battledress of Lieutenant James 'Jimmy' Loring, the signals officer. He pulled the pigeon out and let it go. After circling the battery twice it flew off, in the wrong direction!* The yellow smoke flares were also set off and it was hoped that these would be seen by reconnaissance aircraft from the Fleet Air Arm who were to fly

---

* The pigeon arrived safely back in England the following day.

84

To Gonneville-en-Auge (originally Gonneville-sur-Merville)

To the Merville Battery →

The road along which Otway's assault force gathered.

Point C Map 2, p.79. The track leading to the Merville Battery. Otway's men attacked across the minefield to the right of this track.

Merville Battery

Gonneville-en-Auge

Site of minefield over which Otway led his attack

Track to Battery

View from the machine-gun post on top of No. 1 casemate.

The front of No. 3 casemate.

sorties over the area before the bombardment began.[4] However, nothing could be left to chance. The order was given to evacuate the battery area.[†]

> *Moving back to a bomb crater occupied already by two men, one an officer, name of Parry, I was joined shortly after by a sergeant, who cut open my sleeve with his fighting knife and applied a field dressing to the wound. Shortly after we moved the wounded to a house not far from the battery where I spent some time collecting grenades from the wounded and stacking them outside.*
>
> PRIVATE TOM STROUD, BREN GUNNER, C COY 9 PARA

As the survivors assembled the cost was counted. From the 150 men who attacked the battery only about eighty walked away.[5] The Germans, too, had sustained heavy casualties and later *Oberleutnant* Steiner confirmed that out of the 130 men who had manned the garrison that evening only six remained unwounded and able to continue with their duties.[6]

The speed and ferocity of the assault on the battery left some of those who survived with memories of turmoil, which has through time, taken on an almost dreamlike quality. The resulting flashbacks of the assault, however, will remain etched into their memories forever.

> *The stench of dead cows. Seeing a glider circle the battery before passing over our heads and crashing into an orchard. As we approached the battery two machine-guns opened up on us from our right and a sergeant told me to get them with the Bren. I fired, first from the hip and then on his instructions from the more accurate position on the ground until both machine-guns ceased firing. Running on then into the battery and towards an emplacement on my right, hearing an officer shouting at me to get down and then seeing him immediately get up and kick the backside of a German. Running forward again into the gun emplacement until stopped by a bullet which promptly sat me hard on my backside. My left arm being useless, giving the Bren*

† There was some confusion over orders given with regards HMS *Arethusa* and the naval bombardment of the Merville Battery. Commander Kenneth Edwards, Royal Navy, in his book *OPERATION NEPTUNE,* reports that HMS *Arethusa* was initially told to open fire on the battery unless she received orders stating that it had been captured. Then she was told not to open fire unless she was certain it had been captured. With the issue of the second order she could not be sure of the situation and so, in the event, did not open fire. It would appear Lieutenant Colonel Otway was not aware of the countermanding order and so, without radio contact to confirm the success of his attack, he hastily evacuated the area.

9 Para with some German Prisoners.

to Colville and thinking I must remember his name because I had signed for it.

PRIVATE TOM STROUD, BREN GUNNER, C COY 9 PARA

Having overcome overwhelming odds the men of 9 Para had proved themselves in battle beyond any doubt. Later, the name Merville would be one of many names added to the regiment's battle honours. It is this battle, though, that will provide inspiration to future generations in the armed forces, and particularly to members of The Parachute Regiment, and show what can be achieved by a small, highly trained force whatever odds may be stacked against it.

It was time to pull out as time was limited and, glancing back, the battery area was strangely silent with men moving slowly out, some wounded and others quite still on the ground where they had fallen. The remaining German prisoners were being herded together and taken out of the area. The impression was of all passion spent but I personally felt strangely privileged and maybe a little satisfaction that I had been a member of this unit who had, I feel, achieved all that was asked of them.

COMPANY SERGEANT MAJOR JACK HARRIES, A COY 9 PARA

AFTERMATH

After the battle those who were able to move made their way to the second RV. This was at the Calvary (see Ch. 6, A1) which is situated at the junction of the D223 and D95a about 0.5 miles (0.8km) south of the battery. Once here Otway took stock of the situation and moved on to his next objective which was around the high ground of le Plain (aka le Plein) near Amfréville. On approach to the village it was discovered that it was held strongly by the enemy. Otway's depleted force increased to about 100 men as more stragglers joined his force. However, the Germans inflicted further casualties in the fight for the village. Although Otway had too few men to overpower the German defenders completely, 9 Para were able to take half the village. Thereafter there was a period of watching and waiting by both sides until reinforcements from 3 Cdo arrived. [7]

igadier James Hill DSO MC.

But it had not just been the operation to destroy the guns at Merville that had been severely disrupted because of the disastrous parachute drop the previous night. Otway's own commander had also had great difficulty in reaching his objective. Brigadier James Hill, commander of 3 Para Bde, had landed in several feet of water in a flooded field near Cabourg,[8] several miles away from his intended destination. By 0600hrs he had finally found his way to the DZ near Varaville and made contact with 1 Cdn Para Bn. From there he decided to make his way to where 9 Para should be and find out how their attack on the Merville Battery had gone.

I had with me my brigade defence platoon commander, two parachute sailors who were part of our wireless link with the bombardment ship and one of our parachute Alsatian dogs, together with some thirty-five good chaps. We were making good progress and were encouraged by the tremendous din of the preliminary bombardment which the beach defences were undergoing. We were walking down a lane when I suddenly heard a horrible staccato sound approaching from the seaward side of the hedge. I shouted to everybody to fling themselves down and then we were caught in the middle of a pattern of anti-personnel bombs dropped by a large group of aircraft which appeared to be our own Spitfires... The lane had no ditches to speak of and I flung myself on top of a young officer who had been one of my sergeants when I commanded the 1st Parachute Battalion in North Africa. Something seemed to hit me very hard on the backside and, when the dust and foul stench of cordite had almost disappeared and the shattering din had died down, I looked round and saw a leg lying beside me. I then saw that the boot was a brown one and therefore it could not be mine. After stumbling to my feet, I found one other man who was able to stand, namely my defence platoon commander, and the lane was littered for many yards with the bodies of groaning and badly injured men.

BRIGADIER JAMES HILL, COMMANDER, 3 PARA BDE

The two officers set about injecting the wounded with morphia to ease their suffering. They also removed the morphia phials from the dead and gave them to the wounded to be used later. Then they set off to find 9 Para. Two hours later they found

Major John B.V. Pooley.

Captain 'Harold' Watts, the Medical Officer of 9 Para, who promptly gave the brigadier some temporary first aid treatment and told him about their success at the Merville Battery. It was later discovered that the aircraft that strafed them were Typhoons on sorties to disrupt any enemy movement behind the lines. Unfortunately, the pilot had mistaken the group of British paratroopers for a German patrol.

The following day it was believed that the Germans had managed to get the battery operational again after some shellfire landed on SWORD Beach. Two troops of 3 Cdo were ordered to retake it. Under the command of Lieutenant Colonel Peter Young, twenty-five year old Major John B.V. Pooley, 2ic, stormed the battery with No. 4 and No. 5 Troop. They

Temporary graves of those killed in the 'friendly fire' attack on Brigadier Hill's group.

managed to overpower the small garrison that had retaken the position after Lieutenant Colonel Otway's attack, but within minutes the Germans put in a strong counter-attack with SP guns. The commandos fought bravely, but were outnumbered and forced to retreat back to le Plain. This they did after losing half their men in the action. Major Pooley was one of the last to be killed.[9] He was posthumously awarded the Military Cross and now rests in Bayeux Commonwealth War Cemetery (plot XXIV, row F, grave 2).

Three months later Brigadier James Hill ordered Major Crookenden, who had by that time taken over command of 9 Para, to send a party out to the lane where he had been wounded in an attempt to locate and bury the bodies of the rest of his men. Major Allen Parry, CO of A Coy, went out with a party which included the Padre, Reverend Captain John Gwinnett. The soldiers were soon found, having been roughly

Rev Captain John Gwinnett.

91

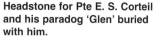

Headstone for Pte E. S. Corteil and his paradog 'Glen' buried with him.

Pte Emile Corteil and his paradog 'Glen'.

buried in a bomb crater. Among them were nineteen year old Private Emile Corteil and his paradog 'Glen'. Having identified nearly all the bodies, they were all reinterred and their location passed on to the graves registration and concentration units. Eventually the remains were moved to their final resting place at Ranville War Cemetery (see Battleground Europe book *Pegasus Bridge & Horsa Bridge* Ch. 7, B1).

Finally, take some time to explore the grounds of the Merville Battery. The four casemates are accessible and now form an integral part of the museum as a whole (see Ch. 5, D).

CHAPTER FIVE

Memorial Tour of the 6th Airborne Division Battlefield No. 1

Sallenelles to Merville Battery

Distance between stops by vehicle: 4.25 miles (6.84km)
Total walking distance at stops: Approx 1.5miles (2.41km)
Recommended time allowed for tour: 3 to 4 hours

If your arrival in France is by ferry at Ouistreham then head for Pegasus Bridge. This can be found by taking the D514 to Bénouville. Alternatively, if you are approaching from Caen, take the D515 (signposted for Ouistreham car ferry) until you see the sign for Bénouville on the D514. Take this road, go straight on at the roundabout and you will see the new Pegasus Bridge in front of you over the Caen Canal. Continue across Pegasus Bridge and across Horsa Bridge and at the next roundabout take the third exit, continuing along the D514 for approximately 2.3 miles (3.7km) until you reach the village of Sallenelles.

This tour begins in the village of Sallenelles. Drive into the village and turn right at the crossroads onto the D37b and drive for approximately 520 yards (475m) up to the top of the hill.

A. Sallenelles

On the left-hand side of the road, on a marble plinth and between two flag poles, is a bronze:

1) Memorial Plaque to No. 4 Special Service Bde. This memorial is dedicated to the men of 4 SS Bde HQ, 41,46,47 & 48 RM Cdo who gave their lives in the fighting, from June to August 1944, while holding positions in this area.

Drive back down into Sallenelles and turn right at the crossroads back onto the D514. Approximately 130 yards (119m) on the left-hand side of the road on the boundary wall between houses No. 13 and No. 15, and beneath a lamppost, there is a:

2) Memorial Plaque to Edouard Gérard. This memorial is in memory of the first Belgian soldier of the *1 Belgian Piron Bde* to be killed in Normandy on 16 August 1944. Only twenty years old he was also the youngest member of the regiment to be killed in Normandy.

Continue to drive along the D514 for about 175 yards (160m) and on the left there is a stone:

3) 1 Belgian Bde and Colonel Jean Piron Memorial. This

Total area covered in four car tours

For simplicity the following four tours are shown as one continuous route. However, with the use of the area titles the tour can easily be picked up at any point. Individual memorials and places of interest can be easily found using the list in Appendix D. This also gives individual satellite navigation coordinates to help with location.

OUISTREHAM

St-Aubin d'Arquonay

D514

Bénouville

Pegasus Bridge

Horsa

D515

Ch6 H

Longueval

D223

D

Ste Hon la Chardro

One of the gliderborne troopers of A Coy 9 Para wi German prisoner on the roa to Sallenelles (D514). Note the skull and crossbones or the front of his smock. This was painted wth luminescer paint to help distinguish A Coy from German troops after their planned glider landing within the Merville Battery.

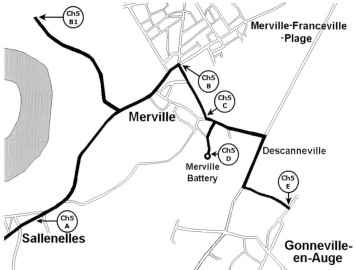

memorial is dedicated to the Belgian and Luxembourg soldiers of *1 Brigade Belge* and their commander Colonel Jean Piron. Otherwise known as the *Brigade Piron*, or *1 Belgian Piron Bde*, they were No. 4 Troop of the multinational 10 (IA) Cdo.

Sallenelles was the scene of heavy fighting for the Piron Bde between 14 August and 17 August. It was during this time they took their first casualties. On the stone memorial there is also a plaque dedicated, in 2004, by the people of Sallenelles to those from *Brigade Piron* who lost their lives for the liberation of Sallenelles. Those named are: Réne de Queker, Henri Duchesnes, Edouard Gérard, Petrus J. L. Harboort, Julius Leysen and Raymond Vanremoortele (see Ch. 5, B5, D21 & Battleground Europe book *Pegasus Bridge & Horsa Bridge* Ch. 7, B1, B8 & B18).

Continue along the D514 for 0.5 miles (0.8km) and on your left you will see some German bunkers that were originally part of a:

4) German Naval Radar Station. These bunkers have now been turned into a nightclub called The Bunker. In 1944 it was one of the objectives assigned to Lieutenant Colonel Otway and the men of 9 Para. However, after the attack on the Merville Battery Otway decided that his remaining force would be put to better use in taking the more important secondary objective of the high ground near Amfréville.

German naval radar station now a nightclub called The Bunker.

B. Merville-Franceville-Plage

Continue along the D514 and at approximately 800 yards (732m) take the next left turning, immediately after the pumping station and signposted Base Nautique de Franceville. Follow the road down to the car park, by the beach, in the Estuaire de L'Orne. Warning! Do not leave any valuables in your car in this area. From the northernmost point of the car park there is, approximately 130 yards (119m) due north, a large German bunker (type *H612*), one of many in this area. Continue past this, turn right and follow the first stretch of open sand that runs between the brushwood-covered sand dunes heading due north-east for a further 200 yards (183m) this will bring you to a reinforced concrete shelter observation post. It is this position that it is most widely believed to have been used as:

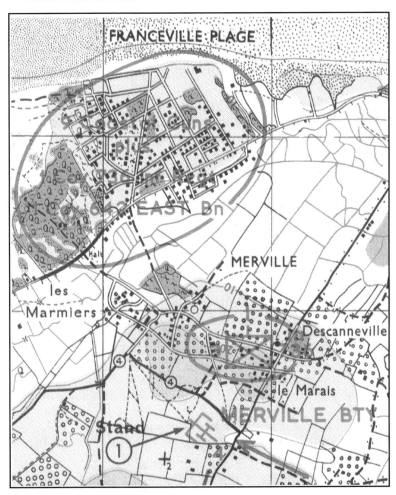

1) *The Merville Battery Observation Post.* From this bunker, in 1944, the Orne Canal locks, Ouistreham, SWORD Beach and, later, the massive Allied naval fleet could be clearly seen. Firing orders would have been passed to the Merville Battery via underground armoured covered telephone cable. On 6 June 1944 *Oberleutnant* Raimund Steiner, commander of the Merville Battery, was in his observation bunker and was awoken by a telephone call in the early hours with news that the battery was under attack (see Ch. 5, D28). This area of beach, east of the Orne Estuary, was not a designated landing beach on D-Day for the Allies. Although the Allies made swift progress on SWORD Beach, the start of which can be seen if you look west to the other side of the Orne Estuary, the bunkers on this side of the Orne Estuary were not abandoned by the Germans until mid-August 1944.

There are many bunkers in this immediate area as it was one of the many large fortified areas that formed part of Hitler's *Festung Europa*. This particular strongpoint had been identified as *Wiederstandnest* (*WN*), aka *Stützpunkt* (*Stp*), *05*. Its position here provided defence for the eastern flank of the Orne Estuary and Ouistreham. Amongst the many reinforced concrete structures are a variety of gun casemates, personnel shelters, tobruk pits and observation bunkers. The fire protection would come from the two type *H506* casemates and the one type *H612*. The latter was positioned to provide enfilade fire across the Orne Estuary. The observation bunker for the Merville Battery was within this fortified complex.

The sand dunes, dense scrub and undergrowth can make access up to some of these positions difficult though and the ever-changing terrain periodically covers and uncovers the many defence positions at different times of the year. All entrances to bunkers are blocked up and so no efforts should be made to try and enter any of them.

Within the area of the German strongpoint complex there is also an ancient coastal defence battery, today surrounded by high sand dunes. Although not an integral part of the German fortifications the Germans had mounted a tank turret on top of the fort and which can be clearly seen today if standing on the surrounding sand dune. It is most likely the Germans would have used the building for storing supplies as well. This impressive fortification is often credited as the work of *Marshal* Sebastien le Pestre de Vauban (1633-1707) and is sometimes

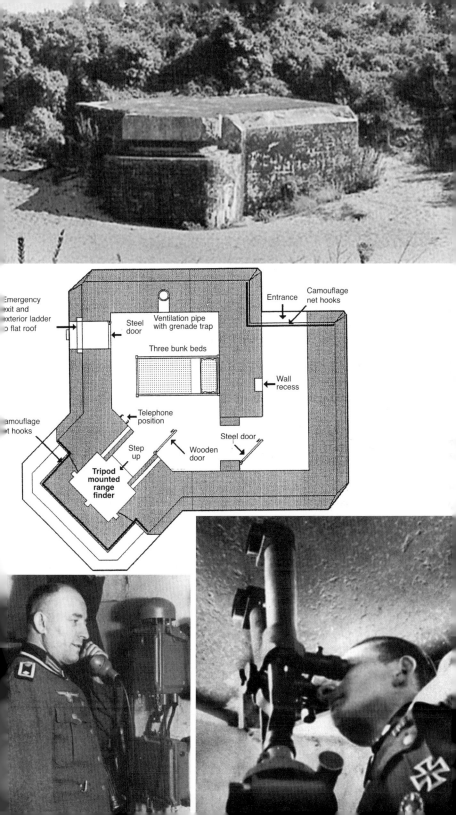

Emergency exit and exterior ladder to flat roof

Entrance

Camouflage net hooks

Steel door

Ventilation pipe with grenade trap

Three bunk beds

Wall recess

Camouflage net hooks

Telephone position

Steel door

Wooden door

Step up

Tripod mounted range finder

referred to as the *Vauban Redoubt de Merville*. It was, however, actually built in the late eighteenth century (1779), many years after the death of the famous military architect, but built in part, to his original designs. Vauban does have another connection with twentieth century warfare as he is also credited with the invention of the bayonet in 1689.

Return to your vehicle and drive back onto the D515 turning left towards Merville-Franceville-Plage. Continue until you reach the roundabout and take the first exit on your right. Parking spaces are available on your left after the turning. On the opposite side of the road you will see a number of memorials between four flagpoles, including from left to right:

2) No. 45 Royal Marine Commando Memorial. This is dedicated to the thirty-five men of 45 RM Cdo who were killed in Merville-Franceville in between 6 and 8 June 1944. Next, to your right, is a:

3) Memorial to Allied Soldiers and Merville-Franceville Civilians. This was presented by the *Comité du Débarquement,* in memory of those civilians and Allied soldiers killed in this area between June and August 1944. To your right there is:

4) Merville-Franceville Village Memorial. This memorial is dedicated to the local inhabitants who lost their lives fighting in both the First and Second World Wars. It has also been placed here in memory of those civilians who lost their lives after being deported or in the fighting during the 1940s. Next on the right is:

5) Belgian Piron Brigade Memorial. Placed in memory of the two Belgian NCOs, *Sergent* Zenon Boon and *Sergent* Francois Raquet, and the two privates, *Soldat* Guy Poncelet and *Soldat* Raymond de Ridder, of *1 Belgian Piron Bde.* All were killed in Merville-Franceville on 18 August 1944 during the fighting for its liberation.

Return to your car and continue to drive through the village and along the *Avenue Alexandre de Lavergne* and follow the signs for *Musée de la Batterie de Merville*. On entering the small village of Merville follow the road around to your left and 50 yards (46m) on your left is:

C. Merville Churchyard

On the right hand gatepost leading into Merville churchyard there is a:

Merville Church.

1) Commonwealth War Graves Commission Plaque. This green plaque with white writing has been placed here by the CWGC to signify that within the churchyard grounds there are buried members of the Commonwealth forces. In this particular churchyard there is an:

2) Unknown First World War Soldier's Headstone. This casualty, with the distinctive white Portland stone headstone, is an unknown soldier of The Great War from the Royal Army Medical Corps. There was no fighting in this area of France during the First World War, and CWGC documents record that this drowned body was found on the 3 August 1917. There is also one other CWGC headstone in this churchyard:

3) Sergeant A.K. Eley and RAF Aircrew Headstone. The only confirmed identified casualty in this burial plot is RAF Lancaster air gunner, Sergeant Alban Kenneth Eley. He is recorded as having died on 18 April 1943. The remaining five unidentified casualties are recorded as having died on 19 April 1943. RAF aircrew records detail all the crew as killed on 18 April 1943.

These six men were part of the seven-man crew of Lancaster Mk I GT-W4849 from No. 156 Sqn RAF. This squadron was part of Pathfinder Force No. 8 Group. At 2121hrs on 18 April 1943 this Lancaster crew, piloted by Sergeant Godfrey S. Cooper, took off from RAF Warboys in Cambridgeshire along with twelve other aircraft. Their objective was la Spezia in the Liguria region on the west coast of northern Italy. During their mission Sergeant Cooper and his crew were reported missing off the French Coast. They had joined No. 156 Sqn less than four weeks previous on 23 March. The remaining twelve aircraft and crew all returned safely from their mission.

Only six of the seven bodies were recovered from Sergeant Cooper's crashed Lancaster, and only one body, Sergeant Eley, was identified. The remaining crew are now commemorated on the RAF Runnymede Memorial in Surrey, UK: Sergeant G.S. Cooper and twenty-one year old Sergeant K. Coulson on Panel 146; twenty-two year old Sgt D.R. Edwards on Panel 148; twenty year old Sergeant R. Harrison on Panel 152, twenty year old Sergeant J.J. Vaulkhard on Panel 168 and twenty-one year old Sergeant N.O. Robinson (RCAF) on Panel 185.

Before D-Day 156 Sqn had lost 132 aircraft and by the end of the war a total of 153 Halifax, Lancaster and Mosquito aircraft had been lost along with a total of 891 aircrew killed.

The Runnymede Memorial is dedicated to the 20,331 airmen who were lost in Second World War operations and who have no known grave.

Although not officially identified as being buried here in Merville Churvh Yard, there is also at the base of Sergeant Eley and his comrades headstone a:

4) Memorial Plaque to Sergeant J.J. Vaulkhard. In the churchyard there are a number of graves to locals who were killed during the war. Among them is:

5) Andre Alexandre's Headstone. Andre was a young nine year old boy who was killed during an Allied bombardment on the 20 April 1944. There is also another grave marked by:

6) Jacques Auradou's Headstone. Master Pilot Auradou served with the French Navy and was killed on 2 May 1945. You will notice in this churchyard a number of identical plaques that have been placed on the graves of certain individuals. These are:

7) Les Anciens Combattants Prisonniers de Guerre Plaques. These memorial plaques have a piece of barbed wire laid over the *tricolore* along the top and are presented by a French organisation of old comrades that were once prisoners of war. They are now placed on the graves of their fellow comrades who have died since the war. On another grave there is:

8) Les Rescapes Du Marquis Des Glières Plaque. This memorial plaque, dedicated to Monsieur Serge Aubert, is placed here in memory of him having survived his involvement with the *Maquis des Glières*, a Free French resistance group, during February and March 1944.

From the churchyard continue driving along for approximately 200 yards (183m) and take the next right turn along *Avenue de la Batterie de Merville*. After another 200 yards (183m) this leads to a circular driveway around which you may park. At the far end of the driveway there is:

D. The Merville Battery Museum

For a detailed explanation of the battle, and alternative tour of the battlefield, see Ch. 3 & 4.

Before you enter the museum, via the wooden building, there are a number of memorials in the gardens and on the grassed area. In addition, in the centre of the circular drive there is:

1) 9 Para Memorial. This memorial commemorates 9 Para and the supporting arms of the Royal Navy, Army and Royal Air Force who attacked the Merville Battery at 0500hrs on 6 June, thus preventing them from firing on the assault beaches. Back towards the entrance and to the left of the wooden building there is:

2) OVERLORD l'Assault Marker No 1. This is one of many markers of a route called *OVERLORD l'Assault* (OVERLORD, The Assault).

9 Para Memorial.

On each marker there is a brief explanation in both French and English of what happened in this particular area. This forms just one of eight such self-guided trails, provided by the *Comité Departemental Du Tourisme Du Calvados* (*CDT Calvados*), *CDT Manche* and *CDT Orne*, that covers the whole area of Normandy that is associated with the Normandy Campaign. A free information booklet/map called The D-Day Landings And The

Battle For Normandy can be picked up at most museums and tourist information outlets in Normandy. This particular trail finishes at the *Musée Mémorial de la Bataille de Normandie* (Memorial for The Battle of Normandy Museum), in Bayeaux.

To the right of the gateway that leads into the Merville Battery, there are some information boards that detail various aspects of the battery. To the right of these are a number of memorials. The first, under an oak tree, is:

3) *Major Charles Strafford Memorial Plaque.* This oak tree was planted, and memorial plaque unveiled, on 5 June 1999 in memory of Major Charles Strafford (see Battleground Europe *Book Pegasus Bridge & Horsa Bridge* Ch. 7, B15 & B19). Next along is a small conifer tree in front of which is:

4) *Sergeant Roy William Wright Memorial Plaque (1).* Sergeant Wright, 9 Para, passed away in 2008. This tree was planted in his memory and the memorial plaque erected. Sergeant Wright had been wounded in Normandy during the fighting around the *Château d'Amfréville* and le Plain. Next along, beneath another tree there is:

5) *Lieutenant Barney Ross Memorial Plaque.* This plaque is dedicated to Lieutenant Ross who was a Company Sergeant Major in 9 Para during the attack on the Merville Battery and who led the attack on No. 3 casemate. He passed away in 2005. Next along, beneath another oak tree is:

6) *Lieutenant Colonel Terence Otway Memorial Plaque.* The oak tree was planted on 6 June 2007 in memory of the CO of 9 Para. Lieutenant Colonel Otway passed away on 23 July 2006, aged ninety-two years. To your right beneath the next tree is:

Sergeant Sidney Frank Capon.

7) *Major William 'Bill' Mills Memorial Plaque (1).* This tree was planted on 5 June 2006 in memory of Major 'Bill' Mills who passed away in 2005. As a captain in Normandy he was engaged in the heavy fighting around the *Bois des Monts* (see Ch. 6, D5) while defending the ridge there. Beneath the next tree to your right there is:

8) *Sergeant Sidney Frank Capon Memorial Plaque.* This tree was planted on 6 June 2007 in memory of Sergeant Sid Capon, 9 Para, who passed away on 9

September 2006, aged eighty-two years. Sergeant Capon was in the party that attacked No. 1 casemate on D-Day. He was later seriously wounded by shrapnel in July 1944 (see Ch. 6, D7). Behind where you now stand are two wooden benches. On the first there is, on the backrest, a second:

9) *Major William 'Bill' Mills Memorial Plaque (2)*. This wooden bench was donated by his wife. Behind this bench is another bench and on the backrest is a second:

10) *Sergeant Roy Wright Memorial Plaque (2)*. This wooden bench was donated by his wife and family. Now make your way through the wooden building and into the small gift shop. A small admission charge is payable at the desk. As you walk through the building follow the footpath that leads to:

11) *No. 1 Casemate.* This is a type *H611* casemate which is the largest of the four casemates on this site. Unusually this battery has three different types of casemates housing its four guns – further information can be found at www.atlanticwall.org. The site itself has been identified as WN01 of Normandy's section of *Festung Europa*. It was occupied by No. 1 Battery of *Artillerie Regiment 1716* of *716 Infanterie Division*. The battery was started in 1941 and although designed for medium calibre guns of approximately 150mm (5.91in), at the time of the attack on the Merville Battery, it housed 100mm (3.94in) guns.

No. 1 casemate.

One of the Czech Skoda 100mm L FH 14/19 (t) field guns inside the Merville Battery.

Inside No. 1 casemate you can experience, at twenty minute intervals, a sound and light show that recreates the attack on the Merville Battery. In between these shows you may have a look around this part of the museum and see the many artefacts and memorabilia, now on display, that have been donated by veterans or excavated from the site during its restoration.

At the far end of the casemate there is a Czechoslovakian Skoda 100mm (3.94in) *L FH* (*Leichte Feldhaubitze*) 14/19 *(t)* field gun. After consultation with German veterans, and with evidence from archive documents and ammunition found in the area, it has now been established that this was representative of the type of artillery piece that was in place at the battery during the raid on 6 June 1944. It had previously been believed, and therefore documented in some publications, that they were French 75mm (2.95in) M 1897 field guns. The Skoda Field Gun in the museum is now positioned as it would have been when ready for firing onto SWORD Beach. These guns had a range of 10,717 yards (9,800m), some 6 miles (9.8km). A well trained crew could fire eight 35lbs (16kg) rounds per minute onto a target.

Display of Belgian equipment.

Because of the size of the concrete casemates, British intelligence had led the paratroopers to believe that they would house guns of approximately 150mm (5.91in). Nevertheless, the Czech 100mm (3.94in) guns had sufficient range to wreak havoc among the troops who landed on SWORD Beach, which is only 4 miles (6.44km) to the north-west of this battery.

Inside No. 1 casemate there would be a crew of nine men to man the gun. Operating on shifts, those off duty would reside in the requisitioned properties of *Château Haras de Retz* (see Ch. 6, A2) and *Château de Merville*. The officers had taken up off duty residence in the *Mairie* in Merville.

On the outside of the casemate, to the left of the entrance, there is a marble:

12) *No. 3 Commando Memorial Plaque.* This plaque commemorates the men of 3 Cdo who fought on this site on 7 June 1944 (see Ch. 4 & Ch. 5, D 18). At the top of the footpath leading down into No. 1 casemate there is the:

13) *Combatants of all Nationalities Memorial.* This memorial is dedicated to all those who fought and died on the site of the Merville Battery. This was dedicated on 5 June 2007.

Nearby there is an information stand one of many along the footpath around the battery, these will provide you with further information about this particular casemate and other points of interest around the battery. Continue along the footpath until

No. 2, 360°, open gun platform. The author's daughter, Hannah, gives a sense of scale. Beyond left, is the area 9 Para launched their attack.

you reach the second information stand. This gives details of:

14) No. 2 360° Open Gun Platform. The concrete platform provided a base for an open gun that was adapted to suit the type of gun that was sited there. With the gun mounted on the raised concrete centre block, the sunken pit of the gun platform was designed to collect spent shell cases so they would not interfere with the movement of the gun. Continue along the footpath until you come to the third information stand for:

15) No. 2 Casemate. This is type *H612*. The information stand provides you with details about the construction of the casemate and the various forms of camouflage used to disguise German bunkers. Today you can still see how the concrete on the exposed part of the bunker was formed to deflect light, in addition camouflage netting, earth banks and grass would cover most of the structure to make it less detectable from the air.

Time should be taken to go inside No. 2 casemate as the interior has now been transformed into a permanent memorial to the men of 9 Para. An audio and visual documentary is shown on two TVs and includes an interview with Lieutenant Colonel Otway as well as information about the daring attack on the battery. In the far centre of the casemate, beneath the distinctive paratrooper's badge, there is a display case with the red beret and medals of Lieutenant Colonel Otway, DSO, *Chevalier de la Légion d'honneur*. These were kindly donated to the museum after he had passed away in 2006. Seat benches provide a quiet place to sit and reflect upon the heroic actions of 9 Para and after the brief documentary a roll of honour is played showing photographs of many of those who took part in the attack on the

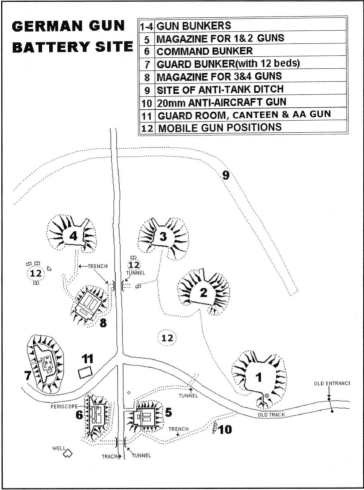

GERMAN GUN BATTERY SITE	1-4	GUN BUNKERS
	5	MAGAZINE FOR 1&2 GUNS
	6	COMMAND BUNKER
	7	GUARD BUNKER(with 12 beds)
	8	MAGAZINE FOR 3&4 GUNS
	9	SITE OF ANTI-TANK DITCH
	10	20mm ANTI-AIRCRAFT GUN
	11	GUARD ROOM, CANTEEN & AA GUN
	12	MOBILE GUN POSITIONS

Merville Battery. It is, without doubt, one of the most respectfully presented and moving memorials one can experience in Normandy.

Outside, on the top of No. 2 casemate accessed by some steps, are a number of orientation tables that provide additional information about the battery and surrounding area. Return and continue along the footpath until you come to a bench seat, just after where the footpath turns right, on the backrest there is a brass:

16) John Gooday Memorial Plaque. This was donated by his wife in memory of her late husband who was in 9 Para. Next along the footpath there is a fourth information stand for:

17) No. 3 Casemate. The second *H612* type casemate, this information stand details the stores system and the extraction and ventilation systems for the casemate. Inside there is a cockpit of a Horsa glider along with a flight simulator and documentary film. It was presented to the Merville Battery on 6 June 2008 by the Glider Pilot Association, in tribute to the glider pilots that took part in the airborne assault on D-Day. Among the other exhibits there is a framed:

18) *Memorial to No. 3 Commando.* This details the action of 3 Cdo on 7 June 1944. After some shellfire was received on SWORD Beach later in the day on 6 June, it was believed that this fire may have come from the Merville Battery. Major James Pooley, 2ic of 3 Cdo, led the attack on the battery and was killed just outside No. 1 casemate. There is now a photograph of him and of some of his troops in this framed memorial. As you walk back towards the main footpath, on your right there is:

19) *No. 3 360° Open Gun Platform.* This platform was linked to No. 3 casemate and around the edge of the circular platform you can still see the concrete ammunition storage shelters. Return to the footpath and walk along and through the tunnel underpass towards the next casemate. Left of the footpath there is a bench:

20) *Private Ronald Sydney Jepp Memorial Plaque.* Private Jepp served in the Machine-Gun Platoon, 9 Para. He was killed in action on the 12 June aged just twenty years. He is now buried in Ranville Commonwealth War Cemetery (IA, G, 15). His older brother, Private Terry Jepp, was a medic in 9 Para. Twenty-four year old Private Terry Jepp was wounded and taken prisoner, but he later escaped his captors and eventually rejoined 9 Para after the Normandy campaign. Continue along the footpath until you come to a fifth information stand for:

21) *No. 4 Casemate.* Again information is provided about the construction of the casemates. This is a type H669 casemate, but very similar in design to No. 2 and No. 3 casemates. The inside of the casemate is dedicated to *Brigade Piron*. There are many interesting exhibits including one of German mines and Allied mine-clearing equipment. Amongst the many photographs of Belgian troops there is one of the first Belgian soldier to be killed, Edouard Gérard (see Ch. 5, A2, A3, B5 and Battleground Europe book *Pegasus Bridge & Horsa Bridge* Ch. 7, B1, B8 & B18). Return to the footpath and continue until you come to the sixth information stand that is for:

22) No. 4 360° Open Gun Platform. This platform was linked to No. 4 casemate. The information board shows how underground tunnels linked the platform to No. 4 casemate and additional information about the artillery. If you walk over to the platform you will see, in the concrete on the centre circular stand, some

German Graffiti on the centre stand of No. 4, 360°, Open Gun Platform.

original German artwork. The large 'V' centred above the laurel leaves represents Fatherland as in the German *Vaterland*. The inscriptions either side of the Third Reich symbol, an eagle holding a Swastika, reads: *Deutschland mub, Leben* on the left and *Wenn auch wir Sterben*, on the right. Translated it reads Germany must live, even if we die. It is a line, with slight paraphrase, from a popular German poem called *Soldatenabschied* (Soldier's Goodbye) written by worker poet Lersch Heinrich (1889-1936). He penned the poem in 1914 after joining the German Army on the Western Front. A Roman Catholic he became an anti-Marxist and in the 1930s supported the Nazi Party. He was also the composer of a number of poems/songs that were published, in a compilation called *German Songs For The People And The Fatherland*, in 1918. Continue walking along the footpath, on the left there is a bench on the backrest is a brass:

23) Louis of 224 Para Fd Amb Memorial Plaque, donated by his wife. Farther along the footpath there is the seventh information stand for:

24) No. 3 and No. 4 Casemate Ammunition Magazine. This bunker had separate areas for storing and for preparing charges and was linked by the battery trench system. Ammunition was transported on sledges. The same sledges were used by 9 Para, after their attack, to evacuate the wounded. Continue along the footpath until you come to the eighth information stand for the:

25) Guard Bunker. Providing accommodation for the men on duty at the battery, this bunker also allowed sheltered movement via the battery trench system between emplacements. It was also protected by a machine-gun Tobruk pit that provided covering fire around this side of the battery. Continue along the footpath until you come, on your right, to a bench. On the backrest there is a brass:

26) 6th Airborne Division Memorial Plaque. This was donated by Tom Laurd to all those of the 6th Airborne Division who lost their lives in Normandy. Opposite the bench is the ninth information stand for the:

27) Canteen, Guard Room and Anti-Aircraft Gun Position. While the building provided the battery personnel with a kitchen and guard room, situated on top was a 20mm (0.79in) flak light anti-aircraft gun. This was the standard dual-purpose light anti-aircraft and anti-tank gun for the German army. It could fire 120-240 rounds per minute at a velocity of 2950 ft/sec (899m/sec). The flak gun would have a vertical range of approximately 4,155 yards (3,799m), some 2.3 miles (3.7km), but an effective target range of 2,400 yards (2,195m).

The twenty round box magazine, required a crew of seven men to keep the gun firing at maximum rate of fire. The flak gun was temporarily, sited on top of the canteen, after its own base was destroyed by an Allied bombing raid in May 1944, before it was moved to the top of the concrete roof of the battery well. Continue along the footpath until you reach the tenth information post for the:

28) Command Post. The nerve centre of the battery, this position contained the telephone exchange that linked the Merville Battery with its forward observation post on the beach near Merville-Franceville (see Ch. 5, B1) and each of the casemates so that their fire could be accurately directed. At the time of the attack on the battery by 9 Para, *Stabsfeldwebel* Johannes 'Hans' Buskotte was inside the bunker and used the periscope inside to observe the attack. He then telephoned through to *Oberleutnant* Raimund Steiner, who was in the OP on the beach to inform him the battery was under attack. *Oberleutnant* Steiner, in turn, telephoned through to other batteries in the area to request help by them laying down fire on the perimeter of the Merville Battery. On the opposite side of the footpath there is a reinforced concrete structure that covers the well that supplied the battery with all its fresh water. It was on this structure that the anti-aircraft gun was situated at the time of the attack on the battery. Continue along the footpath and through the tunnel. As you exit the tunnel, on your left, you will see a:

29) 5.5in (139.7mm) Medium Gun. Used by most of the medium regiments of the Royal Artillery in the Second World War, the 5.5in (139.7mm) calibre gun could fire two to five rounds per minute. Rounds were made up of either 80lb (36kg) or 100lb (45kg) charges. Maximum ranges were 18,100 yards (16,551m), some 10.28 miles (16.55km) for a super charged 80lb (36kg) shell, with a velocity of 1,950ft (594m) per sec. For the 100lbs (45kg) shell, maximum range was 16,200 yards (14,813m), some 9.2 miles (14.8km), with a velocity of 1,675ft (511m) per sec.

The gun's weight in action was 13,646lbs (6,190kg), some 6.09 tons (6.19 tonnes) and was usually towed by a Matador vehicle that would also carry the ammunition and essential mechanical spares and tools. Manned by a crew of ten men, a well trained crew could have this gun firing on target within three minutes of taking up firing positions. The accuracy, at 9 miles (14.48km), was within 6ft (1.83m). When used as an anti-tank weapon the crew would often fire a 100lb (45kg) shell, minus the fuse, but with the transit steel plug still in place. This would, with accurate fire, lift the tank turret from its mount. By the end of the campaign in north-west Europe, between 6 June 1944 and 8 May 1945, 21 Army Group fired 2,610,747 rounds with their 5.5in (139.7mm) medium guns.

This weapon is sited on top of:

30) No. 1 and No. 2 Casemate Ammunition Magazine. The same construction and design as the magazine for No. 3 and No. 4 casemate. Next along the footpath, on the right, is a bench. On the backrest is a brass:

31) Private Frank Delsignore Memorial Plaque. This memorial was donated by his wife. Private Delsignore formed part of the small group of four men that actually made it to No. 1 casemate during the attack by 9 Para. With him were Sergeant Sid Capon, Sergeant Eric Bedford and Private Harold 'Johnnie' Walker. The officer leading them, Lieutenant Alan Jefferson, was wounded by machine-gun fire as they crossed the minefield. His batman, Private Morgan, was also wounded in both legs. Continue along the footpath until you reach the eleventh information post. On this post are a number of interesting quotes from people involved with the Merville Battery. Just behind the post are the remnants of:

32) Anti-Aircraft Position. Positioned here was a 20mm (0.78in) Flak light anti-aircraft gun. (see Ch. 5, D27 for weapon specification). The position was damaged during one of the many bombing raids on the battery. To the left of the anti-aircraft position and information post there is:

33) Bronze Bust of Lieutenant Colonel Terence Otway. This bust

is the third sculptured by Vivien Mallock (see Battleground Europe Book *Pegasus Bridge & Horsa Bridge* Ch. 6, A24 & Ch. 7, B11). This one is dedicated to Lieutenant Colonel Otway and was unveiled here on 7 June 1997. To the left of the bronze bust is a bench. On the backrest is a brass:

34) Lieutenant Colonel Terence Otway Memorial Plaque. This was donated by his wife in his memory. Farther over to the left there is another bench seat. On the backrest is a brass:

Lt-Col Terrance Otway in 1998, next to the bronze bust of himself.

35) Frederick Scott Walker Memorial Plaque. Dedicated to the memory of Fred Walker, 9 Para. Before leaving the museum, via the wooden building, walk over to the far side of No. 1 casemate and to the:

36) Douglas C47 Transport Plane. This is the military version of the DC3 airliner built by Douglas. The most versatile aircraft used in the Second World War, this aircraft was widely used in the D-Day landing to tow gliders, drop paratroopers and parachute in supplies. It was also used throughout the Normandy campaign to evacuate wounded troops and bring in supplies to some of the many temporary airstrips that were built in Normandy during the conflict. It had a crew of three in the flight compartments: pilot, co-pilot/navigator and radio operator. The crew would also consist of one or two dispatchers depending upon what it was transporting. The C47 could transport one of the following: a load of 6,000lbs (2,722kg); approximately twenty-one fully laden paratroopers; or evacuate eighteen stretchered wounded along with a medical crew of three. Approximately 1,000 C47s took part in the British, Canadian and American airborne drops on D-Day.

Many heroic deeds were performed by the pilots and crew flying over Normandy on the night of 5/6 June. The pilots had to slow their aircraft from their cruising speed of 121 knots (139mph or 224kmh) down to approximately 95 knots (109mph or 176kmh), when dropping paratroopers. This was just above

'The SNAFU Special' Douglas C-47 (Dakota) Transport Plane.

stall speed, but was necessary to give the paratroopers less buffeting when they exited the aircraft. They were also flying their aircraft as low as 500-700ft (152m-213m) when dropping the paratroopers so that their precious cargo would present less of a target for the German ground forces as they descended. This, however, came at the expense of their own aircraft becoming more vulnerable to enemy fire at such a slow speed and low altitude.

The C47 Dakota No. 42-15073, on display at the Merville Battery and called The SNAFU Special, actually saw service in all the major airborne operations in Europe during the Second World War. In Operation OVERLORD she was assigned to 440th Troop Carrier Wing (TCW), 95th Troop Carrier Squadron (TCS), United States Army Air Force (USAAF) and dropped the paratroopers of 501 Parachute Infantry Regiment (PIR) 101st Airborne Division, near the ancient market town of Ste-Mère-Église on the night of 5/6 June 1944. Later she saw service in Operations: DRAGOON in southern France; MARKET GARDEN in Holland; REPULSE over Bastogne; and VARSITY in the crossing of the River Rhine.

Its final days of action were in the former Yugoslavia. After being machine-gunned near Sarajevo in 1993 during the war in

Merville Battery ➤

The Crossroads in Gonneville-en-Auge, now called a) *Carrefour du 9ene Bataillon*, from where Lt-Col Otway led his 150 strong assault force towards the Merville Battery. The memorial to 9 Para also marks the area.

the Balkans, she was finally grounded. The association for the management for the Merville Battery found and raised funds for the aircraft to be purchased and restored. It was finally transported and unveiled here at the Merville Battery in 2008. Around the aircraft are positioned several information boards detailing the aircraft's history. Alternatively visit www.the-snafu-special.com.

To exit the museum return to the wooden building, inside there is a small gift and book shop.

Return to your car. Drive down the *Avenue de la Batterie de Merville* and turn right and drive to the next crossroads in Hameau de Descanneville. Turn right at the crossroads onto the D223. After 330 yards (302m) the area to your right, and for the next 200 yards (183m), is now an open field. In June 1944 it was a small wood and the area through which 9 Para launched their assault into the Merville Battery. Approximately 90 yards (82m) after the track on your right, there is a single track road on your left leading down to:

E. *Gonneville-en-Auge*

Continue down a single track road, to the crossroads in Gonneville-en-Auge. This crossroads is now called:

1) Carrefour du 9ème Bataillon, named in honour of 9 Para. To the right of the crossroads there is a:

2) *Memorial to 9 Para,* which marks the spot where Lieutenant Colonel Terence Otway, with only 150 men, met his reconnaissance party and then departed to launch their assault on the Merville Battery.

You can either finish your tour here, or continue, with the next tour, by following the directions in the next chapter.

Memorial Tour of the 6th Airborne Division Battlefield No. 2

The High Ground

Distance between stops by vehicle: 13.5 miles (21.73km)
Total walking distance at stops: 0.8 miles (1.28km)
Recommended time allowed for tour: 3-5 hours

This tour starts at the T junction of D223 and D95a near the village of Gonneville-en-Auge. Alternatively, if you have just completed the previous tour, then return from the crossroads, in your car, to the D223. Turn left and 600 yards (549m) farther on, at the next crossroads, you will see a calvary cross on your right.

The Calvary cross
second RV for 9 Para.

A. The Calvary Cross and Haras de Retz

1) Calvary RV. This Calvary was the RV for 9 Para after their attack on the Merville Battery. It was on the steps leading up to the cross that Lieutenant Colonel Otway sat while he collected his thoughts and made his decision on what he would do next. All that was left of the battalion at this point were eighty men, including about six Canadians from 1 Cdn Para. Apart from small arms Lieutenant Colonel Otway's men had no mortars and only one Vickers medium machine gun.

Although there is no mention of his decision in the war diary, it is reasonable to assume that it was at this point Lieutenant Colonel Otway decided not to proceed with the attack on the Sallenelles German naval radar station (see Ch. 5, A4). Instead, with his severely depleted force he decided to move toward the more important secondary objective of capturing and holding the high ground at le Plain (aka le Plein) and Hameau Oger (aka Hauger or Hoger) around Amfréville.

At 0600hrs Otway began to reorganise his force. At 0730hrs the battalion moved toward le Plain with some of their prisoners. Provisions had also been made for the wounded. As there were only a few medical personnel from 9 Para, more had been found amongst the German ranks. They were instructed to help tend the wounded and move them to a nearby château. Located some 200 yards (183m) due south there is:

2) *Château Haras de Retz.* The château and buildings of this stud farm were assigned as an RAP for 9 Para. The captured German medical officer, his two medical orderlies and two of 9 Paras own medical orderlies set up their RAP here.

B. Bréville (-les-Monts)

Continue to drive along the D223 for 2 miles (3.22km) into Bréville-les-Monts (Bréville officially changed its name to Bréville-les-Monts in 2004) and stop just before you reach the crossroads. As you approach the crossroads on foot you can clearly see in front of you the commanding view that these heights give over the River Orne, Caen Canal and the area across to Caen. The Germans knew only too well the importance of this feature that ran from the area north-north-west of here at Hameau Oger and le Plain around Amfréville, through where you now stand and then due south-east-east to le Mesnil.

Early in 1944 *Generalfeldmarschall* Erwin Rommel had stood at this site to plan his defence of the area. On one of these inspections he was noted as saying; *whoever holds this ground will control the battle.* This Rommel did by using some of his best trained infantry in this postition.

The task of clearing and holding this ground was given to the men of Brigadier James Hill's 3 Para Bde. This, however, was to be done only after their primary objectives had been achieved. In June, 1944, this area become known, and is still referred to in many history books, as the Bréville Gap. Because it was such a dominating feature, the Allies knew they would not be able to expand their bridgehead until this gap was closed and so it was decided that Bréville had to be taken at any cost.

On 11 June at first light, 5 Black Watch, of the 51st Highland Division, put in an attack at 0430hrs towards the crossroads from the direction of the *Château St Côme.* But the assault encountered overwhelming resistance and failed. The battalion's first action in Normandy had cost nearly 200 casualties.

The following day the German infantry, supported by tanks, put in three heavy counter-attacks on the 6th Airborne Division positions. It was after the last attack at 1700hrs that Major General Gale decided drastic action was needed to close the Bréville Gap once and for all. He devised an unorthodox plan to

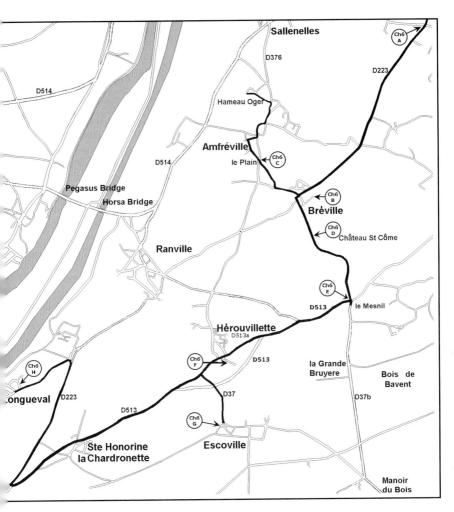

catch the Germans off guard. Instead of the traditional dawn raid it was decided to put in an attack late that same evening at 2200hrs from the direction of Amfréville. After a full day of heavy fighting, it was hoped that the enemy would be exhausted and unprepared for any such attack. In addition it was hoped the diminishing light as dusk settled, would give the assaulting force a little extra advantage as they advanced on the village.

Major General Gale had only 12 Para in reserve. Even though this unit was understrength with only 300 men they were nevertheless brought in from their rest period, along with D Coy of 12 Devons and some tanks from 13/18 Hussars, to prepare for the attack. In support they had four field and one medium artillery regiments from 3 Inf Div. At 2145hrs 100 guns from the

Royal Artillery opened up and pounded the village of Bréville.

Unfortunately the attack did not start well. Some of the artillery shells fell short of their target and amongst the men at the start line. One shell also landed near where a group of senior officers had gathered to watch the assault. Amongst those killed was the commanding officer of 12 Para, thirty-two year old Lieutenant Colonel Alexander P. 'Johnny' Johnson. Now buried in Ranville Commonwealth Cemetery (IVA, C, 10), he was later posthumously awarded the DSO for his action in Normandy. Others also wounded in that incident included 1 SS Bde CO, Brigadier The Lord Lovat, and 6 Airldg Bde CO, Brigadier The Hon Hugh Kindersley.

Nevertheless, at 2215hrs the battle began in earnest and the paratroopers and gliderborne troops moved forward. The crossroads were the first objective after the tanks had destroyed the German strongpoint leading into the village, but the Germans put up fierce resistance by returning fire with mortar bombs and shells. The airborne soldiers did, however, finally overpower the Germans and capture the village. The cost though was high, and 162 men of the 6th Airborne Division were killed in this single battle to close the Bréville Gap.

But their sacrifice was not in vain as the Germans never counter-attacked Bréville again, and the 6th Airborne Division had successfully achieved another of their objectives. Reinforcements from 1 RUR relieved the paratroopers and gliderborne troops at just after noon on 13 June.

As 1 RUR moved up the road (D223) from Ranville, towards the crossroads, Major Edmund Warren of 12 Devons noticed one of the many surreal sights that sometimes face men who have been in battle. The top half of a dead German soldier lay, head and arm first, out of the hedgerow beside the road. As the Irishmen passed by they each took it in turns to shake his hand and pass an amusing remark. It was one example of how, despite being in the most humourless of situations, these men would always find a way to lift their indomitable spirits and keep fighting on.

In the right-hand corner of the crossroads, to the right of the road where 1 RUR made their way in Bréville, you will see the signpost

1) *Carrefour 6th Airborne Division*. That names this crossroads in memory of the 6th Airborne Division. To the right is the:

German equipment abandoned in Bréville.
The same place, present day.

(2) *6th Airborne Division Memorial.* This memorial is dedicated to the memory of the local inhabitants, units of 6th Airborne Division including 12 Para and 12 Devons who were killed in fighting at Bréville. Although 12 Devons formed part of 6 Airldg Bde, all but one of the companies, arrived in Normandy by sea due to a shortage of gliders. To the right of the memorial, just in front of the bus stop, is a:

3) *OVERLORD l'Assault Marker.* This briefly explains the battle that took place here. Across the road, opposite the bus shelter, are the entrance gates to:

4) *Bréville Churchyard.* Again, as with all churchyards that have Commonwealth soldiers, sailors or airmen buried in their grounds, there is a green and white CWGC plaque on the wall next to the gates. The original church was destroyed in the fighting, though part of its ruins can be seen to the right of the footpath as you enter the churchyard. In this churchyard rest two men of the 6th Airborne Division, thirty-four year old Captain Hugh William Ward of 53 (WY) Airldg Lt Regt RA, and twenty-one year old Private Charles J.B. Masters of 12 Para, both killed on 12 June 1944, and buried near where they fell. On leaving the cemetery walk back towards the crossroads and turn left along the D223, the next road on your left is:

5) *Rue du Général Gale.* This road was named in honour of Major General Gale, GOC of 6 Airborne Division. Continue down the road for some 80yds (73m) until you come to the rebuilt church. On the wall, between the stained glass windows there is:

6) *Civilian and Military Victim's Memorial.* Dedicated by the people of Bréville, this memorial is in remembrance of the children, civilians and military personnel who became victims in the First World War, Second World War and the war in Indochina.

C. Amfréville

Return to your vehicle and turn right at the crossroads, past the churchyard, and continue to Amfréville along the D37b *Rue de Sallenelles* and *Route du Moutier*. After 700 yards (640m) turn right onto *Rue Mesaise* 300 yards (274m) on your right is a gravelled roadway next to an open area of grass. This is before the fork in the road that encircles the village green and church. Park on the right and on the gravel near the white fencing that surrounds the:

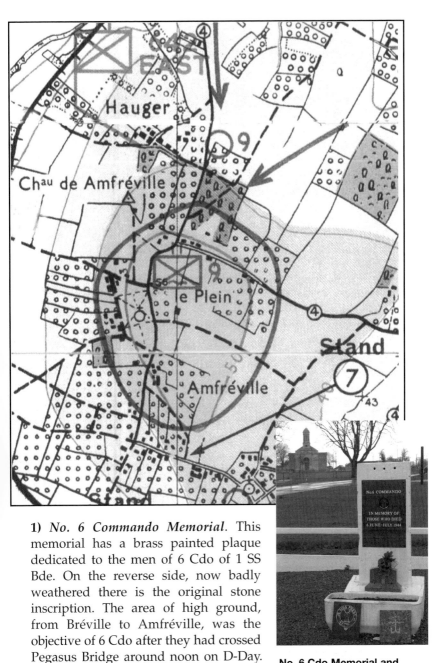

1) *No. 6 Commando Memorial.* This memorial has a brass painted plaque dedicated to the men of 6 Cdo of 1 SS Bde. On the reverse side, now badly weathered there is the original stone inscription. The area of high ground, from Bréville to Amfréville, was the objective of 6 Cdo after they had crossed Pegasus Bridge around noon on D-Day. The area was taken and held by the morning of 7 June, but the commandos

No. 6 Cdo Memorial and Amfréville Church in background.

suffered heavily from German artillery fire during and after the attack. When 5 Black Watch failed in their attack on Bréville four days later, 12 Para then led their attack on Bréville through the commando positions around here.

It was just to the east of here, beyond the village buildings, that the three senior officers became casualties. Despite the serious shrapnel wounds Brigadier The Lord Lovat received, he nevertheless sent the following message to his men; *I have become a casualty, but I can rely upon you not to take one step back. You are making history.* The buildings near the memorial belonged to *Monsieur* Bernard Saulnier, a local farmer, who helped tend the wounded who took shelter in one of his barns. On the building adjacent to the commando memorial, on the left of the gates leading into the farmyard, above the narrow window there is a small wooden and brass:

2) *Commando Commemorative Plaque*. This was placed here in recognition of the commandos using the farm buildings as a base during their operations in this area. Some 35 yards (32m) due north from the memorial, towards the church there is a:

3) *OVERLORD l'Assault Marker*. This gives a brief explanation of events in this area.

Return to your vehicle and drive along the gravelled path towards the church. At the road junction drive across the road *Rue Mesaise* and take the left fork where the road divides around either side of the village green. After 200 yards (183m) on your right hand side is:

4) *Memorial Cross and Plaques to First Special Service Brigade*. After Lord Lovat's wound put him out of action, Lieutenant Colonel Derek Mills-Roberts, who had also been wounded in Normandy, but not as seriously, took over command of the 1 SS Bde and stayed in command of the brigade until the end of the war. Major Lewis took over Lieutenant Colonel Mills-Roberts' former position as commander of 6 Cdo. Beneath the memorial cross there is a brass plaque dedicating this memorial to the officers and men of 1 SS Bde; made up of the following units: HQ 1 SS Bde, 3 Cdo, 4 Cdo, 6 Cdo, 45 RM Cdo and 10 (IA) Cdo, who lost their lives in the fighting in Normandy during June and July 1944. The bronze plaques to the left and right of the memorial explain, in French and English, the memorial dedication. Some 60 yards (55m) behind the memorial in the centre of the village green there is:

5) *Amfréville Church*. By 0900hrs on 6 June 9 Para were approaching Amfréville from the north-east in order to take its secondary objective of the high ground around le Plain (aka le Plein) which is the name given to the large village green on the heights and east side of Amfréville and also to take the area of Hameau Oger (aka Hauger or Hoger) which was a separate small village in 1944. At this time Lieutenant Colonel Otway's force was up to about 100 men having been reinforced by a few stragglers and some of the troops who were on board the glider that had crash-landed near the Merville Battery.

On their approach to Hameau Oger 9 Para were warned by a local French man that the village was occupied by about 200 Russians, all of whom had been captured on the Eastern Front and had been impressed into the *Wehrmacht*. Otway decided to avoid the area and instead approach Amfréville from the east and towards le Plain.

As 9 Para approached a road junction to the north east of le Plain they came under fire. Continuing with their advance 9 Para managed to force the enemy back to their main defensive line at the road junction some 200 yards (182m) north-north-east of the church. Having now occupied some of the buildings to the north-east of the village themselves, 9 Para were soon counter-attacked by the German forces. This however, was met with 9 Paras only Vickers machine-gun which managed to decimate and stop the attack.

Lieutenant Colonel Otway realised that the Germans had set

No. 1 SS Bde Memorial and Amfréville Church.

up too strong a defence for his own depleted force to attack and decided to leave one section of his men at the north-east road junction and take his main force around to the western side of the village and occupy the *Château d'Amfréville* which was situated between the le Plain and Hameau Oger (today all that remains of the château is part of its perimeter wall). The prisoners that 9 Para had collected from the Merville Battery were kept within the secured fenced tennis courts of the château.

At this point both sides settled into a period of sporadic firing and sniping, although the better equipped and more numerous Germans continued to use their machine guns and mortar fire against 9 Para they didn't launch another counter-attack. The German snipers were taking a steady toll on Lieutenant Colonel Otway's men, so priority for the dwindling supply of ammunition was given to 9 Para snipers in order to deal with the German snipers. Although some of the German snipers were skilful in concealing themselves, others were less experienced in their tactics. An entry in 9 Para's war diary for 6 June explains how the problem was dealt with:

> *Their standard of shooting varied... In one instance they appeared incapable of learning any lessons from the fate of their comrades. They persistently sniped from the church tower although one man after another was killed in doing so. Subsequently, six dead snipers were found in the tower. The most effective way of dealing with the sniping proved to be the 'set a thief to catch a thief' method. Our own snipers, by carefully watching, located enemy snipers and eliminated them in turn.*

APPENDIX C REPORT ON OPERATIONS OF 9 PARA 6-12 JUNE 1944,
9 PARA WAR DIARY

It was No. 3 Troop of 3 Cdo, of Brigadier The Lord Lovat's commandos that were first to reach the hard pressed men of 9 Para on D-Day. Arriving by bicycle they met with 9 Para at just after 1400hrs at the Écarde crossroads to the east of Amfréville. Soon after, a troop from 45 RM Cdo arrived. After a meeting with Lieutenant Colonel Otway it was a decided that an attack would be launched against the Germans positions at le Plain in Amfréville. After a reconnaissance by the commandos the plan was decided. With 9 Para providing covering fire from the château and along the left flank, the commandos would launch their attack from the direction of Écarde.

Just before the attack Brigadier The Lord Lovat arrived and

126

ordered No. 3 Troop of 3 Cdo to continue with the assault. The commandos soon took a number of casualties and it became clear that this route of advance into Amfréville was not possible. After withdrawing to cover, the commandos regrouped and reorganised their attack plan. With some troops left to cover the route they had just tried to use, another squad was sent around on the right flank, due south, to cause a diversion for the main attack that would be towards the centre of the village. This attack was more successful and managed to eventually rout the Germans from the building along this side of the village green.

It was not until the following day that 9 Para were eventually relieved by the rest of 1 SS Bde. The church was also used by Brigadier The Lord Lovat and his men, as a means of shelter, during the night of 8 June. This was after experiencing fierce fighting around the village of Bréville.

Continue along the road and 100 yards (91m) after the memorial, turn right onto the short road that leads to the *Mairie* and:

**Commandant
Philippe Kieffer.**

6) *Place du Commandant Kieffer*. This area is named in honour of *Commandant* (aka *Capitaine de Corvette*, the naval equivalent to lieutenant commander and army equivalent of Major) Philippe Kieffer who was the commander of *1er Bataillon de Fusiliers Marins Commandos* (1 BFMC). Also known as the Free French Commandos. This unit formed part of the multi-national No. 10 (Inter Allied) Commando [10 (IA) Cdo]. For the Normandy Landings, *Commandant* Kieffer and his force of 177 men, divided into No. 1 and No. 8 Troop, were attached to 4 Cdo of 1 SS Bde for the Normandy landings.

Having been recently promoted to lieutenant commander just before D-Day, *Commandant* Kiefer led his men onto SWORD Beach near la Brèche at just after 0730hrs on 6 June. Landing around the same time were the rest of 1 SS Bde.

I carried my rucksack, tommy gun, a thirty round magazine, 200 spare rounds and four hand grenades... In addition everyone had been assigned an extra payload, a 200 ft hemp rope with which to swim across the Caen Canal and Orne River, in case the enemy had blown the bridges.

Lance Corporal Peter Masters, 3 Brit Tp, 10 (IA) Cdo, 1 SS Bde

After attacking and destroying the German gun emplacement at Ouistreham, *Commandant* Kieffer and his men passed over Pegasus and Horsa Bridges at just after noon and went on to occupy the high ground feature at Amfréville, taking over from 9 Para, in the evening of 6 June. By this time *1 BFM Cdo* had sustained a twenty-five per cent casualty rate.

Return and continue along the road, 25 yards (23m) farther on the road forks. Take the left-hand fork and 50 yards (46m) on your right is a short path leading to:

7) *No. 3 Commando Memorial*. Sited on le Plain, this memorial has been sited here in dedication of those of 3 Cdo who liberated Amfréville on 6 June 1944. It is also dedicated to the memory of those who died.

Continue to drive for another 30 yards (27m) to the junction onto *Rue Morice*. Turn right at the corner where the sign is for *le Plain* and continue along *Rue Morice* for 145 yards (133m) until you reach the T junction. Turn left onto *Route de Sallenelles* (D37b) and continue to drive through Amfréville for 640 yards (585m). On the left there is a street called *Rue Patra*. If you continue for a further 25 yards (23m), on your right there is:

8) *Rue du 4ème Commando*. This street is named in honour of 4 Cdo with which *Commandant* Philippe Kieffer and the Free French Commandos were attached.

Return and drive down *Rue Patra*. 275yds (251m) on your left there is a small track that leads around a small triangle area of grassed area. This area is now known as:

9) *Place Colonel Robert Dawson*. This part of Hameau Oger (aka Hauger or Hoger) is now named after the commanding officer of 4 Cdo. It was in this area, in the nearby farm buildings, that 4 Cdo dug in and established their HQ at 2130hrs on the evening of 6 June. This HQ, however, was all but destroyed during an artillery barrage just prior to a heavy German counter-attack on the 10 June. At this time 4 Cdo HQ was moved into, and around, the grounds of the château and its farm buildings situated just 40 yards (37m) away, due north-east, from this place. For four days and nights 4 Cdo had no rest and were in continuous contact with the enemy. In the centre of the grassed triangle area there is:

10) *No. 4 Commando Memorial*. The white stone cross is now worn with age but engraved upon it is No. 4 Commando 1944 and the combined operations badge of the commandos. Below there is a brass plaque with a short verse penned by the Marquis of Montrose. It was a verse that had been quoted as part of the speech, to all the troops, by the Commander of the 21st Army Group on D-Day.

> *We have a great and righteous cause. Let us pray that the Lord, mighty in Battle, will go forth with our armies and that His special providence will aid us in the struggle. I want every soldier to know that I have complete confidence in the successful outcome of the operations that we are now about to begin. With stout hearts and with enthusiasm for the contest, let us go forward to victory; and, as we enter the battle, let us recall the words of a famous soldier spoken many years ago. These are the words he said:*
>
> > *'He either fears his fate too much,*
> > *Or his deserts are small,*
> > *That puts it not unto the touch,*
> > *To win or lose it all.'*
>
> *Good luck to each one of you – and good hunting on the mainland of Europe.*
>
> GENERAL SIR BERNARD MONTGOMERY, C-IN-C 21ST ARMY GROUP

The casualties for 4 Cdo had been high during the first five days of fighting. Starting out with 434 officers and men, by 10 June, only 160 had not been killed or wounded.

D. Château St Côme and Bois des Mont

Drive back up *Rue Patra* and turn right back onto the *Route de Sallenelles* (D37b). Continue to drive through Amfréville, past the church and village green on your right, and along the main road back to the village of Bréville (although still the D37b the road name changes to *Rue Mesaise* then to *Rue du Moutier* then back to *Route de Sallenelles*). At the crossroads, after the church, in Bréville continue straight on along *Rue de Arbre Martin*. Some 300 yards (274m) on your left-hand side there is a fence and hedgerow that is at the end of a long paddock. The paddock runs at 45 degrees, away from the road, to your right and is flanked by a row of trees. At the far end of this field is the *Château St Côme*. Continue to drive for a further 370 yards (338m) and park on the area in front of the water tower on your right. Across the road, to your left, is the main entrance that leads to:

1) Château St Côme. This Château is private property. To the left of the entrance lane leading to the Château there is:

Château St Côme after the fighting in June 1944.

The Château today.

2) *Princess Irene Brigade Memorial.* This memorial was unveiled in December 2003 and is dedicated to the Dutch armed force that was attached to the 6th Airborne Division in August 1944. Initially formed in England in 1940, it was made up of Dutch military personnel who had escaped from the Netherlands or Dutch volunteers from England, America, Canada and South Africa.

Memorial to *Princess Irene Brigade*.

In January 1941 the brigade became officially known as Royal Dutch Brigade and then on 27 August 1941 Queen Wilhelmina of the Netherlands conferred the title *De Koninklijke Nederlandsche Brigade Prinses Irene*, the Royal Dutch *Princess Irene Brigade*, in honour of her grandchild. The brigade had 1,205 personnel and was made up of an HQ, three combat teams, a reconnaissance unit, an artillery battery and a brigade supply train. The unit formed No. 2 Troop of the multinational 10 (IA) Cdo.

Princess Irene Brigade landed on JUNO Beach on 7 and 8 August and took up frontline positions around the *Château St Côme* on 12 August. The unit later took part in Operation PADDLE on 17 August and became the first unit to occupy Pont Audemer on 26 August. The brigade was then assigned to the First Canadian Army for the crossing of the River Seine. The *Princess Irene Brigade's* involvement was appreciated by the GOC of the 6th Airborne Division, as the following message to the *Brigadecommandant, Luitenant Kolonel Artillerie* A. C. de Ruyter van Steveninck, expresses:

My Dear Colonel,
I cannot say, how sorry I am, that the command of your gallant brigade should so soon pass from me. It will always be with great pride, that the Royal Dutch contingent first fought in this great battle for liberation under my command.

Your men fought splendidly throughout this time, culminating in your splendid dash for Pont Audemer. It has been an honour to have fought besides you.

May God Speed you in your advance to your great country.
Yours very sincerely
(SIGNED) Richard N. Gale
Major General

Further information on the *Princess Irene Brigade* on www.prinsesirenebrigade.nl

On the right-hand corner of the lane leading to the *Château St Côme*, in front a large tree there is:

3) 9th Parachute Battalion Memorial. The plaque on this memorial also pays homage to the men of 5 Black Watch, Royal Armoured Corps and 1 Cdn Para who took part in the fighting around the *Château St Côme* and the *Bois des Monts*.

Major General Richard Gale.

Lieutenant Colonel Otway was ordered on the evening of 7 June to take the ground around here. 9 Para arrived by making a detour around Bréville as the Germans had the village strongly defended. Just near here, some 100 yards (91m) due south-south-west, across the road, there is a small villa called *Bois des Monts*. Lieutenant Colonel

The lane opposite the *Château St Côme* where Lieutenant Christie was killed and Lieutenant Colonel Otway (pictured left) was concussed.

Otway decided that he had insufficient men and equipment to occupy both the château and the villa. As the thick woods and dense bocage around the *Bois des Monts* provided a better defensive position he decided to use this, and its adjacent buildings, as his HQ and RAP. Its occupant turned out to be the Mayor of Bréville, Monsieur Magninet, who also happened to be a member of the local French Resistance. It was when using the Mayor's secret radio that Otway heard on the BBC news service a mention of his raid on the Merville Battery.

Lieutenant Colonel Otway still only had a fraction of his original battalion when he arrived in this area. Even though he had lost several men in the fighting around Amfréville, some paratroopers, despite some being dropped miles from their DZ, had by this time managed to find their bearings and make their way back to their units. Still desperately undermanned with only ninety men, and still without much of their heavy equipment, the paratroopers dug in around this area ready to carry out their orders which were to deny the enemy the use of the château and the high ground which lay between the château and le Mesnil and the area towards Bréville. With such a depleted force 9 Para were destined to have a rough time over the next five days.

As you stand in front of the 9 Para Memorial, to your left is the driveway leading to the château. To your right is a hedgerow running, due south, and curving due east that runs adjacent to the road that leads to le Mesnil. It was from this point and down along that hedgerow for about 50 yards (46m) that Lieutenant Colonel Otway concentrated his limited firepower by positioning some men from A Coy so they were facing the open field and driveway. This would provide the first line of defence against an enemy attack from the direction of the château. In addition the remainder of part of A Coy also took up positions along a ditch that bordered the woods, beyond the field, some 170 yards (155m) due south-east.

Walk across the road and beyond the wide gateway along the hedgerow there is a sunken lane, flanked by high hedgerows. This is where the anti-tank platoon, with their PIAT, covered both the Bréville to le Mesnil road and the château driveway. About halfway down the sunken lane, just beyond the hedgerow on the right, B Coy was given the task of protecting the north-west approach to the *Bois des Monts*. Continue, due south and some 15 yards (14m) on your right there is:

4) *51st Highland Division Memorial* This bronze statue of a highland piper is dedicated to the 51st (Highland) Infantry Division and to the 110 men who were killed near here in their first attack on Bréville and their defence of the château. Although the engraved plinth states that the 51st (Highland) Division made its first attack on 10 June, the actual attack took place at 0430hrs on the morning of Sunday 11 June by 5 Black Watch with artillery support from 63 Med Regt RA.

Walk back towards the gate leading to the sunken lane.

Despite a warning from Lieutenant Colonel Otway, not to attack Bréville toward the heavily defended German positions to the west of the château, he was overruled by a brigadier from the Black Watch. On 10 June Lieutenant Colonel Otway was ordered to take the château and he detailed C Coy

51st (Highland) Division Memorial.

to do so at 2300hrs. They managed to successfully take the château but were subjected to numerous probing attacks by the Germans throughout the night. During the night 5 Black Watch moved up to take their start positions along the sunken lane next to the *Bois des Monts*.

Walk for 25 yards (23m), past the gateway leading down the sunken lane. Just after the water towers (that were not here in 1944) on your left, stop by the fence that overlooks the fields to the south of Bréville.

D Coy and HQ Coy of 5 Black Watch relieved C Coy of 9 Para at the château in the early hours of Sunday. At 0430hrs, 5 Black Watch started their assault with A Coy leaving the protection of the trees and hedgerow along the length of the sunken lane down the slope to your left. A Coy had a distance of approximately 720 yards (658m) to reach Bréville crossroads. Farther over to the east B Coy and C Coy approached Bréville from the bottom of the sunken lane and covered the left flank towards Bréville. Using the natural cover of a hedgerow (no longer there today) down towards the bottom of the hill, B and C Coy had approximately 1,000 yards (914m) of ground to cover to reach the crossroads.

After about 250 yards (229m) A Coy came to another hedgerow (no longer there today but it ran across the field where

134

the building now stands along the hedgerow to your right). This hedgerow ran east to west from the Bréville to le Mesnil road for approximately 170 yards (155m). When the company had advanced about 130 yards (119m) across into the next field the Germans laid down withering mortar and machine-gun fire wiping out most of A Coy. B Coy and then C Coy both tried to outflank the German positions to the left, but to no avail. By 0900hrs the battalion had sustained some 200 casualties with fifty men killed. With no armoured support and with the 5.5in (139.7mm) guns of the artillery medium regiment having missed their target 5 Black Watch had to withdraw bringing back with them as many of the wounded as they could.

From your position here you are also able to better appreciate the strategic importance of this part of the high ground and the area up to Bréville. The commanding view of the village of Ranville, the area around Pegasus Bridge and Horsa Bridge, and the plains leading to Caen from SWORD Beach soon also became apparent to Lieutenant Colonel Otway on the morning of 8 June when 9 Para initially occupied this area.

Walk back towards the 51st (Highland) Infantry Division memorial and some 10 yards (9m) beyond the memorial there are the gates leading into the grounds of the:

5) *Bois des Monts*. Please note this is now private property. Within the gardens though, the most recent owners have respectfully preserved some of the undergrowth and wooded areas leaving them pretty much as they were back in 1944. In parts, the slit trenches and protective earth banks can still be clearly seen. The debris of the battlefield has been removed for preservation and safety; as well as to deter unauthorised collectors of militaria. Nevertheless, some items have been protected and left in situ, including:

6) *Captain Wilkinson's Stone Cross Headstone*. This is located 30 yards (27m) south-east of the villa and 10 yards (9m) north-east of the tool shed and wood store. This stone cross was made by Corporal Tilley, a former stone mason, who was a member of Captain Wilkinson's section. It was the original headstone for Captain Wilkinson's grave

Captain Wilkinson's stone cross headstone.

after he was killed (see Ch. 6, D8). He was later reinterred in Ranville Commonwealth War Cemetery (IA, C, 20).

A large part of the grassed area between the villa and around Captain Wilkinson's stone cross became a temporary cemetery during the summer of 1944. These bodies were also later reinterred in Ranville Commonwealth War Cemetery. Also situated nearby in the grounds of the *Bois des Monts* is a wooden bench seat, on the back of which there are two brasses:

7) *Memorial Plaques to Sergeant S.F. 'Sid' Capon*. One is dedicated to his memory, by his friends and comrades from 9 Para (see Ch. 5, D8). Some 40 yards (37m) south-east of the villa, there is a:

8) *Tool Shed and Wood Store (Dressing Station)*. Inside, scribed upon the wall in chalk, there is still visible a list of soldiers names. No one, however, has been able to determine who these soldiers are, or why and when their names were written.

After Lieutenant Colonel Otway deployed part of A Coy along the other side of the hedgerow across the road from the *Bois des Monts*, his anti-tank platoon at the top of, and B Coy to the north-east of, the sunken lane; the area and buildings in the grounds of the *Bois des Monts* became 9 Para's HQ and RAP.

Part of HQ Coy dug in along the hedgerow and trees that continues after the gates, and which runs parallel to the Bréville and le Mesnil road. The remainder of A Coy took up positions amongst the woods in the eastern part of the *Bois des Monts* and the barn (now converted to a house), sited some 140 yards (128m) due east from the villa, was used as A Coy's HQ. The south-west of the grounds were protected by C Coy who were also tasked with forming a mobile reserve so that in the event of a counter-attack they could be deployed where they would be most needed.

Meanwhile, one room in the villa was used as the battalion HQ and the kitchen was used as a first aid treatment room. Between the barn and the villa, some 40 yards (37m) away, is a tool shed and wood store. This was turned into a dressing station. Holding a tight defensive line around the *Bois des Monts*

The graves around the villa in *le Bois des Monts*.
Bois des Monts today.

fighting patrols were sent out to reconnoitre and probe enemy positions. The Germans, too, were constantly probing with the inevitable skirmishes taking a toll on both both sides.

It was on one of these patrols, led by Lieutenant Dennis Slade, that some men entered the château to see if it was being occupied by the Germans. Inside they found ample evidence that the enemy had indeed been using the building. It seemed they were also in a bit of a hurry to leave as there was clothing and overturned chairs strewn about the place, along with half-eaten meals still left on the table.

> *On the first floor, with Lieutenant Slade, we entered an office. There was a large desk near the large window that overlooked open fields to Bréville. On this desk was a cash box with a lid partially open. To me this seemed to be a classic booby trap, but Lieutenant Slade decided to look and I left the room in a hurry. Later it was found to contain a German pay roll and the money was handed over to Lieutenant Colonel Otway.*
>
> PRIVATE KEN E. WALKER, 9 PARA

Before leaving, the men helped themselves to some of the spoils of war, Lieutenant Slade taking a German officer's sword in addition to the substantial sum of money. (Reports of the exact amount vary between 500 and 150,000 Francs!) Whatever the true amount, it was said that Lieutenant Colonel Otway was later ordered to hand over the money to the Corps HQ. But he had decided to ignore the order and instead 'donated' the money to his Quartermaster so that fresh food and drink could be bought for his men.

Later that day, around noon, a German patrol was fought off when they approached from the north-east towards A Coy. This was then followed by two attacks on A and C Coy's positions, but as the Germans did not use any artillery or mortar support during these attacks they were soon stopped.

Since early morning both 3 Para Bde and 1 Cdn Para HQ, had been subjected to heavy German attacks. So intense was the action that Brigadier James Hill at one point radioed 9 Para requesting reinforcements. As some of the German troops had redirected their attack farther north, towards the area between le Mesnil and the *Bois des Monts*, Lieutenant Colonel Otway organised an assault group to make a left flanking attack towards the rear of the German attack.

Meanwhile, Major George Smith led a small group armed with two machine-guns, forward along the wood bordering the road to le Mesnil in order to lay down covering fire. Also joining the group was twenty-four year old Captain Anthony Wilkinson, an intelligence officer with 3 Para Bde HQ who had been with Lieutenant Colonel Otway when the request for help came from 3 Para Bde HQ. Seizing the opportunity to possibly get a German prisoner for interrogation, he had requested to join the covering party.

As they approached a corner along a roadside ditch Lieutenant Colonel Otway, who had also moved up with the group, looked around the corner to observe the Germans. Immediately he was fired upon. Moving back along the ditch he warned Captain Wilkinson to move back also. But Captain Wilkinson also looked around the corner before withdrawing and was hit in the head by a sniper's bullet. Within minutes he died of his wound.

Continuing with their task Major Smith and his men successfully pushed forward and forced the Germans to withdraw into the line of fire of the assault group. As well as relieving the pressure on 3 Para Bde HQ, it also prevented the Germans from breaking the vital road connection between the *Bois des Monts* and le Mesnil. Captain Wilkinson's body was taken back and buried in the grounds of the *Bois des Monts* (see Ch. 6, D6).

The fighting continued into the following days with the Germans laying down heavy mortar and artillery fire on 9 Para positions at frequent intervals. In addition, these bombardments were often followed by infantry assaults.

> *We were well dug into our trenches in the thick undergrowth, and the Germans did not know where until it was too late. We killed them all at very close range, so as not to miss, but they still came, till there was so many dead bodies that there was a horrible putrid smell. The bodies started to swell up and were covered with bluebottles and other flies which came in a black cloud to descend on them.*
>
> PRIVATE RON TUCKER, 9 PARA

It was on one of the many bodies that orders were found commanding that no airborne or commando troops should be taken alive. To give the order more impact, the German soldiers were misinformed by the Nazi Propaganda Minister, Goebbels, that Allied paratroopers had also been ordered not to take any prisoners.

In the early hours of 9 June, at first light, the Germans attacked in strength. At this stage two companies of 9 Para were dug in either side of the road and by the entrance of the lane leading to the château Sergeant McGeever and Corporal McGuinness manned a Vickers machine-gun. As the enemy approached from the direction of the château and Bréville, the paratroopers held their fire until the Germans were within 50 yards (46m) of their positions.

Opening fire with machine-guns, mortars and rifles they stopped the Germans in their tracks. Most were killed or wounded, while those who survived fled back into the woods by the château. At about this time news came in from a reconnaissance patrol that the Germans were constantly being reinforced at Bréville and that they already had an estimated strength of about 500 men.

Meanwhile, in the opposite direction, at le Mesnil, more men were needed and about a dozen men were taken from the *Bois des Monts* up to the crossroads by Major Ian Dyer to help reinforce brigade headquarters. The day continued to take its toll with the loss of Lieutenant Gordon Parfitt, 2ic of 9 Para, Major Charlton, Sergeant Rose, Signalman Courtney and three others who were killed while out on patrol.

Next day, on 10 June, the battalion reached its maximum strength so far, as more stragglers reached their respective companies. But this still left Lieutenant Colonel Otway with only 270 men to continue with his tasks. At noon, a new company of approximately fifty Germans walked into the open and prepared to dig in just to the north by the wood alongside the road leading to Bréville. This was in full view of 9 Para positions. The paratroopers waited until the troops had discarded most of their weapons and equipment. Then, as the Germans began digging in, the paratroopers opened fire with Vickers and Bren guns, wiping out the company.

Meanwhile, the Germans had launched an attack on Ranville. Although this attack failed, they had also moved and reoccupied the *Château St Côme* during the morning and were beginning to concentrate their efforts against 9 Para positions with even greater force. Brigadier James Hill by now knew that his men on this ridge were up against Germans from *Infanterie Regiment 857* of *346 Infanterie Division*. In addition to the mortars and artillery support the Germans were also using armour to support their attacks.

It was a desperate time for the paratroopers, which called for desperate measures. Lieutenant Colonel Otway, during a particularly heavy attack against his position at 1700hrs, decided it was necessary to ignore the 1,000 yard safety limit for fire support from HMS *Arethusa*. Calling the FOB at 3 Para Bde HQ, the message and coordinates for support were relayed to HMS *Arethusa*. Within minutes the 6in (152.4mm) guns of HMS *Arethusa* opened up on the attacking Germans while they were only 500 yards (457m) away from 9 Para.

Directing the fire was Captain The Honourable Paul Greenway, despite being in full view of the enemy, he shouted corrective fire coordinates to Lieutenant Colonel Otway who in turn had them radioed through to the FOB at 3 Para Bde HQ. The accurate and devastating fire power of HMS *Arethusa's* guns decimated the German attack. It also raised morale amongst 9 Para. After some close hand-to-hand fighting with the remaining Germans that had managed to reach some of 9 para's slit trenches, the attack was thwarted.

After the failed attack on Bréville by 5 Black Watch on the morning of 11 June, the remnants of A, B, and C Coys joined D Coy and HQ Coy in and around the *Château St Côme*. Throughout the night 5 Black Watch were reinforced with machine guns from a platoon from 1/7 Middlesex Regiment and 6pdr anti-tank guns from the 51st (Highland) Infantry Division.

Tanks from the 13/18 Hussars had also been brought up from the south and west and through the *Bois des Monts* to help reinforce the highlanders' position. But, as three tanks made their way down the driveway toward the château, a German SP gun hidden some 300 yards (274m) away in the woods blew the turret off the first tank and then knocked out the next two tanks in quick succession. The remaining tanks were then withdrawn after realising that the woods, close-knit fields and high hedgerows of the *bocage* were not suitable for tank warfare. The evening of 11 June passed with relative quiet, but patrols from both sides continued to probe each other's defences.

On the morning of 12 June, just after first light, the Germans continued with sporadic shell and mortar fire. By noon, this had intensified and the whole area was being subjected to continuous enemy fire. At 1500hrs the bombardment intensified and lasted for a further forty-five minutes. This was followed immediately by a determined infantry attack supported by armour and Mk IV tanks and SP guns.

Troops from 5 Black Watch and 1/7 Middlesex were in danger of being overrun as the German armour and tanks advanced across the fields to the west of the château. For the next three hours the highlanders lost most of their Bren gun carriers and anti-tank guns, but they held tenaciously onto the château building.

In the woods to the east of the château though, events were taking a turn for the worse. Routed by the Germans, confusion reigned as those who survived the German onslaught began to withdraw towards the *Bois des Monts*. As some highland troops withdrew toward 9 Para lines they had to be hastily reorganised to form a defensive line.

Lieutenant Colonel Otway had already called 3 Para Bde HQ for additional support and more ammunition. Brigadier James Hill knew that the situation must indeed be critical for Otway to convey such a message. He immediately led the reserve company of about sixty Canadian paratroopers of A Coy 1 Cdn Para, from le Mesnil, to help the beleaguered troops.

The Germans continued with concentrated mortar and artillery fire in support of their infantry and armoured attack. During this shelling Lieutenant Slade was seen walking about boosting the men's morale by waving the sword he had taken from the château. He gave the order to *Stand fast and make all shots count.* The Padre, the Reverend Captain John Gwinnett, also raised morale when he came out from the cover of the *Bois des Monts* driveway crossed the road and hung the battalion's flag on the trunk of the tree situated on the right-hand corner of the entrance leading to the château.

Château St Côme driveway (left) and tree (right) on which Reverend Gwinnett hung the battalion flag. Memorial to 9 Para in foreground.

Entrance to the *Château St Côme*.
Private Peter Sanderson.

By now two German tanks were also starting to come up the road from Bréville in support of the infantry that was advancing before them. They were heading directly for the 9 Para positions around the entrance to the château and the top of the sunken lane. When the Germans were within 20 yards (18m) 9 Para let loose with everything they had left. The machine-guns, positioned by the entrance to the château and along the sunken lane, opened up, along with mortar bombs, grenades, PIAT projectiles and small arms fire into the German lines.

Corporal McGuinness had his machine gun positioned near the driveway entrance to the château and Corporal Bailey's machine gun was in the wood, both facing Bréville. Opposite, Private Peter Sanderson had his gun covering the château. His position unfortunately received a direct hit from a mortar round killing nineteen year old Private Sanderson and wounding his comrades.

One tank had its track blown off with a PIAT and began to retreat and fire its high explosive rounds into 9 Para's defences. It was estimated that the tank accounted for at least twenty-two casualties. The tank was soon finished off when Corporal McGuinness helped man a 6pdr and put three rounds into the tank stopping it completely. Later, the second tank was fired upon when Company Sergeant Major 'Wally' Beckwith and Regimental Sergeant Major Bill Cunningham manned an abandoned 6pdr gun that was positioned some 30 yards (27m)

143

down along the château driveway. Although it was not damaged by the artillery rounds the tank commander thought better of continuing his attack and withdrew.

At one point though, the German infantry had actually managed to break through the defences of 9 Para but were beaten back by bloody hand-to-hand fighting with bayonets and knives. Small probing patrols also managed to infiltrate 9 Para positions:

> *Just how close they could get without being seen was brought home to me. I was crouched over a spirit stove, brewing up, when something made me look at my companion. Before I could speak he motioned me to silence and pointed just over my head, I looked up to see the bushes part and the head and shoulders of a German soldier came into view. How he failed to see us I will never know as we were right beneath him. All his attention was on the Vickers position. He raised his arm and in his hand was a stick grenade; before he could throw it my companion shot him and as he fell his helmet came off striking me on the shoulder. We immediately fired bursts into the undergrowth but he was alone. In his wallet were photos of his wife and two small children who had just lost their father.*

> SERGEANT DOUG WOODCRAFT, 9 PARA

Brigadier James Hill himself led a detachment from A Coy 1 Cdn Para to the area south-east of the château as reinforcements. They were met by the Black Watch and Germans engaged in confused fighting in the woods. Clearing the woods of Germans Brigadier Hill and the Canadians pushed on towards the château. Their arrival was much appreciated by the beleaguered men of 5 Black Watch who were still holding out.

Finally, fire support from HMS *Arethusa* was called upon again. Anchored some 12 miles (19.31km) away its 6in (152.4mm) guns pounded the German positions just as they were regrouping for another attack. By 2000hrs the Germans had finally had enough and withdrew.

As the German and British dead piled up, two or three high in places, there was a nauseating stench of decaying and burnt flesh. Combined with the smell of cordite, unwashed bodies and human excrement a sickening odour was created that hung heavily in the air all around the château and the *Bois des Monts*. It was an unwelcome addition to the horrific sight of the battlefield.

144

The RAP in the villa was also a grotesque scene, overflowing with the wounded that lay wherever space could be found. The growing mound of amputated limbs and soiled dressings continued to pile up next to the building adding to the shocking, gruesome and desperate image of the sharp end of battle. In the back garden the ever increasing numbers of dead were laid out in rows, close together, so as to make use of every available inch of space.

> *At one time we had 183 wounded in there... In fact, at one time, the Germans were not taking their wounded in, and so I asked the Padre if he would mind going out with stretcher-bearers and bringing them in. He went out but got very angry because we had arranged a sort of truce, not to fire, and there was a single shot... He always had a big shepherd's crook and he stood up, pointed at his dog collar and in a very un-Christian language, in English, asked the Germans if they couldn't see it. He was a very brave man... We had people walking around here with bandaged legs, bandaged arms, bandaged heads, still fighting. They went to the RAP, they were patched up, came out and made room for the other people... I think, from memory, I ended up losing 120 killed here, plus wounded.*
>
> LIEUTENANT COLONEL TERENCE OTWAY, COMMANDER, 9 PARA

In July 1944, the Padre, the Reverend Captain John Gwinnett, received the Military Cross for his actions during the many battles fought by 9 Para around the *Château St Côme*.

That day, 12 June, had seen the final desperate attacks by the Germans to dominate the high ground at the château and le Mesnil. In the evening at 2100hrs, just prior to the attack on Bréville by 12 Para and 12 Devons, Lieutenant Colonel Otway was out inspecting his positions with several of his officers. As they stood on the bank of the sunken lane (see p. 132), opposite the château drive, the Germans opened up with an intense artillery barrage that lasted for ten minutes. One shell landed beside the group of officers. Lieutenant Christie was killed instantly, Sergeant McGeever was wounded and Lieutenant Colonel Otway, Captain The Honourable Paul Greenway and Lieutenant Hugh Pond were all concussed, the latter two severely.

In the early hours of 13 June, after the successful capture of Bréville by 6th Airborne Division, 9 Para received orders that they were to be relieved by 2 Oxf Bucks. For the paratroopers around the château it was a great relief for they thought that they would have, at last, a chance to get some much needed and well deserved rest.

But there was to be no respite yet for the men of 9 Para as Lieutenant Colonel Otway had been ordered to take his men, ten officers and 218 other ranks, straight back into the front line near where 1 Cdn Para were deployed. At 1100hrs 9 Para reported to the HQ of 3 Para Bde at le Mesnil.

That evening, at 1735hrs, 9 Para received an unwelcome reception in their new positions, when 3 Para Bde HQ and the MDS for 224 Para Fd Amb were strafed in an air attack. This attack was not by the Germans though, it was a mistaken friendly fire attack by Typhoons firing their 20mm (0.79in) cannons and launching their rocket projectiles. During the attack two Canadian officers were wounded and a French female civilian was killed. 9 Para did not suffer any casualties.

On 17 June, 9 Para moved to Ranville, before, finally, being moved to Écarde on 20 June where the battalion spent the next four days in rest and recuperation. With the background echo of gunfire they were also provided with entertainment by a group of performers from ENSA. After the brief respite the battalion were reclothed and re-equipped, and on 25 June 9 Para moved back to the front line and relieved 13 Para at le Mesnil.

After experiencing some after-effects from the explosion in the sunken lane, including a brief period of blindness, Lieutenant Colonel Otway was paid a visit by Major Alastair D. Young, the commanding officer of 224 Para Fd Amb, and his ADMS, on 23 July. He decided that Otway had to be evacuated and on 24 July Otway went to attend a medical examination at the general hospital in Bayeux where he was declared unfit for further active service.

It was a terrible blow for the twenty-nine year old officer, just as it was for the men of 9 Para who were now less than 200 strong. They had come to trust implicitly the orders and actions of their Commanding Officer and his loss was a great blow to their morale. For his efforts during the first crucial weeks of the Battle of Normandy Lieutenant Colonel Otway was subsequently awarded the Distinguished Service Order. Command of 9 Para then passed to Major Allen Parry for the remainder of the battalion's time in Normandy. Later, on 16 September, Lieutenant Colonel Napier Crookenden assumed command of 9 Para for its future deployments and operations in north-west Europe.

E. le Mesnil

Return to your vehicle and continue along the D37b for 0.75 miles (1.21km) until you reach the next crossroads at le Mesnil. Continue straight across and pull into the picnic area 100 yards (91m) on the right. Drive down the short gravel driveway and park. Over the grassed area beneath the three flag poles is a concrete memorial surrounded by gravel. This area is known as:

1) *Brigadier James Hill DSO MC Square.* On the grassed area beneath the three flagpoles there is a concrete memorial surrounded by gravel. The top blue plaque, with white lettering, names this square in honour of Brigadier James Hill, Commander of 3 Para Bde. He set up 3 Para Bde HQ some 200 yards (182m) south-west-west of here in the nearby buildings of the *Potérie de Bavent*. These buildings were known as the brickworks by the paratroopers.

Beneath, there is a black marble plaque with gold lettering:

2) *3 Para Bde Memorial Plaque.* This memorial is dedicated to the units of 1 Cdn Para, 8 Para, 9 Para, 3 Para Sqn RE and 224 Para Fd Amb who all formed 3 Para Bde and were in action in this area. To the left of this memorial some 10 yards (9m) away there is a large stone:

3) *1st Canadian Parachute Battalion Memorial* which pays tribute to the Canadians who defended this particular area, around le Mesnil crossroads, on the eastern flank of the Allied invasion force. Leaving Down Ampney Airfield on the evening of 5 June, A Coy and B Coy flew and dropped from C-47 Dakotas while C Coy flew in Albemarles. 1 Cdn Para was assigned to land at DZ V, near Varaville, with each of the three companies given the following tasks:

A Coy was to protect the left flank of 9 Para while they attacked the Merville Battery and cover their advance towards Amfréville, after which they would then move up to the crossroads at le Mesnil.

B Coy was to destroy the road bridge near Robehomme, with one section of 3 Para Sqn RE, and then take and hold the high ground at Robehomme until orders were received to move back to the crossroads at le Mesnil.

C Coy dropped thirty minutes prior to the main 3 Para Bde landing, as part of the pathfinder group, and secure the DZ by destroying the German HQ and strongpoint around the *Château de Varaville* which was known to be towards the south-east corner of the DZ. They would then destroy the bridge over the Divette, some 500 yards (457m) east of the DZ, on the eastern side of Varaville and the nearby German signal exchange approximately 1,000 yards (914m) west of the southern end of DZ V. Their final task was to then join the rest of the battalion at le Mesnil crossroads.

HQ Coy including Intelligence section, signal section and elements of 224 Para Fd Amb were to proceed towards le Mesnil after landing, and meet at their RV point.

The wide dispersion of the main drop meant that less than twenty men of A Company managed to make the RV. This group, led by Lieutenant John Clancy, were able only to join 9 Para after their attack on the Merville Battery, whereupon they provided a rearguard for part of 9 Para's advance towards Amfréville.

At 0900hrs they left 9 Para and made it to le Mesnil by 1530hrs on the afternoon of 6 June. As with 9 Para, stragglers rejoined their respective companies over the next week or so. In some instances, men were absorbed into other battalions if there was a need for their services.

B Coy with only thirty men managed to take their objective of Robehomme and destroy the nearby bridge. Two companies of B Coy had been dropped wide of the DZ and had landed in the marsh and wetlands south and west of Robehomme.

C Coy were also widely dispersed, with one stick landing west of the River Orne over 3.5 miles (5.6km) away from the DZ and some landing in the flooded plains around the River Dives. Despite this, one platoon managed to successfully take up defensive positions around the bridge over the River Divette so that it could be blown up by the engineers.

The remaining troops along with elements from 3 Para Bde HQ and RE, managed to take the German strongpoint at the *Château de Varaville*, take Varaville and set up defensive positions around the village. At just after 1500hrs the Canadians were relieved by 6 Cdo, at which point they moved on to le Mesnil.

By 1100hrs Headquarters Company arrived and set up 1 Cdn Para HQ in the 'brickworks'. By noon, on D-Day, 1 Cdn Para had achieved all of its primary objectives. From then on the lightly equipped paratroopers were dug into slit trenches fighting as infantry. Their remaining task was now to deny the enemy the use of this ridge. This could only be achieved by having well prepared defences and by maintaining a constant static offensive to ensure that the Germans were kept on the defensive. During this time continual reconnaissance patrols, night and day, would keep the battalion and brigade HQ informed of enemy strengths and defence positions.

In the early hours of 7 June German troops from *Infanterie Regiment 857* and *858* of *346 Infanterie Division*, launched a determined counter-attack with Mk IV tanks and SP guns in support. They approached in tight formation along the road leading to the crossroads from Varaville. As the Germans formed up paratroopers sent several salvoes of mortar rounds down between the tanks, killing and maiming many of the tightly packed infantry soldiers.

Undeterred, the Germans continued their attack. One tank managed to penetrate to within 100 yards (91m) of C Coy defences, but was soon forced back when fired upon with a PIAT. As the tank retreated the German infantry were left exposed. B Coy took advantage of the retreat by fixing bayonets and charging the Germans in a counter-attack. This surprised the Germans enough to force them back, some 250 yards (229m), to where they had set up a heavily defended position in a farmhouse at l'Abre Martin, on the right-hand side of the road.

The next day, on 8 June, B Coy rejoined the battalion from Robehomme. With the extra men now available it was decided that the Germans should be removed from the farmhouse and adjacent buildings. Following a preliminary naval bombardment Captain Peter Griffin led a force of seventy-five men, made up from HQ Coy and B Coy, towards the farm buildings under the cover of the battalion's mortar fire. Split into two sections, the main body led by Captain Peter Griffin attacked the enemy head-on, the second section protected the right flank to the north-east of their objective heading through the orchards and woods toward the Bavent road (now the D224).

Catching the Germans by surprise the Canadians managed to overrun the German outer defence positions about 200 yards (183m) from the farmhouse. Despite the Germans having six to eight machine guns set up in the hedgerows to the front of the farmhouse, Captain Griffin continued with the attack. With bayonets fixed, the Canadian paratroopers charged the enemy. Men began to fall almost immediately as the German machine-gun bullets ripped through the advancing body of men. Despite the casualties the Canadians pressed forward. As they approached the enemy lines the German machine-gunners abandoned their positions and withdrew to prepared trenches behind the farmhouse. Entering the building the Canadians used their weapons to deal with the remaining enemy troops.

At this point Captain Griffin discovered that the outbuildings and farmyard were occupied by too large a number of enemy troops, along with armoured vehicles, to make any further advance worth considering. Almost immediately the Germans had regrouped and launched a counter-attack. With mortar fire raining down and a large group of German infantry supported by a tank moving towards the farmhouse Captain Griffin ordered a withdrawal to the battalion's lines.

As the Germans moved forward, part of the section sent to protect the right flank were well positioned to deal with the counter-attack. Private Russell Geddes and Private William Novel were among the Bren gun group and sniper group and opened up with enfilade fire on the advancing Germans. Private Noval's citation for the Military Medal explains the effect this had on the enemy:

> At le Mesnil on 8 June 1944 in a company attack this man with his Bren gun and a sniper were detached to give covering fire to his section crossing open ground to the objective. When the company were counter-attacked he and the sniper were cut off but kept fighting and finally found their way into the company positions. Twenty-five dead Germans were accounted for by him and the sniper.
>
> CITATION FOR MILITARY MEDAL, PRIVATE WILLIAM 'BILL' NOVAL, B COY 1 CDN PARA

The Canadians had sustained some twenty-one casualties, eight of whom were killed. The Germans lost at least fifty killed, along with an unknown number wounded. As the Germans withdrew they left snipers posted in the trees and hedgerows who would continue to cause problems for the Canadians in the coming days.

However, the attack by 1 Cdn Para had the desired effect and the Germans did not reoccupy the farmhouse again. There were several awards for gallantry to the Canadians for their action at le Mesnil among them were Private Noval and Private Geddes who received the Military Medal and Captain Griffin who was awarded the Military Cross.

The Canadians successfully held on to their positions and beat off several more German attacks in the following days.

Casualties sustained by 1 Cdn Para amounted to over 150 in the first three weeks of fighting alone. By the end of the Normandy Campaign this figure had more than doubled to 328.

Return, in your vehicle, to the crossroads. Turn left onto the D513, signposted Hérouvillette, and stop 300 yards (274m) on your right in the narrow dirt parking space opposite the splendid old, timber and brick building. This building is called:

4) *Potérie de Bavent*, also known as the brickworks by the paratroopers it was the site of the 1 Cdn Para HQ and RAP. Opposite the pottery, is the white fenced and gated entrance to:

5) *le Ferme de Mesnil*. This farm is private property. In 1944 it was the HQ of 3 Para Bde from 6 June until 17 June. After a brief move to Ranville and three days respite at Écardes, 3 Para Bde HQ again returned to le Mesnil on 25 June and remained until 4 July. It was also the Main Dressing Station (MDS) for 224 Para Fld Amb RAMC. They were stationed here, on the front line, from 6 June until 21 June. The unit was then moved to Écarde

The *Potérie de Bavent* today. Back in 1944 it was 1 Cdn Para HQ and known as 'the brickworks'.

The lane leading to *le Ferme de Mesnil* where 224 Para Fd Amb set up the Main Dressing Station.

until 7 August and then to Riva-Bella. On 21 August they moved to Dozule for the end of the Normandy campaign.

In the grounds, attached to the farm building, there is:

6) *224 Para Fd Amb RAMC Memorial Plaque*. This was dedicated in 1989 and commemorates the 112 major life-saving operations that were carried out and the 822 serious casualties that were treated in these farm buildings between 6 and 19 June 1944. It also pays homage to the officers and other ranks of the unit who became casualties. The farm was in use as a MDS within the first day of the landings.

There were 129 men, all ranks, who made up 224 Para Fd Amb. Each parachute battalion had a medical section of nineteen medical orderlies and a RMO that would jump with them: No. 1 Section with 1 Cdn Para; No. 2 Section with 8 Para and No. 3 Section with 9 Para. The majority of the MDS Party, including administrative staff and surgical teams, would parachute in with 3 Para Bde HQ along with the five-man Casualty Clearance Station (CCS) Party.

In addition five gliders were also allocated to 224 Para Fd Amb, each with a jeep, trailer and additional medical supplies. Each of the battalion medical sections would have the use of one of the gliders, and the remaining two gliders would supply the MDS.

After landing on their DZ, the plan for the 224 Para Fd Amb was to initially help clear the area of wounded and allow the Regimental Medical Officers (RMO) and sections to move off with their respective battalions. Then a temporary Advance Dressing Station (ADS) was to be set up to care for the casualties brought in from the RAP and DZ areas. Finally all those casualties needing further treatment or evacuation would be transferred to the MDS once it had been established. All heavy transport, further medical equipment, blood supplies and the remaining twenty-eight MDS personnel were to be brought in by sea to reach the MDS by 8 June.

Like many of the parachute drops that night, things did not go quite as planned for 224 Para Fd Amb. Widely scattered, the brigade MO, two RMOs, one section MO, the senior surgeon and the CO, Lieutenant Colonel D. Thompson, were all taken prisoner soon after landing. Another two section MOs were also reported missing. Subsequently command was taken over by the 2ic Major Alastair D. Young.

The dispersed drop of the medics also meant that many of the decisions made in the field, before the casualties were sent to the MDS, were made by the RAMC medical orderlies. An interesting fact is that thirty per cent of the orderlies were actually conscientious objectors. These men, despite their moral refusal to bear arms, nevertheless underwent the arduous training to become airborne troops and risked their own lives to provide medical services during the heat of battle.

By 0830hrs on D-Day Major Young had arrived at le Mesnil Farm with some RASC staff, the junior surgeon, a section MO and twenty-seven RAMC orderlies. They had made it to the farm, from the DZ, under the protection of some men from B Coy 1 Cdn Para. Upon meeting the farmer at le Mesnil, *Monsieur* Barberot, and explaining their medical facility plans, the French farmer immediately set about arranging accommodation for the wounded paratroopers. One room, the *fromagérie*, was converted into an operating theatre where a large wooden table, normally used for making cheese, was used as an operating table (the table is still at the farm).

Originally intended as 8 Para ADS, Major Young was convinced that this was a better site for the MDS, than their intended position further east. Major Young then sought and received permission from brigade HQ to set up his MDS here. By

Pte Wildman, 224 Para Fd Amb, and his Jeep at the *Ferme de Mesnil*. Note the casualty laid on a stretcher across the front of bonnet and two more wounded laid on the back of the jeep.

the end of the first day though, only one-third of the medical staff had arrived at the MDS. Seventy-five per cent of their equipment was still missing with much of it lost in the flooded fields of the River Dives valley.

In one instance, after a glider had landed in the wrong place, an undaunted RASC driver, Lance Corporal W. Young, was preparing to drive his jeep and trailer over enemy held territory to le Mesnil; to what he thought was 8 Para's ADS. Before he could, Major Tim Roseveare CO of 3 Para Sqn RE, commandeered his vehicle so that he and his sappers could advance quickly towards Troarn and destroy the bridge there. All the medical equipment and vital supplies of plasma were removed from the vehicle and trailer and left on the ground.

Using his initiative, Lance Corporal Young persuaded a nearby group of captured Germans, with their bicycles, to help him take the supplies over 1.5 miles (2.41km) to *le Ferme de Mesnil*. This ensured that during the first day of battle resuscitation of the wounded was able to continue at the MDS. For his enterprise and sense of duty he undoubtedly saved many lives and was later Mentioned in Despatches for his dedication to duty.

Captain 'Hal' Hudson.

With just one junior surgeon and one surgically trained orderly, only minor procedures were initially carried out. By 1700 hrs though, the anaesthetist had arrived and, despite the limited medical equipment, major surgery was carried out on those with the most desperate need. Captain 'Hal' Hudson, 9 Para Adjutant, who was wounded in the stomach during the raid on the Merville Battery was one of those operated on:

By the end of D-Day ten operations had been performed. 'Hal' Hudson was among those whose abdomen had been opened up with a cut-throat razor, the gut wound sutured and his life saved by timely surgery. When the le Mesnil results of such operations were later analysed the survival rate exceeded both expectations and previous wartime experience – a tribute both to surgical skill on site and the promptitude of casualty clearance.

Lieutenant Richard 'Bobby' Marquis, No. 2 Section MO, 224 Para Fd Amb

Brigadier James Hill had also received a wound, to his buttock, after his landing. After surgery at the Divisional HQ he later used his authority as brigade commander to refuse any further surgery which would immobilize him and might have resulted in his evacuation. Instead he took alternative treatment in the form of a large dose of anti-gas serum to prevent gas gangrene. The treatment worked. Ironically, the surgeon later received a reprimand from his own CO for not insisting on obtaining a second opinion.

All but the most urgent cases had to wait, sometimes up to twenty-four hours, before they could receive treatment. The arrival of a second surgeon and anaesthetist on 8 June helped reduce the waiting time. Plasma and blood were always in short supply and blood was not brought in with supplies until several days after D-Day. On three occasions the orderlies themselves volunteered as blood donors. One of these volunteer patients was a German medical orderly *Obergefreiter* Hans Kehlenbach who had been taken prisoner at the Merville Battery. All three patients to whom the blood was donated survived.

Previous to this, *Obergefreiter* Kehlenbach had led an RASC driver to a German strongpoint where he knew that casualties had been left. In recognition of his medical integrity Major Alastair Young recommended him for the Iron Cross Class II and passed the citation to a wounded German officer. Once again, during the fighting the British and German medical orderlies worked together tending the wounded of both sides until the eight German orderlies were eventually taken to the POW camps on 14 June.

The front line and German forces were only 500 yards (457m) away during this period. British and Canadian para-troopers were constantly engaged with the enemy by probing patrols, snipers or sporadic shell, mortar, machine-gun and small arms fire. It was therefore little surprise that, as they also shared the

Obergefreiter Hans Kehlenbach, the German medical orderly who helped tend the wounded at The Merville Battery and at the le Mesnil Main Dressing Station.

same building with 3 Para Bde HQ, they would be on the receiving end of enemy fire. At 1730hrs while the Germans were launching a concentrated attack towards Hérouvillette and Ranville on 9 June, machine-gun bullets were flying between the farm buildings during the two hour attack. On the following day heavy machine-gun and mortar fire meant all but essential personnel had to take cover in their slit trenches.

On 11 and 12 June the medical personnel had to deal with the heaviest number of casualties so far, some 313 in a forty-eight hour period, mostly as a result of the attacks around the *Château St Côme* and Bréville. To add to their woes they were also strafed with anti-personnel bombs by the Luftwaffe as well. So close was the fighting to the MDS, during the first of these days, that 224 Para Fd Amb were unable to use their vehicle to move the wounded and had to rely on hand carriage of the wounded to the MDS.

But attacks on the MDS were not confined to enemy attacks, on 13 June, RAF Typhoon pilots circled the area and, apparently not seeing the 2ft by 20ft (0.6m by 6.1m) Geneva crosses that were prominently displayed, returned twice to strafe the MDS area with their 20mm cannons and rockets. Miraculously there was only one fatal casualty. Unfortunately it was a civilian, and the wife of the farmer who had welcomed the medical staff into his home.

Events eventually escalated into a concentrated and full blown artillery attack on the MDS by 105mm (4.14in) guns on 19 June. Taking three direct hits, two of the captured German vehicles and all their own transport, except for one ambulance car, were destroyed or put out of action. Twenty-nine year old Corporal Ben Wade, RASC, was also killed in the attack. It was then decided that the *Ferme de Mesnil* had served its purpose and all the medical staff and wounded were evacuated the following day.

Major Alastair Young was officially appointed Acting Lieutenant Colonel on 29 June which was to take effect, and backdated to, 7 June. He was also awarded the DSO for his service during the first month of the Normandy Campaign and officially appointed as CO of 224 Para Fd Amb.

In the first fourteen days of setting up their field ambulance at le Mesnil the surgeons and medical staff performed 112 major operations on casualties. In total 822 wounded were treated in the first two weeks of battle. Fifty-four of those treated were

German POWs. Despite the problems caused by the dispersed drop and lost equipment, in the first two days only a few known casualties did not receive medical treatment at the MDS within the first twenty-four hours of D-Day. From 8 June many were being treated at the MDS within one hour of being wounded, most were treated within ten hours.

The hazardous task of recovering and treating the wounded in the heat of a battlefield inevitably took its toll on 224 Para Fd Amb. Some sixty-eight members of the unit became casualties themselves, seven of whom were reported killed. As a testament to the skill of the surgeons and medical staff only twenty-four, less than three per cent, of the 822 casualties treated by 224 Para Fd Amb died as a result of their wounds before they were able to be evacuated. For the most seriously wounded, those requiring life-saving operations, the survival rate was more than eighty-four percent. Abdominal wounds counted for over fifty per cent of fatalities.

By the end of the Normandy Campaign, on 29 August 1944, 195 Airldg Fd Amb along with 224 and 225 Para Fd Amb RAMC had performed in their respective MDS, 397 major operations in the field. Of these the majority were compound fractures, of which 108 were treated. There were also seventy-two amputations, sixty-three abdominal wounds and even an appendicitis to take care of. The three medical units treated some 7,123 wounded during the twelve weeks of fighting. Of these, a staggering 4,850 were from 6th Airborne Division alone. A total of 821 men of the division were killed, or died of wounds, and now rest in the Commonwealth war cemeteries or local churchyards in Normandy (see page Ch. 8, C).

Return to your vehicle and continue to drive along the D513 for 0.75 miles (1.21km), down the hill from the high ground, towards Hérouvillette. Take the second turning on your right onto the D513a. Some 120 yards (110m) from the junction, on your right, there is a sharp turning into a gravelled parking area. Continue along here and 60 yards (55m) on your left there is:

F. Hérouvillette

1) *'The Pegasus Trail' Orientation Table (3)*. This is the third and final table of the AANT 'Pegasus Trail' (see Battleground Europe book *Pegasus Bridge & Horsa Bridge* Ch. 6, A22 & Ch. 7, A). Look at the map on the table and this will help you identify the local

landmarks. You are now standing facing north-north-west. Some 700 yards (640m) to your front, just across the D224 that runs from east to west across the open fields, is the south-eastern most sector of DZ/LZ N.

To your right, due NE, you can make out the water tower on the ridge. This is 1 mile (1.61km) away on the high ground, and 350 yards (320m) south-west from the *Château St Côme*. The building some 80 yards (73m) to the right of the water tower is the *Bois des Monts*. The tree line running downhill some 250 yards (229m) and due south-west, to the left of the water tower, is the sunken lane opposite the entrance to the *Château St Côme*.

Farther to the left, approximately 800 yards (731m) along the horizon from the water tower, you can see the new church tower in Bréville-les-Monts. To your front left, due north-west, the village of Ranville is approximately 1 mile (1.61km) away. To your left, due west is Hérouvillette and beyond this village, just over 2 miles (3.22km) away is the village of Longueval.

It was land between Longueval and where you now stand that was the southern front of the 6th Airborne Division's bridgehead. The task of holding and expanding this territory was given to the men of 6 Airldg Bde who landed, at 2100hrs on the evening of D-Day, in just over 170 Horsa gliders and thirty Hamilcar gliders, on the LZ to the front of you. On landing 1

A Tetrarch tank being secured inside a Hamilcar glider.

Hamilcar gliders landing on DZ/LZ N at 2100hrs on D-Day.

'The Pegasus Trail' Orientation Table near Hérouvillette overlooking the south-eastern side of DZ/LZ N.

RUR moved towards their objective of Longueval while 2 Oxf Bucks prepared for their attack on the village of Hérouvillette.

The British airborne troops in this sector were up against *21 Panzer Division* which had among its equipment a selection of armoured half-tracks, Mk IV *Panzer* tanks, SP guns and *Nebelwerfers* (multiple-barrelled rocket launchers). Initially, the only heavy fire that the lightly armed British airborne soldiers had in response to this was naval artillery support from two battleships and two destroyers anchored several miles off the coast. Later, 3rd Infantry Division, landing on SWORD Beach, would provide further artillery support.

There was also an additional armoured group that landed in the resupply mission at 2100hrs on D-Day. This was made up of Tetrarch tanks from 6 AARR, 75mm (2.95in) pack howitzers of

211 Airldg Lt Bty and one company of infantry from 12 Devons. This group was designated to move south after landing on LZ/DZ N, and intercept any approaching German armour.

On landing 6 AARR and 211 Airldg Lt Bty went into the history books as being the first units to ever land tanks and an artillery battery in battle by air. However, things did not go quite as planned. After landing, it was decided that the company of 12 Devons were needed more urgently elsewhere on the front. Furthermore, eleven of the Tetrarch tanks also became temporarily immobilized on landing when the discarded parachutes on the DZ became entangled around the sprockets on their tracks as they drove across the fields. These had to be burnt off through the night using blowlamps. Another incident that did not help the situation was when one Hamilcar glider crash-landed into a tank just as it was exiting from its glider, thus putting another two tanks out of action. Instead of their intended plan, 6 AARR then received orders to move off the following morning in the direction of le Mesnil and join 8 Para in the *Bois de Bavent*. The recce force was also used to set up a series of OPs watching the area between Ranville, Caen, Escoville and Troarn.

At 0230hrs on 7 June, 2 Oxf Bucks moved forward of 13 Para lines in Ranville to occupy Hérouvillete. C Coy occupied the western side while A and B Coy moved to occupy the eastern side. The sight that greeted the airborne troops was not pleasant.

A Tetrarch tank disabled after being struck by a landing Hamilcar glider.

Some of the paratroopers who had overshot their LZ/DZ were seen still dangling from buildings in the village where they had been shot on landing. Nevertheless, 2 Oxf Bucks managed to take their objectives by 0830hrs without encountering any enemy resistance.

Return to your vehicle and drive into Hérouvillette for some 475 yards (434m) along the D513. Take the first left turn immediately after the church. Approximately 100 yards (91m) on your left there are some parking spaces. On the wall to the right of the gateway there is a stone;

2) *Memorial Plaque to 2 Oxf Bucks.* This plaque was unveiled in June 1947 and is dedicated to the men of 2 Oxf Bucks who fought at Pegasus Bridge, Escoville, Hérouvillette, Bréville-les-Monts and the advance to the River Seine. It also pays homage to the local French people who helped this unit. The gateway to the left leads into:

3) *Hérouvillette Communal Cemetery.* Enter the cemetery and follow the footpath to your right. At the far end of the cemetery are twenty-seven graves of men from the 6th Airborne Division. Thirteen of these men are from 2 Oxf Bucks killed on 7, 9, 10 and 25 June, Two are from the RASC killed on 8 and 12 June and twelve are from The Parachute Regiment; eleven killed on 6 June and one from 7 Para killed on 16 June.

Of those killed on 6 June four were from 12 Para, three from 8 Para and one from 7 Para. Seven of those who are now buried here were the subject of a war crimes trial in 1947. Although the identities of the victims have remained unknown, *Unteroffizer* Karl Finkenrath was initially trialled for the murder of five unarmed prisoners in the grounds of the nearby stud farm *le Ferme du Lieu Haras*, situated 450 yards (411m) to the north-west of the communal cemetery, on the edge of Hérouvillette (the farm is still there today).

The trial was the result of eyewitness accounts and statements from local villagers and, later sworn statements from other members of *Unteroffizier* Finkenrath's own unit the 223 man strong *Pionier Battalon 716*. However, although he admitted to only shooting two prisoners he also offered mitigating circumstances in that he was acting under orders. With insufficient evidence to prove that he was responsible for all five murders, he was nevertheless convicted of the two murders he admitted to; after the presiding judges dismissed his claim that he was acting under orders. He was sentenced to death by hanging and after his appeal failed he was executed on 9 June 1948 in Germany.

Return to your vehicle and to the junction onto the D513a. Turn left and at the next junction, some 90 yards (82m) along the road, continue left along the D513a. After 310 yards (283m) turn left onto the *Rue d'Escoville* (D37) and continue for 1,000 yards (914m) into Escoville. Stop after the church on your right. This area is named:

G. Escoville

1) *Place Six Juin 1944*. In front of the church on the grassed area there is the black granite:

2) *Escoville Memorial to the British Liberators*. Escoville was the most southerly objective of 2 Oxf Bucks. The CO, Lieutenant Colonel Michael W. Roberts, badly damaged his leg during his glider landing and his 2ic, Major Mark Darrell-Brown, assumed command of the regiment. At 2300hrs on 6 June orders were received for 2 Oxf Bucks to move up to Ranville which was presently occupied by 13 Para ready for moving forward into Hérouvillette and Escoville. After occupying Hérouvillette in the early hours of 7 June, C Coy remained in the village while patrols from A and B Coy moved up towards Escoville from the north at 0830hrs. Expecting heavy resistance, they were initially surprised that the village was clear except for some snipers. By 1030hrs the two leading companies had reached the village and were digging in. They were followed by Major John Howard's D Coy and RHQ. C Coy continued to remain in Hérouvillette.

It was as 2 Oxf Bucks tried to advance and take the château, situated to the north-west side of the village (it was later destroyed in the fighting and has not been rebuilt), that they came under heavy fire from mortars and SP guns. The château was to be RHQ but they were only able to get about 100 yards (91m) north of the building.

The men of 2 Oxf Bucks did not have enough time to

Escoville Church and Memorial.

Grenadiers of *22 Regiment, 21 Panzer Division* in action near Cabourg.

establish coordinated defensive positions, before the Germans put in a heavy counter-attack at 1500hrs. An infantry attack, supported by armoured vehicles and tanks, was added to the mortar and SP gun fire. But the ground 2 Oxf Bucks was holding was not suitable for defence. The situation was becoming desperate as the two forward companies became heavily engaged with the advancing armoured German attack. In addition, there was also a possibility that 2 Oxf Bucks positions could be outflanked as Ste-Honerine-la-Chardronette, just over 1 mile (1.61km) to the west, was still under enemy control.

After requesting, and being granted, permission from 6 Airldg Bde the regiment withdrew to the highest piece of ground in Hérouvillette. C Coy acted as rearguard protection while parts of A and D Coy remained engaged with the enemy. For a short period the two companies became cut off. In response, B Coy reformed some 400yds (366m) north of the village and launched their own counter-attack on the German lines to help the two forward companies withdraw. By 1700hrs the regiment had taken up its defensive positions in Hérouvillette and were digging in.

C Coy launched another attack into Escoville at just after noon on 9 June. Again, after some initial heavy fighting, the Germans counter-attacked in force at 1730hrs with infantry, tanks, and armoured cars supported by SP and mortar fire. Enemy *ME109* aircraft also made an appearance and carried out a strafing attack on 2 Oxf Bucks. Two German tanks were knocked out in the battle and were left smouldering as both sides eventually withdrew from the village leaving it a No Man's Land. The day's engagement on 9 June cost 2 Oxf Bucks forty casualties. By 10 June, after just five days of fighting, 2 Oxf Bucks had sustained a total of 218 casualties.

Major John Howard, commanding D Coy, had initially come under the command of 7 Para during the early hours of 6 June, after they had successfully taken the river and canal bridges. Later that evening, control and command of the bridges was relinquished to the seaborne unit of 2nd Battalion The Royal Warwickshire Regiment (2 Warwicks) of 3rd Infantry Division that had landed on SWORD Beach.

When Major Howard joined the rest of the regiment at Ranville he was pleased to be greeted by the remainder of the *coup de main* force from glider No. 4 (see Ch. 8, A). They had managed, despite accidently landing at the bridge over the River Dives near Varaville, to make their way to their rendezvous at Ranville. After leaving the captured bridges Major Howard and his men, like all the other specialized units after D-Day, found themselves fighting the war as infantry. Paying the inevitable costs and enduring the suffering that befell all infantrymen at the sharp end.

Of the 180 men Major Howard had in his *coup de main* party on D-Day, all the sappers were returned to their respective units. The glider pilots were sent back to England and No. 14 and No. 17 Platoon were returned to B Coy. This left Major Howard down to some 100 men. In the next four days of fighting his company was reduced to less than fifty.

Major Howard was also wounded during the fighting. The first time was during the fighting for Escoville on 7 June. While visiting his forward platoon to establish the situation Major Howard peered out from behind a stone wall with his binoculars. There was a loud sharp crack of gunfire and Major Howard was thrown back onto the ground. Blood immediately began to pour from beneath his helmet. Still alive he was quickly manhandled back to the RAP for treatment. The bullet had amazingly only grazed the top of his head with a superficial, if very bloody, wound.

Major Howard, in his published work *The Pegasus Diaries*, put his lucky escape down to the length of his hair:

> *The sniper's fatal accuracy had pierced my helmet from front to back, the bullet actually grazing the top of my head. Photographs of me 'in the field' would show that my hair was particularly abundant on the top of my head at that time. A man with less hair would have been killed. As it was I could legitimately claim to have had my hair parted for me by the Germans*
>
> MAJOR JOHN HOWARD, D COY 2 OXF BUCKS

Major John Howard.

His steel helmet can now be seen in the Memorial Pegasus Museum (see Battleground Europe book *Pegasus Bridge & Horsa Bridge* Ch. 6, B). Beyond the memorial there is:

3) *Escoville Church & Churchyard*. In the churchyard there is a single grave of twenty-two year old Private William Sydney Wilkins, of 2 Oxf Bucks, who was killed in the fighting on 7 June.

Drive back for 1,000 yards (914m) along *Rue d'Escoville* (D37) into Hérouvillette and turn left onto the *Avenue de Caen* (D513a). After 450 yards (411m) take the first exit at the roundabout and continue due

A knocked-out Panzer IV.

south-west along the D514. After 1 mile (1.61km) you will pass through the village of St-Honorine-la-Chardronette. Continue for 700 yards (640m) and take the next right onto *Avenue Léon Blum* (D223). Continue for over 1 mile (1.61km) towards the factory with the red and white marked chimney and take the next left before the factory onto the *Route du Park*. Approximately 1,100 yards (1005m) on your right, in Longueval, beside the road, there is:

H. Longueval

1) *1st Battalion Royal Ulster Rifles Memorial*. This memorial is one of two memorials in Normandy that were erected as part of The Royal Ulster Rifles Memorials Project in 1996. Organised and conducted by Belfastman David Ashe, the project was conceived as a result of discussions with 1 RUR veteran Bill McConnell and 2 RUR veterans Tommy Sharpe and Stanley Burrows; during which they had expressed their sadness that there were no memorials in Normandy to their regiment and fallen comrades.

166

With the assistance of Billy Sharpe, Sam Topping, Paul Higginson and Fionnuala Rogan the project group raised funding for the memorials within several months through the generosity of many people in Northern Ireland and through the support of the RUR Association, Royal British Legion and ex-service organisations. The black marble plaques on the memorials were made and donated by stonemason John Gamble from Ballymena, the home town of the RUR, in County Antrim.

In France, Marc Jacquinot, the former director of the Memorial Pegasus Memorial Museum, liaised with the local mayors and secured the support of local residents and the final location of the memorials. A retired local stonemason, Raymond Hamard, made the memorials from locally quarried granite; as a young boy in 1944 he had witnessed the glider landings on the evening of D-Day.

The memorial at Longueval was unveiled and dedicated on 7 June 1996 by 1 RUR veteran Rifleman Bill McConnell and other veterans along with: *Monsieur* M Bouilly, Mayor of Longueval; Major General Purdon, CBE MC CPM, Honorary Colonel of the regiment; The RUR Memorial Project Group, Marc Jacquinot and many others.

The second memorial, dedicated to 2 RUR, was unveiled on 9 June near the CWGC Cemetery at Cambes-en-Plaine.

1 RUR, under the command of Lieutenant Colonel Carson, landed on the evening of D-Day as part of Brigadier The Hon Hugh Kindersley's 6 Airldg Bde. It was imperative that this low ridge starting on the bank of the River Orne at Longueval was taken, since the Germans who held this position had a clear view of the River Orne Valley and the two bridges over the river and canal between Bénouville and Ranville.

Attacking during the night 1 RUR had taken the village by first light on 7 June. Later that morning an attack was put in towards the village of Ste-Honorine-la-Chardronette, but elements of *21 Panzer Division* forced them back with a counter-attack using tanks and SP guns. 1 RUR took up defensive positions around Longueval and continued to defend this isolated area for the next seven days, during which time they were under near constant shell and mortar fire from the Germans who held the ground to their front and both flanks.

Casualties for 1 RUR were heavy during their first full day in action sustaining a total of 142 casualties. Eventually, on 13 June, 1 RUR began to relocate and moved up to relieve 12 Para and 12

Devons at the Bréville crossroads. Their move was completed by the following day by which stage they had sustained a total of 226 casualties since landing in Normandy.

During the fighting, all along the front, operational communications had to be maintained by the Royal Signals. This was required in order to provide adequate artillery and mortar support for the infantry. Twenty-two year old Captain Geoffrey Proudman, Royal Signals, had nearly fifty men in his troop and was tasked with providing part of this communication link. During the first day Captain Proudman lost twelve men during the fighting, but was nevertheless still able to establish, and maintain, the vital lines between the battalions.

In total they laid nearly eighty miles of assault cable during the first forty-eight hours of the battle alone. This small unit also set up a direct Morse code link back to Britain to help with resupply. Finally the signallers attempted to utilize the existing telephone lines.

> *During the Battle for Bréville I decided to see if the French P&T wires were working and perhaps could be used. On climbing a telegraph pole on the edge of town we keyed in and heard Germans from 21 Panzer Division speaking; we cut the wire and connected a pedal-driven generator – someone got a huge shock!*
>
> CAPTAIN GEOFFREY PROUDMAN, ROYAL SIGNALS, 6 AIRLDG BDE

Captain Proudman was later temporarily blinded and severely concussed after a mortar bomb landed near him. Having already received a MID for his conduct on D-Day, he was also later awarded the Military Cross for his actions.

The tour can be continued by following the directions in the next chapter.

168

Memorial Tour of the 6th Airborne Division Battlefield No. 3

The Bridges Over the River Dives and Divette

Distance between stops by vehicle: 24.8 miles (39.91km)
Total walking distance at stops: 1.7 miles (2.74km)
Recommended time allowed for tour: 5-7 hours

A. DZ/LZ N (South)

This tour starts on the south and towards the eastern side of DZ/LZ N. Alternatively, if you have just completed the previous tour, return to the junction by the factory. Turn left on to the D233 and continue into Ranville. At the crossroads in Ranville with 13 Para Memorial on the wall to your right (see Battleground Europe Book *Pegasus Bridge & Horsa Bridge* Ch. 7, B13), turn right onto (D37):

1) *Rue des Airbornes*. This road is dedicated to all the airborne troops and runs along the south side of DZ/LZ N. After 845 yards (773m) you come to a crossroads. It was at this crossroads Major C.A.'Tim' Roseveare, CO of 3 Para Sqn RE, gathered his men after landing on the wrong DZ.

His record in the squadron's war diary explains the chaos and confusion of the landing and why they had landed here instead of on DZ/LZ K some 1.5 miles (2.41km) to the south of here:

On landing I suspected we were in the wrong position as I could see no high ground to the east and Stirling aircraft were running in from all directions dropping paratroopers. Several gliders landed close by – they were not RE ones. My stick commander Lieutenant [Andrew] Lack and the SSM set about collecting the stick at the containers which were well concentrated and illuminated by the THOMAS devices which worked well. Paratroopers dropping around appeared to belong to every para battalion in the division. I contacted Captain [Ian] Tait of the 22 (Ind) Para Coy who said he had been dropped in the wrong place.
WAR DIARY, 3 PARA SQN RE

Major Roseveare was also able to meet up with Captain 'Tim' Juckes, CO of No. 2 Troop, and Lieutenants John S. R. Shave, George A. J. Wade, Alan N. D. Forster and David Breeze, who had also been dropped on the wrong DZ. In addition he had some sixty sappers and NCOs and some twenty plus ORs from 8 Para.

The group also had a recce boat, 400 to 500lbs (181 to 227kg) of plastic explosives, forty-five General Wade charges, demolition and cratering equipment, two radio communication sets and an adequate number of accessories. Although they only had six trolleys to carry the equipment, Major Roseveare deemed it enough to carry out some form of demolition on their three objectives; the bridges near Troarn and at Bures.

Major Roseveare organised his men and began moving off towards their objectives at 0230hrs. He, along with Captain Juckes and a few sappers, led the way. The route they took was approximately 2.5 miles (4.02km) and went due south, via Hérouvillette, then south-east via Escoville and towards a road junction, on the D37 road from Escoville to Troarn.

Sapper Charlie Willbourne was one of Major Roseveare's 3 Para Sqn RE men to land at DZ N. Unfortunately though, he had dislocated his hip on landing. Another casualty, Sapper Thomas, had been shot in the foot on the way down from his aircraft. Both men were initially carried on one of the stores trolleys that were used to carry the heavy explosives. It was soon clear however, that the two casualties would impede the group's progress and might jeopardise the operation to blow the bridges. It was decided that they would have to find their own way to 3 Para Bde HQ at le Mesnil, from where they could be transferred and treated at the nearest RAP or MDS for their injuries. As the rest of the group were initially heading in that direction they would leave arrows made of twigs to indicate the correct direction for the casualties to travel.

Using their upturned rifles as a crutch both men continued their painful journey, by daybreak they were suddenly joined by another straggler, this time from 8 Para, who had become detached from his stick. The paratrooper joined the two casualties, who welcomed having a fit companion along in the likely event of them coming into contact with any enemy.

Their journey continued, by now to the distant sound of the massive Allied naval bombardment that was heard coming from the direction of the beaches. The noise announced the start of the seaborne landings. Eventually the twig arrows ran out and the men soon became lost. While standing on a metalled road, deciding which direction to take, they suddenly had another problem to contend with; an armoured German patrol spotted and opened fire at the three paratroopers.

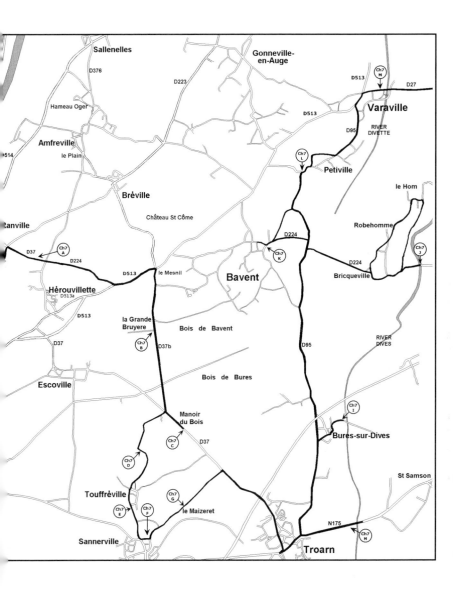

Sapper Thomas ran across the road to our right and dived over a low wall into the front garden of a house. And that was the last I saw of him! Me and the 8 Para man had committed ourselves to the track and as we moved I could see the brickwork of the 7ft [2.13m] high wall splintering as the bullets hit it. The Germans were now about 120 yards [110m] away when we found a five-

171

barred gate by the hedge leading into a large field. How I climbed that gate I don't know but I suppose blind panic helped. I tried to run alongside the hedge for cover when suddenly the machine gun on the Germans' vehicle opened up and began sweeping the hedge... I could see the tracers whizzing through the hedge no more than a foot in front of me.

The 8 Para man was now way ahead of me and out of sight and I never saw him again – so much for infantry support! I dropped to the ground trying to make myself look part of the hedge and the two German soldiers had reached the five-barred gate. The machine gun had ceased firing and surprisingly they made no attempt to scale the gate and I could hear them talking… Amazingly they turned around and went back the way they had come.

SAPPER CHARLIE WILLBOURNE,

NO. 1 SECTION, NO. 1 TROOP, 3 PARA SQN RE

Alone, Sapper Willbourne moved slowly along the hedgerow. When four Frenchmen appeared he used his own limited French to explain he was a British soldier. Then, using his army issued French phrasebook, he showed them the translated sentence *I am wounded, can you take me to a barn?* Indicating that they would come back later the Frenchmen left the field.

Panzergrenadiere of **21 Panzer Division** looking for British paratroopers among the hedgerows.

Unsure as to whether he could trust the men, Sapper Willbourne crawled to the opposite side of the field from where he had a better view of the immediate area and prepared himself a defensive position. In the shade of another hedge he began to clean out the mud from his rifle. Unable to move any further and with only his rifle and two primed No. 36 grenades as his defence, he could do nothing more than wait and see what would happen next.

After some time, he heard English voices nearby on the opposite side of the hedgerow. Shouting out *8 Para* to get their attention, he thought it may be his companion returning with his comrades. To his astonishment, when the hedge parted it was the face of his own section commander Captain 'Freddy Fox' and some of his own troop returning from their demolition task. With the aid of a 'liberated' French bicycle, they helped Sapper Willbourne reach le Mesnil MDS by evening on D-Day where his dislocated hip was treated.

On 6 June 3 Para Sqn RE had seventeen officers and 123 other ranks parachuted into Normandy, a further fifteen troops landed in gliders and twenty-one came in by sea. By the end of June, 3 Para Sqn RE had sustained thirty-six casualties from the 176 that had started out on D-Day. By the end of the campaign in Normandy this had risen to ninety-four casualties.

B. Bois de Bavent

Continue straight on at the crossroads onto the *Route de Cabourg*, along the D224, (the D37 continues off to the right at the crossroads). This crossroads is the point at which Major Tim Roseveare and his men began their journey to the bridges at Bures and Traorn. The area approximately 150 yards (137m) away on your left and along this road for the next 635 yards (581m), continues to be the southern edge of DZ/LZ N. At the point where you reach a dirt track (that is heading due north-north-east) on your left, this track marks the approximate south-eastern edge of DZ/LZ N.

Continue along the road for just under 880 yards (805m) and at the junction with the D513 turn left, and continue for 880yds (805m) along and up the hill and past the white gates of le Mesnil Farm (224 Para Fd Amb MDS) until you reach le Mesnil crossroads. Turn right onto the D37b and after 900 yards (822m) there is a road on your right called:

1) *Chemin du 8ème Para Britannique*. Dedicated to 8 Para and in the area of *la Grande Bruyère*. To your left, on the opposite side of the road, this heavily wooded area is the *Bois de Bavent*. The area immediately south of this is the *Bois de Bures* which continues

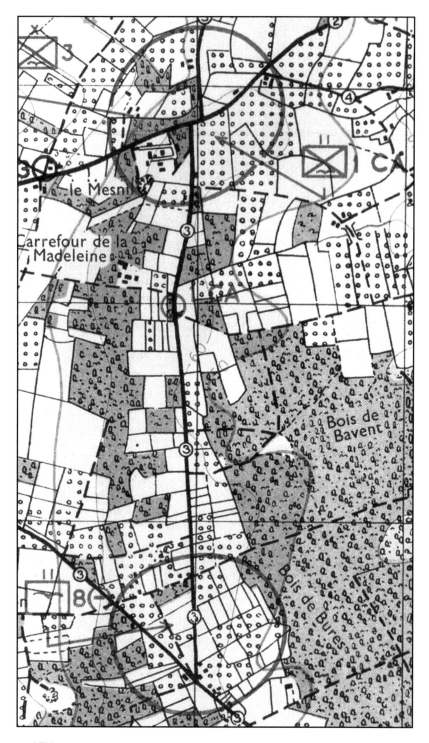

le Mesnil

Carrefour de la
Madeleine

Bois de
Bavent

Bois de Bures

down and across due south-east towards Troarn.

Under the command of Lieutenant Colonel Alastair Pearson, 8 Para had the primary task of helping 3 Para Sqn RE, less No. 3 Troop, destroy the bridges at Bures and St Samson near Troarn. In addition, they also had the task of occupying and denying the Germans the use of the heavily wooded land between le Mesnil and Troarn, which was the south and eastern approach to the high ground.

The main body of 8 Para were expected to land at 0050hrs on DZ K, the northern most part of which is located some 1.25 miles (2.01km) south-west of where you are now. However, and again partially due to some pathfinders being dropped in the wrong place and setting up their beacons and lights on the wrong DZ, some of 8 Para, along with the Royal Engineers, ended up landing on DZ N. This was some 1.5 miles (2.41km) to the north of their designated DZ. Needless to say, this severely disrupted their organisation on landing.

Initially the recce party from 8 Para had been successful in landing on the correct DZ at 0020hrs. The slight opposition they met at the DZ was quickly dealt with and in doing so they managed to take one German prisoner. They later reported in the battalion's war diary as having seen, when the main body arrived, aircraft flying in every direction, at different altitudes and all flying well above the dropping speed.

By 0120hrs, when Lieutenant Colonel Pearson arrived at the DZ, there were only thirty men present and one of the Royal Engineers Jeep and trailer. To add to the confusion the battalion's RV signal, a red and green Verey light, had been seen over 2.5 miles (4.02km) away over DZ N, near Ranville.

As a result, by 0330hrs only 140 to 150 men from the 750 men, who set out with 8 Para, had assembled at their correct RV, near Touffréville. The majority had been scattered far and wide with only a few actually landing on their appointed DZ.

Subsequently, by the evening of 6 June after some more stragglers had arrived, 8 Para strength was still only seventeen officers and 300 other ranks. Nevertheless, the battalion had been able to take up all its positions and fulfil its primary objectives. In the following days, to convince the Germans that there was a greater force occupying this area, Lieutenant Colonel Pearson ensured that his men kept up constant patrolling into the surrounding villages during the night. He also set up defensive positions by the roads and tracks in the

A wounded British paratrooper cared for by his captors.

woods to intercept any German vehicles.

The positions in these woods held by 8 Para were also constantly under attack from German patrols and mortar fire. In addition to the close-quarter fighting in the *Bois de Bavent* the general conditions endured by the men in this area proved to be most uncomfortable; since the heavily shaded ground was permanently wet the slit trenches were turned into quagmires of mud and water. To add to their discomfort, the whole area was also infested with mosquitoes and flies.

The men who occupied the ditches and hedgerows on either side of both this road (D37b), and the road (D37) leading into Troarn, were armed with anti-tank weapons and machine-guns.

This enabled them to deny the Germans the use of this main thoroughfare from Troarn to le Mesnil. For the next eleven days they managed to resist all German attacks to reach and occupy the high ground. The cost was sixty-four men of 8 Para, who were killed in the period up to 17 June.

Continue to drive down the D37b for 1.1 miles (1.77km) until you reach the crossroads with the D37. This was:

2) *8 Para Firm Base.* Major Roseveare, 3 Para Sqn RE, and his men who had landed on DZ N, reached this road junction by 0400 hrs after a one and a half hour march with their heavy equipment. It was later reported in the squadron's war diary that many were limping as a result of DZ injuries but, in a feat of endurance, all had pulled their weight on the long uphill march. Fortunately, the group met no enemy resistance on their journey to the crossroads.

At around the same time a mortar platoon commander, Lieutenant R. Thompson, arrived along with another wounded officer. With him were some fifty personnel, mainly from A Coy, and twelve medium machine-guns and six mortar detachments. He had also been dropped over DZ N, at 0100hrs, and had been helped and guided to the road junction by a Frenchman he had met in Ranville.

Taking command of the party on their arrival, Major Roseveare ordered them to set up a Firm Base at the road junction. As the most senior 8 Para officer present, Lieutenant Thompson began setting up defensive positions around the crossroads and also organised a recce patrol to move along the road (D37) heading due south-east towards Troarn.

Major Roseveare had acquired a medical jeep and trailer at DZ N. The RASC driver, Lance Corporal Young, had his jeep and trailer loaded with medical supplies and had been ready to make his way toward le Mesnil (see Ch. 6, E6) until Major Roseveare commandeered the vehicle.

Upon reaching this road junction, Major Roseveare ordered all the medical equipment unloaded into a nearby timber yard and reloaded the jeep and trailer with the heavy General Wade explosive charges. These were needed for the largest of the six bridges which the engineers had to destroy on D-Day, the 110ft (33.53m), five span masonry arch bridge on the far side of Troarn near St Samson.

From this point Captain Tim Juckes went off with the

majority of the sappers to destroy the two bridges, both 80ft (24.38m) steel lattice girder constructions at Bures (see Ch. 7, I). For this they had the use of all the plastic explosives that were loaded on the trolleys.

That left Major Roseveare, Lieutenant David Breese and seven NCOs and sappers, along with some thirty-nine General Wade charges, to complete the task of destroying the masonry bridge near St Samson. All but one climbed aboard the jeep. The remaining soldier, Sapper Sam Peachey, set up his Bren gun on top of the explosives in the heavily laden trailer. They then set off down the D37 towards Troarn to destroy the main bridge over the River Dives near St Samson. (see Ch. 7, H).

C. Manoir du Bois

Turn left at the crossroads onto the D37. some 350 yards (320m) on your left is a fenced driveway leading to the *Manoir du Bois.*

To the right of the driveway, approximately 30 yards (27m) away along the roadside, there is:

1) *8th Parachute Battalion Memorial.* This marble headstone is dedicated to all those who fought and died with 8 Para, between 6 June and August 1944, during the Normandy Campaign. At the base of the headstone there is a small bronze:

2) *Memorial Plaque to Sergeant Fred Collett.* Dedicated to the memory of Sgt Collett, who was in HQ Coy, 8 Para, and who passed away in 2002. To the right of this memorial is:

3) *Memorial Plaque to Brigadier Alastair Pearson CB DSO (&3 bars) OBE MC KstJ TD.* This is to the memory of the former Commanding Officer of 8 Para who died in 1996. From his humble beginning as a Glasgow baker and son of a grain merchant, Pearson had soon established himself as a natural leader in the army. For his service in North Africa and Sicily he was awarded the DSO plus two bars and a MC, all for leadership and bravery while in action. The twenty-nine year old Scot would later receive a fourth bar to his DSO while serving in Normandy. His unquestionable ability and daring won him many admirers, one of whom is the present Colonel-in-Chief of The Parachute Regiment, His Royal Highness The Prince of Wales, who described Colonel Pearson *as one of the great leaders of the Second World War.*

Lieutenant Colonel Pearson never suffered fools gladly and

had a total disregard for rank with his outspoken views. It was a characteristic that no doubt hindered his promotional prospects. But he was always able to resolve situations and deal with problems in his own unique way. In one instance, while he was personally leading a party over the River Dives to rescue some members of a crashed Dakota, one of his men jumped into his dinghy bayonet first; with the inevitable result. As the drenched soldier climbed out of the water Pearson sent him back into the river with a kick up the backside.

The soldier complained, as he pulled himself out of the river for the second time, and threatened to report the lieutenant colonel to the brigadier for his treatment which most certainly was not in King's Regulations. Pearson was quick to reply in his broad Scots accent:

> You can complain to General-bloody-Montgomery himself... For your stupidity, you can stay here until we come back, and guide us across the river again. And if a German patrol comes to find out what all this bloody row is about, then good luck!

The mission turned out to be a complete success, with the rescue of fourteen survivors from the crashed Dakota.

Turn your vehicle around in the driveway and return to the crossroads 350 yards (320m) back along the D37. Take the left turning and continue for 0.73 miles (1.17km) along the road. Just after the second left-hand bend there is, on the left-hand side of the road, a:

D. Memorial to Private Thomas W. Billington and Private Arthur Platt

Twenty-one year old Thomas Billington and twenty-four year old Arthur Platt of 8 Para Signal Platoon were taken prisoner, in the early hours of 6 June. However, instead of being treated as prisoners of war the two men were unceremoniously brought down this lane and shot through the back of the head.

The grim discovery was made by a local lady from Touffréville, *Mme* Yveline Langevin, as she walked down the lane later that morning. As a result of extensive work on 8 Para by Dr Tony Leake, a retired general practitioner, and William J. Lewis Platt, son of Private Platt, further information about this incident has come to light.

The troops occupying the area that evening were from *Panzergrenadier-Regiment 125, 21 Panzer Division* and were billeted in the nearby village of Touffréville. Several days later, around 10 June, the Germans moved the bodies in an attempt to cover up their crimes and any incriminating evidence. The body of Private Platt, and it is believed that of Private Billington as well, were moved and buried 1.83 miles (2.94km) south-west of here in the fields midway between Démouville and the small hamlet of Lirose west of Sannerville.

Private Platt was later found and his body reinterred in

Ranville Commonwealth War Cemetery (IIA, N, 8). The body of Private Billington has never been discovered. Dr Leake believes this may possibly be a result of the heavy bombing and shelling of this area at the start of Operation GOODWOOD on 18 July. It is an event Dr Leake remembers well as he was then a private in 8 Para and he witnessed the bombardment from his position in the *Bois des Monts*.

It is believed that while this bombardment left Private Platt's grave untouched, Private Billington's grave may have been destroyed. As

Above left: Thomas W. Billington, murdered with Arthur Platt after capture.

Above: The only known surviving photograph of Arthur Platt (arrowed). General Montgomery speaks with Major J. B. Marshall. Lieutenant Colonel Alastair Pearson is to his right.

Memorial to Thomas W. Billington and Arthur Platt.

no body has been recovered. His name is now listed, along with another 1,807 men of the Commonwealth forces who have no known grave, on the Bayeux Memorial (Panel 18, Column 1). This memorial to the missing is situated opposite the entrance to Bayeaux Commonwealth War Cemetery.

The people of Touffreville erected this roadside memorial, at the spot where the two men were murdered by the Nazis, on 6 June 1988. The perpetrators of the crime remain unknown and have therefore never been caught or brought to trial.

E. Touffréville

Continue along the road for 655 yards (599m) until you reach crossroads in the village of Touffréville. Turn right onto the road towards Escoville (D227) and stop on the dirt track 180 yards (164m) on your left-hand side. The corner of the field to your right, due north-east, is the site of:

1) *8 Para RV.* The intended rendezvous for all 8 Para on D-Day.

Turn around and drive back to the crossroads, in Touffréville, and turn right onto what is still the D227. This road is also known as:

2) *Rue du 8ème Para Bn.* Named in honour of 8 Para.

Continue along *Rue du 8ème Para Bn* and after 325 yards (297m) turn left down *Rue de L'Eglise*. Turn left after 100 yards (91m) into parking area opposite the church. This area is called:

3) *Place Caporal E. D. O'Sullivan.* Named in honour of twenty-two year old Lance Corporal Edward D. O'Sullivan, a pathfinder, who served with 22 (Ind) Para Coy. He landed on DZ K, with his commander Lieutenant Robert 'Bob' Midwood and most of the men from his stick.

Because of the heavy loads the pathfinders were carrying, their exit from the aircraft was slower than less heavily burdened paratroopers. Subsequently five of the stick, overshot the DZ and did not manage to report to the stick's RV. Amongst the missing troops was Lance Sergeant Boardman who was carrying one of the stick's two EUREKA sets.

As soon as the pathfinders landed, at 0020hrs, they came under enemy fire. Lance Corporal O'Sullivan was killed during the ensuing firefight. By 0035hrs Lieutenant Bob Midwood and his men had activated the remaining EUREKA set along with a holophane lamp. At 0130hrs the pathfinders gathered at 8 Para RV. They then began a thorough search of the DZ to try and locate the missing EUREKA. This was without success. After the

EUREKA they had activated had fulfilled its purpose, and because of continuing enemy activity all around DZ K, Lieutenant Midwood destroyed and abandoned the set. At 0530 hrs they withdrew from the DZ and made their way to the company's concentration area, over 3 miles (4.83km) away due north-west, at *le Bas de Ranville*. Across the road are some stone steps leading into:

4) *Touffréville Churchyard.* On the left-hand stone gatepost there is a green and white CWGC plaque. Just through the gates on the right-hand side there is the grave of a twenty year old French soldier *Soldat* Emile Hamel. On the far side of the church, in the churchyard, there is the grave of the twenty-two year old pathfinder, Lance Corporal Edward D. O'Sullivan.

F. Sannerville

Return to your vehicle and back along *Rue de L'Eglise*. Turn left onto *Rue du 8ème Para Bn* and continue for 700 yards (640m) until you reach the next junction in Sannerville. Turn left onto *Rue de la Liberation* (D266) and after only 40 yards (37m), turn left again onto *Rue Pasteur.* Continue along this road for 190 yards (174m) until you come to the next junction. Turn left and after 50 yards (46m) on your left-hand side, in *Place de L'Eglise*, and along the churchyard wall of Sannerville Church there is:

1) *3rd British Infantry Division Memorial.* This memorial was erected by the people of Sannerville to perpetuate the memory of the British 3rd Infantry Division who gave their lives in Operation GOODWOOD between 18 and 21 July 1944 and the subsequent battles leading up to the liberation of Europe.

Between 6 June 1944 and the end of hostilities in Europe in May 1945, the 3rd Infantry Division sustained over 11,000 casualties. These included 2,585 killed in action, 8,039 wounded and 1,363 missing. This memorial was the idea of Alain Buzuel and made possible by the work of the *Anciens Combattants et Bénévoles*. It was unveiled on 7 June 2004. On the wall to the right of the memorial, there is:

2) *Group Captain Charles Appleton CBE DSO DFC CDG. Memorial Plaque.* Thirty-eight year old Group Captain Appleton was commanding officer of No. 124 Wing, No. 83 Group, 2nd TAF. This RAF unit comprised of 181, 182 and 247 Squadrons flying Typhoon 1B aircraft. The wing had been transferred to a temporary airstrip near Caen in June 1944.

Left to right: Lieutenants Bobby de Lautour, Don Wells, John Vischer and 'Bob' Midwood, Pathfinders of 22 (Ind) Para Coy, synchronize watches prior to emplaning at RAF Harwell.

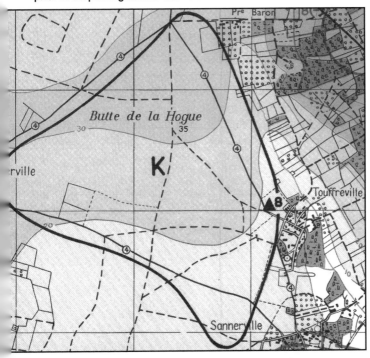

Group Captain Appleton had already lost a leg in action as a result of shrapnel wounds received in a German strafing attack while serving in Algiers, North Africa. When he was appointed CO of No. 124 Wing he was responsible for part of the offensive air to ground attack operations from D-Day onwards, providing valuable help to the Allied ground forces.

Despite his senior rank he regularly participated in operational sorties. On 12 August he was flying Typhoon MN928 G of 247 Sqn. While leading the flight his aircraft received a direct hit from German anti-aircraft fire and his aircraft plummeted to earth killing him instantly. He is now buried in Banneville-la-Campagne Commonwealth War Cemetery (IV, C, 14)

Between 6 August and 21 August No. 124 Wing lost a further eight pilots killed and four shot down and taken prisoner. From 6 June to the end of the Normandy Campaign in August 1944, 161 Typhoon pilots lost their lives. A memorial to all those pilots killed is in the village of Noyers-Bocage.

G. le Maizeret

Continue from *Place de L'Eglise* and along *Rue du Muguet* for 0.73 miles (1.17km) climbing the hill into the small hamlet of le Maizeret. On the right-hand side of the road, just after a left-hand bend in the road there is:

1) *41, 46, 47 & 48 Royal Marine Commando Memorial*. This memorial is dedicated to the Royal Marine units of 4 SS Bde. Under the command of Brigadier B. W. 'Jumbo' Leicester, the brigade was actively patrolling this area between 7 and 17 August 1944 during which time they helped liberate Sannerville and Troarn.

There were five Royal Marine commando units that landed in Normandy on 6 June 1944. 45 RM Cdo was grouped with the three army commando units of 3 Cdo, 4 Cdo and 6 Cdo, to form 1 SS Bde. Meanwhile the remaining Royal Marine units formed 4 SS Bde.

On D-Day 41 RM Cdo landed on SWORD Beach at la Bréche d'Hermanville and fought their way west towards Lion-sur-Mer and Luc-sur-Mer. At the same time 48 RM Cdo landed on JUNO Beach at St-Aubin-sur-Mer and pressed on due east into Langrune-sur-Mer. Meanwhile, 47 RM Cdo landed on GOLD Beach and were tasked with heading farther west to take the coastal village of Port-en-Bessin. On 7 June 46 RM Cdo landed on JUNO Beach as 4 SS Bde reserve. They then helped form the link-up between 41 and 48 RM Cdo. On D-Day the Royal Marines lost over ninety men killed in action.

Later, in June, 4 SS Bde came under the command of 6th Airborne Division. The brigade helped reinforce the left flank of the Allied forces, while General Montgomery continued with his battle to take Caen. Although they formed part of the defences to hold the line along the high ground on the east side of the River Orne, the commandos, along with paratroopers, continued to launch probing and reconnaissance patrols deep into enemy territory.

After the capture of northern Caen in Operation CHARNWOOD on 8 July and the southern part of the city by the end of Operation GOODWOOD on 21 July, the Allied forces continued preparing for a breakout.

The Americans in the west of Normandy launched Operation COBRA on 25 July and began pushing the German forces east towards Falaise. Meanwhile, the British launched Operation BLUECOAT on 30 July on their right flank and on their boundary with the US 1st Army.

On 7 August Operation TOTALIZE began to the south of Caen with the Canadians and Poles pushing the Germans down towards Falaise and out on the south-east flank. As this battle progressed Major General Gale was told by the CO of I Corps, Lieutenant General J. T. Crocker, that the Germans were preparing to withdraw along the 6th Airborne Division front.

Major General Gale, reinforced with the *Dutch Princess Irene Brigade, Belgian Piron Brigade* and commandos from 4 SS Bde, prepared to launch an offensive across the flooded meadows and river of the Dives valley. This would not only protect the left flank of the Canadian and Polish forces but also, by keeping the pressure on the retreating Germans, it would enable the Canadians to accelerate their advance towards Falaise and aid the Canadian and Polish advance eastward. News finally arrived that the commandos would soon be launching an all-out offensive.

We'd been prodding at the Hun for a week or so, speeding the parting guest if you like, but, though one front after another seemed to be dropping back, our own particular and pet German unit – Fusilier Bataillon 346 – *just didn't want to budge. Then one morning I was called with my colonel to the usual O Group of commanding officers at headquarters of 4 SS Bde, and there we heard it. 'Gentlemen,' said Brigadier Leicester, 'the enemy on our front is starting to retire.' That was for me my most inspiring moment.*

LIEUTENANT D.F. MURRAY, 41 RM CDO

On 14 August, the Canadians launched Operation TRACTABLE reaching Falaise two days later. In the meantime Major General Gale had been preparing his own offensive for the 6th Airborne Division and on 17 August the aptly named Operation PADDLE began.

General Gale chose to make his main advance along a route that ran from Troarn towards Putot-en-Auge and Dozulé. From here he would continue the offensive over the River Touques at Pont l'Evêque, on through Beuzeville and the River Risle at Pont Audemer, which was less than 6 miles (9.66km) from the River Seine. Meanwhile, 6 Airldg Bde, the *Dutch Princess Irene Brigade* and *Belgian Piron Brigade* would clear the Germans from along the coast through Cabourg.

This offensive began with 6 Airldg Bde, *Princess Irene Brigade* and *Piron Brigade* attacking north and east of Sallenelles through Merville-Franceville-Plage, No. 1 SS Bde attacked north-east through Bavent and 1 Cdn Para pushing south-east from le Mesnil through the *Bois de Bavent*. To the east 3 Para Bde launched their offensive over the River Dives at Bures and 4 SS Bde went on from the area around this memorial to take Troarn.

H. Troarn (and St Samson)

Continue uphill through le Maizeret, for a further 750 yards (686m) until you reach a T junction. Turn right onto *Rue du Bois* (D37) and across the flyover the A13 (*L'Autoroute de Normandie*) into Troarn. After 800 yards (731m) you will reach a roundabout. Back in 1944 this was the site of the:

1) *Troarn 1944 Railway Level Crossing*. The fourth exit off the roundabout, to your left, is called *Rue du Chanoine Longuet*. This road follows the path of the old railway line that ran, in 1944, east of Troarn and onto Bures where it crossed over the River Dives some 1.88 miles (3.02km) to the north-east. This was a vital supply line for the Germans. The 80ft (24.38m) steel lattice girder railway bridge in Bures that supported the railway was one of the two primary objectives in the village of Bures for Captain Juckes of 3 Para Sqn RE to destroy (see Ch. 7, I).

The road along which you have just travelled, *Rue du Bois* (D37), is the same road that Major Roseveare travelled with eight

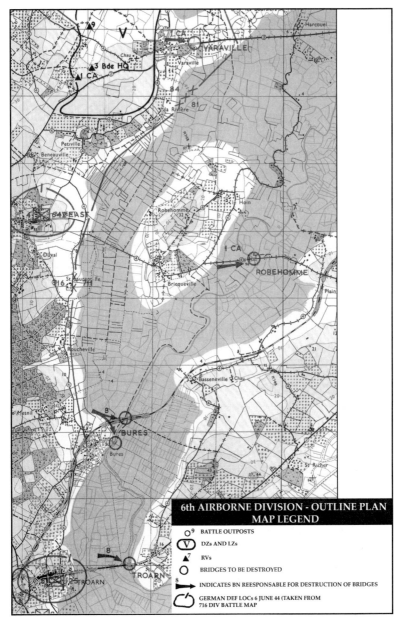

6th AIRBORNE DIVISION - OUTLINE PLAN
MAP LEGEND

O⁹	BATTLE OUTPOSTS
Ⓥ	DZs AND LZs
▲⁷	RVs
O	BRIDGES TO BE DESTROYED
→⁸	INDICATES BN REESPONSABLE FOR DESTRUCTION OF BRIDGES
↻	GERMAN DEF LOCs 6 JUNE 44 (TAKEN FROM 716 DIV BATTLE MAP

men in the heavily laden Jeep and trailer, after he left 8 Para Firm Base at the D37 crossroads and junction with the D37b (see Ch. 7, B2). The roundabout, which was a level crossing back in 1944, was the place where Major Roseveare and his team ran into a German roadblock. His account in the squadron's war diary

187

explains what happened;

> We had set off down the road at a moderate pace with everyone
> ready with a Bren and several Stens ready for any trouble. Just
> before the level crossing we ran slap into a barbed wire knife rest
> road block. One Bosche fired a shot and then went off. It took
> twenty minutes hard work with wire cutters before the jeep was
> freed. We then proceeded on, leaving behind it transpired later,
> Sapper Moon.
>
> MAJOR TIM ROSEVEARE, CO, 3 PARA SQN RE

Proceeding with slightly more caution, Major Roseveare had
sent two scouts ahead to the next crossroads as they untangled
the jeep.

Continue along the *Rue du Bois* (D37) for 350 yards (320m) until you
come to the next roundabout with a calvary to your right, Take the third
exit off the roundabout, on your left, and onto the *Rue de Rouen* (D675).
Find a suitable place to park. Immediately on your right, off the
roundabout, is:

2) Troarn Communal Cemetery. On the wall to the left of the
gateway entrance into the cemetery, is the now familiar green
and white Commonwealth war graves plaque. Inside the walled
cemetery, over to the far right along the west boundary wall,
there are three commonwealth headstones of paratroopers from
8 Para all killed on the 6 June 1944. These are twenty-two year
old Sergeant John Davies from HQ Coy, twenty-three year old
Private Henry M. Carter from A Coy, and twenty-six year old
Sergeant John A. Iliffe from A Coy. The circumstances
surrounding their deaths are unknown.

Also in this cemetery are the graves of Mme Suzanne Lamy
and her one year old son Philippe, both local civilians killed
during the fighting around here.

Outside the entrance of the cemetery, to your left, is:

3) Troarn Eastern Crossroads. Although a roundabout has been
put in today, back in 1944 this was where Major Roseveare's two
scouts were heading for after leaving the level crossing. As they
approached the crossroads, from the direction from which you
approached in your vehicle, a German soldier armed with a rifle
cycled across the intersection. By now the jeep and trailer had
been freed and was heading for the crossroads. It was quickly
decided the German should be dealt with:

On being dragged from his bicycle he protested volubly and we made the mistake of silencing him with a Sten gun instead of a knife. The town was now getting roused so we lost no time and everyone jumped aboard while I tried to make the best speed possible. As the total load was about 3,000lbs [1360kg] we only made about 35mph [56kmh].

MAJOR TIM ROSEVEARE, CO, 3 PARA SQN RE

Return to your vehicle and continue along the *Rue du Rouen* (D675) into Troarn. This is the same route Major Roseveare took as he drove straight through the centre of the village. Some 420 yards (384m) from the roundabout the road starts to bend to the right. On the corner, to your right, there is a car park behind the building that has the *Syndicat d'Initiative* (Tourist Information Office) and *Police Municipale* (town Police station). Park here.

This area where you have parked is known as:

4) *Place Paul Quellec* named after one of the French heroes of the Resistance who were killed in 1944. Above on the right-hand side of the *Police Municipale* building there is a plaque dedicating

The road in Troarn down which Major Roseveare sped in his jeep and trailer; on the left is Troarn Church.

the area to him. Also in front of the building there is a statue of a First World War soldier. Behind this on the wall there is:

5) *Troarn War Memorial.* This memorial lists twenty local men who were killed in the First World War, four local men who were killed in the Second World War and the six local civilians who lost their lives in the Second World War. To the right of the plaque there is a:

6) *Memorial Plaque to 3 Para Sqn RE*. The plaque reads, when translated: *Erected by the people of Troarn in honour of the officers and men of 3 Para Sqn RE who, on information given by the Resistance, destroyed the bridges over the Dives to protect the left-flank of the landings at daybreak on 6 June 1944.* Walk out of the car park and turn right. 40 yards (37m) along the *Rue du Rouen* (D675) there is another crossroads. Cross the road and on the corner of the building above you there is a street sign naming this road:

7) *Voie Major J.C.A. Roseveare*. You may wish to walk further along the *Rue du Rouen* (D675), to see the area along which Major Roseveare raced while under fire, before returning to your vehicle.

As the jeep rounded the corner in Troarn, the Germans, were alert having been roused by the sound of the Sten gunfire from the eastern crossroads. Spread-eagled with a Bren-gun, on top of the General Wade charges in the trailer, was Sapper Sam Peachey, he had taken up the position as rear gunner as the Jeep accelerated through the town. In the Jeep Major Roseveare was driving, Lieutenant Dave Breeze, Lance Sergeant Bill Irving, Corporal John Windeatt, Lance Corporal Bill Fellows and Sapper Tom Price were all on board, some returning fire with their Sten guns. Perched precariously on the tow bar between the jeep and trailer was Sergeant Joe Henderson

> *At the corner here the fun started. There seemed to be a Bosche in every doorway shooting like mad. However, the boys got to work with their Sten guns and Sapper Peachey did very good work as rear gunner with the Bren gun. What saved the day was the steep hill down the main street. As the speed rose rapidly and we careered from side to side of the road, as the heavy trailer was swinging violently, we were chased out of the town by a MG 34 which fired tracer just over our heads.*
>
> MAJOR TIM ROSEVEARE, CO, 3 PARA SQN RE

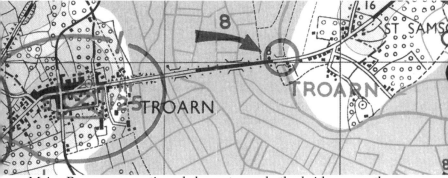

Major Roseveare continued down towards the bridge over the River Dives.

Return to your vehicle and turn right out of the car park onto the *Rue du Rouen* (D675). Continue for just over 0.75 miles (1.21km) through the town, past the church on your left, and downhill following the route Major Roseveare took towards St Samson. Park your vehicle on the dirt track on the right-hand side of the road just before the:

8) *Site of Troarn's 110ft (33.53m) Five Span Masonry Arch Road Bridge.* Today this new bridge is built on the same site. When Major Roseveare and his men arrived at the bridge they found that there were no Germans guarding it. They also discovered that they had lost Sapper Peachey and his Bren gun. He had been thrown off the trailer as they came down the hill. Injured by his fall Sapper Peachey was taken prisoner.

Lieutenant Breese and Lance Sergeant Henderson ran back a short way along the road towards Troarn and set up an ambush in case the Germans followed. The rest of the men unloaded the trailer and set about laying the General Wade charges across the central span of the bridge. This completed, a detonation cord was fixed up and the charges detonated.

The centre span of the 110ft (33.53m) five span masonry arch bridge gave way under the explosion and a breach of 15-20ft (4.75-6.1m) was created. The demolition had taken about five minutes to complete. A second demolition party extended this gap to 35-40ft (10.67-12.19m) later in the day (see Ch. 7, I5). Next to the bridge on the south-west side there is a:

9) *Memorial to Major J.C.A. Roseveare.* This memorial was dedicated on 5 June 1986 by the people of Troarn and pays tribute to Major Roseveare and his men who successfully blew up the bridge in the early hours of 6 June 1944.

After the successful demolition of the bridge, Major Roseveare decided to avoid Troarn and instead headed due

The original five span, 110 ft (33.53m) masonry arch bridge at Troarn (near St Samson) that Major Roseveare demolished.

north, up a farm track beside the river, in the direction of Bures. When the track came to an end the jeep was dumped and the men set off on foot. Lieutenant Breese made a reconnaissance of Bures before the group approached, but he believed that the Germans were occupying the village.

It was some time between 0500hrs and 0540hrs and Major Roseveare decided they should head due west towards the road junction and Firm Base held by 8 Para and from where they started their journey to the bridge near Troarn.

As they neared the road junction the sound of heavy machine-gun fire was heard coming from around the area, Major Roseveare decided to change plans and divert straight to

Memorial to Major J.C.A. Roseveare beside the new bridge at Troarn (St Samson) over the River Dives.

brigade headquarters at le Mesnil.

He reached HQ at 1300hrs and only after he and his men had swum across several streams and found their way through the dense woods in the *Bois de Bavent*. Major Roseveare was later awarded the Distinguished Service Order for his actions in the field.

About thirty minutes before Major Roseveare arrived at battalion HQ, Colonel Pearson, not having received any news on the Troarn Bridge, decided to send another demolition party to destroy the bridge. They were under orders to destroy the bridge or, if they found the bridge had already been, destroyed, then they were to try and widen the breach.

I. Bures sur Dives

Drive for just over 0.66 miles (1.06km) back into Troarn on the *Rue du Rouen* (D675) and at the first crossroads turn right onto the *Rue du 6 juin*. Continue for 473 yards (432m) until you reach the junction with the *Route des Marais* (D95). This junction is where 3 Para Sqn RE set up a Firm Base for a second attack on the Troarn Bridge (see Ch. 7, I5) later on D-Day. Turn right, and continue along the *Route des Marais* (D95) for 0.75 miles (1.21km) until you reach the village of Bures. Take the first turning on your right. This is called:

1) *Rue du Capitaine Juckes*. This street was named in honour of Captain Thomas 'Tim' Roland Juckes who led the demolition party into Bures to destroy the two bridges.

Follow the road for some 350 yards (320m) until you reach, on your left:

2) *Bures War Memorial*. This memorial is dedicated to the local people who were killed in both the First World War and Second World War.

Turn right in front of the war memorial and follow the road, *Rue du Port*, for 480 yards (439m) until you reach a small bridge over the River Dives. This is the:

3) *Site of Bures 80ft (24.38m) Steel Lattice Girder Farm Track Bridge*. This brick farm track bridge, now called *Pont du Capitaine Juckes* (Captain Juckes Bridge) was built to replace the steel lattice girder bridge that was destroyed by Captain Juckes, CO of No. 2 Troop 3 Para Sqn RE. To the left of the bridge is a stone plinth with a bronze plaque that forms:

4) *Capitaine Juckes Memorial*. This memorial dedicates the bridge to the memory of 24 year old Captain Thomas 'Tim' R.

Juckes. On 28 June 1944, Captain Juckes, was reporting to the HQ of 1 Cdn Para at the brickworks at le Mesnil, when a mortar bomb landed next to his jeep. He was knocked unconscious and received a severe chest wound. His driver immediately took him to the RAP from where he was then taken down to the MDS in Ranville.

He never recovered consciousness and died of his wounds soon after. The following day he was buried in the cemetery in Ranville (IIIA, H, 9). The last rites were performed by his friend, and 9 Para Chaplain, the Reverend Captain John Gwinnett. For his action in Normandy Captain Juckes received the MC. His troop was taken over by Lieutenant John S.R. Shave who would also receive an MC for his action in Normandy.

Some 450 yards (411m) downstream, due north-north-east, on the other side of the River Dives and along a dirt track that runs parallel to the river, there is the:

Farm bridge over the River Dives at Bures blown up by Captain Juckes.

Juckes Bridge, the new bridge that replaces the one blown by Captain Juckes.

5) *Site of Bures 80ft (24.38m) Steel Lattice Girder Railway Bridge*. Although the 80ft (24.38m) steel lattice girder railway bridge and railway line no longer exist, part of the bridges concrete foundations are clearly evident today on the east bank of the river. This is all that remains of the second bridge Captain Juckes and No. 2 Troop 3 Para Sqn RE were tasked with destroying on D-Day.

The railway signalman's house is still visible and located 35 yards (32m) from the west bank of the river. Some 100 yards (91m) farther downstream, beyond the remnants of the railway bridge, you can see the bridge carrying the *Autoroute de Normandie* (A13) over the River Dives.

In the early hours of 6 June, as Captain Juckes and his men approached the village of Bures, they heard the massive explosion caused by Major Roseveare's detonation of the General Wade charges at the bridge near Troarn. When they reached Bures, at approximately 0545hrs, they were met by a Trowbridge party from 8 Para led by Captain Charles Shoppee. This group had also been dropped in the wrong place and landed some 1.5 miles (2.41km) to the north near Bricqueville. After landing, they made straight for the bridges at Bures to reconnoitre the area.

A recce patrol from 8 Para also arrived at Bures around this time. A runner was then sent to bring up a platoon to provide further protection for the Royal Engineers and also to bring the jeeps with RE stores. By 0630hrs Captain Juckes had arrived at the bridges, completing their 2 mile (3.22km) journey with their heavily loaded trolleys from 8 Para's Firm Base at the crossroads.

RAF reconnaissance photograph showing the 80ft (24.38m) steel lattice girder railway bridge over the River Dives at Bures.

Stone support pillar, all that remains of the railway bridge at Bures. In the distance is a new bridge that is part of the *Autoroute de Normandie* (A 13).

The 80ft (24.38m) bridge was a steel lattice girder bridge and used primarily, like the concrete bridge that has replaced it today, as a farm track. Captain Juckes split his group, totalling about one and a half sections, into two parties. Lieutenant John Shave and one section of No. 2 Troop started arranging the demolition charges at this bridge, Captain Juckes, with Lieutenant Alan Forster and the remaining men of No. 2 Troop, went to deal with the railway bridge. This was located some 450 yards (411m), downstream. While this, too, was an 80ft (24.38m) steel lattice girder bridge, it was of heavier construction so that it could withstand the railway line.

In the meantime men of No. 1 Troop were on guard to provide local protection for the engineers while they went about their tasks. Lieutenant George Anthony 'Tony' Wade was sent back to help find Lieutenant Andrew Lack and his trolley party. They had fallen behind due to several of the sappers having sustained injuries at the DZ. On his journey he met some of No. 1 Troop in a jeep and trailer. They had landed on the correct DZ/LZ K, along with some of 8 Para. The CO of 8 Para, Lieutenant Colonel Alastair Pearson, had sent the men to Bures with the extra supplies after hearing that Captain Juckes was there.

Lieutenant Wade took the jeep and decided to proceed on to Troarn. However, some French locals alerted him to the fact that Troarn was occupied by the Germans and that he would not be able to get through. He decided to return to Bures with the Jeep and trailer and carried out a reconnaissance of the bridge near Troarn on foot which was just over 1 mile (1.61km) away. On his way to the bridge he came across the jeep and trailer that had been used by Major Roseveare and his men. He also found the bridge had been demolished across its central span. With no sign of any engineers he returned to Bures to report his findings.

Lieutenant Shave and his section had prepared the farm track bridge for demolition in just over thirty minutes. However, during their preparations Captain Juckes returned to report some complications had arisen and that detonation of the charges on the farm track bridge should wait until these had been resolved.

The first problem was that some 350 yards (320m) downstream, between the two bridges there was a crashed glider. This had landed and come to a halt on the embankment with part of the glider actually in the river. Inside there was one of the glider pilots, Sgt F Carpenter, with two broken legs. Also injured were gunners from 4 Airldg A Tk Bty that had been part of the three man crew travelling with the glider's cargo of a jeep and 6pdr anti-tank gun. The remaining gun crew member and pilot, Capt J.M. Walker had tried to remove the jeep and trailer but without success. After ensuring the glider pilot and other casualties were as comfortable as possible, they left the scene and moved on towards their objective which had been LZ N.

The second problem was that the railway bridge was of an even heavier construction than had been anticipated. Captain Juckes decided that this bridge should be blown first and then, once that had been successful accomplished; they would withdraw over the farm track and then destroy the second bridge.

With the return of the jeep and trailer by Lieutenant Wade it was decided the jeep, now free of its cargo of explosives, could be used as a temporary ambulance to evacuate the glider pilot and gun crew. They were carefully extracted from the crashed glider and loaded onto the jeep and evacuated back to 8 Para, in the *Bois de Bures*, some 2 miles (3.22km) to the east, for further medical treatment.

With the farm track bridge ready for demolition, Lieutenant Shave and his men initially tried to salvage the anti-tank gun and jeep from the glider. But, despite working for over an hour trying to untangle the lashing chains, they were unable to free the cargo from the half-submerged glider. Instead, Lieutenant Shave and his men moved to help form part of the defences around the area while Captain Juckes and his team completed final preparations for the demolition of the railway bridge.

At just after 0900hrs Captain Juckes ordered everyone back over to the west side of the River Dives across the farm track bridge. Only Lieutenant Alan Forster remained on the east side ready to detonate the charges. Men were sent to evacuate the local inhabitants of the houses and farm buildings near the river and move them towards the centre of the village. Captain Juckes also allowed a local farmer to move some cattle from the fields back into the village.

Once the area was clear Lieutenant Forster detonated the explosives. A terrific explosion announced the demolition of the railway bridge. After inspecting the damage and ensuring the bridge was destroyed, Lieutenant Forster returned to the farm track bridge and withdrew to the west side of the River Dives.

Lieutenant Shave then detonated the charges on the farm track bridge. Also destroyed and sunk was a steel punt that was anchored in the river. By 0930hrs the engineers had successfully completed another of their objectives. In his book, *'Go To It' The Story of the 3rd Parachute Squadron RE*, published after his promotion to Major, Lieutenant Shave recalls the timing; *this was some four hours later than we had hoped, but in view of the unexpected events, we thought quite justifiable.*

With his primary objective achieved, Captain Juckes decided his men needed some sustenance before they moved off. With sentries still posted, to guard the village, Captain Juckes ordered his men to sit down in the street, brew up some tea and have breakfast from their ration packs. For half an hour the men relaxed, smoked, ate and chatted between themselves almost as though they had just completed a training exercise back in the UK. Not everyone was so relaxed about the situation:

While we were smoking and talking, the villagers, who by now had lost their first shyness, were very anxious lest in our seeming folly we should allow the 'Salles Boches' to fall upon us and destroy us. [Captain] 'Tim' [Juckes], however, was fully aware of the risk and knew it was outweighed by the need for a short rest.
LIEUTENANT JOHN S.R. SHAVE, COMMANDER, NO. 6 SECTION
NO. 2 TROOP 3 PARA SQN RE

Once rested, the men of 3 Para Sqn RE moved off towards the *Bois de Bures* to search out 8 Para HQ. The troops from 8 Para remained in the village. Captain Juckes went on ahead in one of the jeeps and reported to the CO of 8 Para, Lieutenant Colonel Alastair Pearson, at 1000hrs.

Lieutenant Colonel Pearson organised a party and personally led them back to Bures in an attempt to salvage the jeep and anti-tank gun in the glider. This proved to be impossible and so they withdrew back to the *Bois de Bures*. By 1215hrs both Captain Juckes' men and Lieutenant Colonel Pearson were back at battalion HQ.

The CO of 8 Para decided that an attempt should be made to widen the breach of the main road bridge at Troarn. The force, under the command of Captain Juckes, consisted of a demolition party with Lieutenant Tony Wade and six sappers from No. 1 Troop in a jeep and trailer. There was also a rearguard party led by Lieutenant Shave and No. 6 Section of No. 2 Troop, and a protection party formed by No. 9 Platoon of 8 Para commanded by Lieutenant William Brown. There was also a detachment of Royal Engineers, under the command of Sergeant Shrubsole, for added protection.

The party moved first east to Bures and then south down to Troarn, along the *Route des Marais* (D95) at the junction of the track leading south into Troarn (now called *Rue du 6 Juin*) a Firm Base was established for the demolition party and rearguard party.

Despite some warnings that were received from the local inhabitants and sniper fire from the Germans in the village, a decision was made to continue. The protection party from 8 Para pushed south into Troarn and reached the crossroads. Lieutenant Brown's men then forced the Germans west through the village, while Sergeant Shrubsole's detachment pushed east and down the hill towards the bridge. During the battle several German prisoners were taken and were later identified as being from *21 Panzer Division*. Meanwhile, the rearguard party took up positions in the area, then an orchard, between the houses and the Firm Base.

Once the road was clear, the demolition party raced through Troarn in the jeep and trailer and down to the bridge. Charges were laid across the span next to the one already destroyed previously by Major Roseveare and his men. By 1500hrs, a second section was successfully demolished and one of the supporting piers almost completely destroyed. The gap in the bridge was now some 35-40ft (10.67-12.19m). The party also destroyed some boats and punts on the river but left the sluice as this did not allow any vehicle traffic. The demolition party then withdrew through Troarn via the route they had come and Captain Juckes force was back at 8 Para HQ by 1630hrs.

J. Robehomme

Drive back along *Rue du Port* and *Rue du Capitaine Juckes* and turn right onto *Route des Marais* (D95). Continue along for some 2.2 miles (3.54km) then turn right at the T junction onto the D224. Continue for 0.75 miles (1.21km) into Bricqueville. Follow the road through the village that bends round to the right and then after 100 yards (91m) it bends to the left. Continue for 700 yards (640m) and take the right-hand fork in the road (still the D224). Continue for 850 yards (777m) down this straight road until you reach the River Dives and the:

1) *Site of Robehomme 80ft (24.38m) Steel Lattice Girder Bridge.* Today a similar bridge has replaced the bridge destroyed by the engineers of No. 3 Troop 3 Para Sqn RE, under the command of Captain Geoff Smith and B Coy from 1 Cdn Para, in the early hours of D-Day. Although Robehomme is nearly 0.75 miles (1.21km) away it was the nearest main village to this bridge, hence the reason it is referred to as the Robehomme Bridge. On the brick wall on the south-west corner, before the bridge, there is:

2) *Memorial Plaque to 3 Para Sqn RE and 1 Cdn Para.* This memorial is dedicated to the men tasked with destroying this bridge over the River Dives, and Varaville Bridge just over 2 miles (3.22km) to the north over the River Divette. The troops were scheduled to land on DZ V located west of Varaville. The same DZ that 9 Para were designated. However, like 9 Para, men from 1 Cdn Para and 3 Para Sqn RE were spread over a much wider area. 3 Para Sqn RE later reported that the majority had been dropped 0.6 miles (0.97km) east of the DZ.

200

The 80ft (24.38m) steel lattice girder bridge that has replaced the one destroyed by 3 Para Sqn RE and 1 Cdn Para. On the south-west corner of the bridge is a memorial plaque.

In one instance, a pilot's evasive action resulted in the paratroopers, from a small HQ party, being thrown to the floor of the aircraft, by the time they got to their feet and exited the aircraft the stick was spread from Varaville to Robehomme, a distance of over 1.8 miles (2.9km). Furthermore, because all the low-lying marshland around in this area had been flooded by the Germans, the majority of the men from 3 Para Sqn RE landed in water or on sodden ground.

British intelligence had estimated that the depth of the flooded areas would be about 9 inches (22.86). In reality it proved to be about an average of 3ft (0.91m) in depth. There were also underwater hazards such as the drainage ditches to contend with. These could add an extra 6ft (1.83m) more to the depth. Many barbed wire entanglements had also been laid as part of Rommel's defences against airborne operations. Any paratrooper who had the misfortune to land in the floods would almost certainly have jettisoned most of his equipment for fear of drowning. The floods also meant it was more difficult to

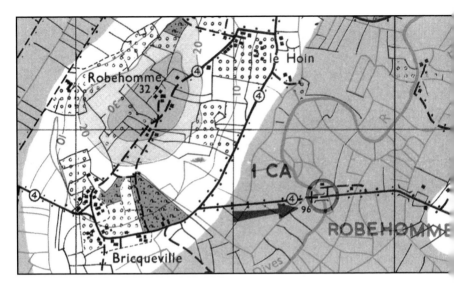

locate the containers, carrying heavier equipment and explosives. However, the THOMAS illuminated locating devices they were fitted with, did offer some help as they had been designed to work underwater.

Lieutenant Jack Inman, No. 10 Section leader from No. 3 Troop 3 Para Sqn RE, was fortunate to find three containers carrying explosives and to make contact with twelve sappers. They then proceeded towards Varaville and the bridge over the River Divette.

After navigating the crossing of several ditches he and his men arrived at the Varaville Bridge and were met by Lieutenant Edward 'Ted' Baillie, No. 9 Section leader from No. 3 Troop 3 Para Sqn RE. He was, however, on his own having not been able to locate the rest of his men from his stick.

Lieutenant Inman left five sappers and 200lbs (90.72kg) of explosives with Lieutenant Baillie. He took the remaining seven sappers and using a single trolley, began heading off towards Robehomme. In the southern part of Varaville Lieutenant Inman contacted the CO of No. 3 Troop, Captain Geoff Smith. Also with him was Lieutenant Beverley 'Bev' Holloway, CO of No. 11 Section of No. 3 Troop and three sappers.

Captain Smith went onto the bridge at Varaville (see Ch. 7, M6) while Lieutenant Inman, Lieutenant Holloway and the remaining seven sappers continued towards Robehomme. On reaching Petiville they obtained information that Bavent was occupied by the Germans, so the party took to the flooded fields. After 0.6 miles (0.97km), the trolley full of explosives was proving difficult to manage, so each man took a load and carried the explosives on their backs.

At 0900 hrs the party of seven men reached Robehomme where they made contact with Sergeant Bill Poole of 3 Troop 3 Para Sqn RE. He had landed near the bridge and had successfully managed to destroy it with the help of a number of Canadian paratroopers. Major Clayton Fuller, CO of B Coy 1 Cdn Para, had been one of the first to reach the bridge, along with his 2ic, Captain Peter Griffin and another thirty men from the battalion. Joining them soon after was Lieutenant Norman Toseland and a group of another twenty-nine men from B Coy. They had been guided safely through the marshes and German minefields, to the bridge, by a local French woman.

Although Sergeant Poole didn't have any of the engineers' explosives, he improvised by using the 2lbs (0.91kg) of plastic explosives some of the paratroopers carried for their No. 82 Gammon Grenade. He managed to collect approximately 30lbs (13.61kg) of explosives and placed it precisely where it would have most effect.

Major Fuller left to find 1 Cdn Para HQ while Captain Griffin and his men waited to see if any other Royal Engineers would arrive with additional explosives. At 0630hrs none had arrived so Sergeant Poole detonated the explosives and successfully destroyed the bridge.

A guard was set up at the bridge and the rest of the paratroopers moved to the high ground in the village of Robehomme some 0.7 miles (1.13km) away.

Lieutenant Inman, having spoken with Sergeant Poole, decided that after his men had taken a short rest he would continue down to the bridge and try to further extend the damage. At 1100hrs his party were preparing to blow two craters in the road next to the bridge when German infantry moved up on the other side of the river in several lorries. Although pinned down by the German fire, they managed to detonate the explosives and withdrew to Robehomme under the cover of their Bren gunners.

At Robehomme the Royal Engineers and Canadians dug in and prepared their defences. The high ground in the village gave them a good view of the surrounding countryside and area up to the bridge they had just destroyed.

Drive back along the D224 for 850 yards (777m) until you reach the junction with the D95. Turn right onto *Chemin de Bas* (D95) and continue for 0.75 miles (1.21km) until you reach the road junction at le Hom:

3) *Site of le Hom (aka le Hoin & le Hain) Objective.*

By 7 June only one of the primary tasks for 3 Para Sqn RE had yet to be completed. This was the blowing of the culvert, a small bridge, at le Hom (referred to as le Hoin on the maps issued to the paratroopers and le Hain in the War Diaries).

This objective, however, was abandoned as the position could not be located due to the extensive flooding. Instead it was decided that two craters would be blown at this road junction as this would have the same effect on enemy movement. This lies some 850 yards (777m) north-east of the church at Robehomme. At 1600hrs on 7 June, Lance Sergeant Wren and seven sappers successfully made this junction unfit for traffic.

Continue along this road for a further 1.1 miles (1.77km), through la Londe and along *Chemin de l'Anguille* to the culvert, over the unnamed waterway. It is most likely that this is the culvert that the Royal Engineer paratroopers were tasked with destroying but were unable to locate because of the floods. This however cannot be confirmed as the map reference on the orders issued incorrectly placed the culvert some 150 yards (137m) to the north-east in a place where there is no roadway or culvert.

Return to the junction at le Hom and turn right onto *Rue du Robehomme*. Continue for 900 yards (823m) until you reach:

4) *Robehomme Church.* It was on this hill, just south of the church that Lieutenant F. Williams landed. He was the last man out of the aircraft with the small HQ party from 3 Para Sqn RE, that had been dropped in the stick that extended for over 1.8 miles (2.9km) between Robehomme and Varaville.

His experience, and the problems encountered as a result of his poor drop, was similar to many other paratroopers that night. After landing he managed to contact two sappers and initially proceeded, due north, towards the bridge over the River Divette in Varaville. However, because of the flooded marshland in the Dives valley, he had to first head east via Bavent. Finding this village held by the Germans, he decided to head south and then west, through the *Bois de Bures* and towards le Mesnil.

Picking up stragglers from 8 Para, 13 Para and 1 Cdn Para along the way, He finally made it to 3 Para Bde HQ at 0900hrs, after a journey of over 4 miles (6.44km).

The task of holding the high feature of Robehomme had been assigned to B Coy 1 Cdn Para, along with a section from No. 3 Troop 3 Para Sqn RE. The church spire here in Robehomme was used as an OP by 1 Cdn Para, as it offered an excellent view of the surrounding countryside. Beside the road on a wall to the left of the church, there is:

Robehomme Church and Memorial plaques.

5) *Robehomme Memorial Plaque*. This bronze plaque was dedicated in June 1997, to the inhabitants of Robehomme, by the veterans of 1 Cdn Para. The plaque also acknowledges the work of the Royal Engineers and was given to the village in gratitude to the citizens of the Bavent area for the risks they took to assist the battalion. To the right of the plaque there is a seat bench. On the backrest there is a:

6) *1 Cdn Para Memorial Plaque*. This plaque dedicates this seat to all ranks of 1 Cdn Para who gave their lives for freedom while serving with 3 Para Bde.

There were no Germans in the village when elements of 1 Cdn Para first entered Robehomme, although there were several skirmishes throughout the day as the Germans attempted to infiltrate the village. The nearby school building, to the left of the church, was turned into a temporary dressing station by the medical orderlies.

By midday on D-Day the strength of troops at Robehomme was about 120 men all ranks and made up of both British engineers and British and Canadian paratroopers. The village was secured and guarded by using available cover or by digging slit trenches.

During the day an attempt was made by some men from 1 Cdn Para to recover a jeep and trailer from a nearby glider. This had crash-landed in 3ft (0.91m) of water just over 900 yards (823m) away to the south-south-west of Robehomme Church and just to the east of Bricqueville. However, initial attempts were frustrated by enemy fire.

A detachment of thirty-two men from 12 Para also made an attempt to move through the village of Bavent, but they were captured. The OP in the church spire allowed the Canadians to observe the Germans' movement along the road (D27), some 2 miles (3.22km) to the north-east, between the bridge over the River Dives and the bridge over the Divette at Varaville. This went on for many hours with the Germans bringing infantry and artillery up towards Varaville. Unfortunately, with no radio equipment 1 Cdn Para were unable to relay details of enemy movement to 3 Para Bde HQ at le Mesnil. With the Germans holding Bavent, the troops here were almost completely isolated.

By 7 June Captain Griffin had organised the mixed groups of sappers and paratroopers into three platoons. At noon a reconnaissance party was also despatched to establish a safe route to battalion HQ at le Mesnil. The beleaguered troops at Robehomme did slowly grow in strength, as throughout the day stragglers continued to find their way to the village. This brought the total number up to over 150 all ranks.

An attack on Bavent was launched, but proved unsuccessful. In the meantime Lance Corporal Hill led another party, at 0100hrs, in another attempt to salvage the equipment from the nearby crashed glider. This attempt proved more successful and the group returned with much of the equipment from the glider seven hours later.

As Lance Sergeant Wren was blowing the road junction to the north-east at le Hom, the two remaining roads leading up to the village from the south-south-west were also being blocked. Situated approximately 600 yards (549m) from the church, road blocks were created using rows of Mk V anti-tank mines, thus denying the use of the road to any enemy vehicles.

At 2000hrs the reconnaissance party returned from le Mesnil, reporting the route clear of enemy. They also returned with orders to prepare for withdrawal to battalion and brigade HQ. Lieutenant I. Wilson, IO for 1 Cdn Para, came to guide the party back. Sappers were immediately sent out to lift the anti-tank mine road blocks. In addition, a German machine-gun post situated just over a mile away to the south-west of Robehomme, and south of Bavent, was dealt with at 2300hrs by one of the Canadian platoons.

At 2330hrs the paratroopers, now 162 men strong, began their withdrawal from Robehomme. They began by heading down the hill towards Bricqueville. To transport the wounded the local parish priest had given the paratroopers his car. In addition a local farmer also gave the troops his horse and cart. There were many occasions where the local inhabitants took risks to help the airborne troops. This generosity and kindness by the local people did not go unnoticed, even at the highest level:

> *Here is an incident, one of many, which I think indicates the courage of the French. A farmer who had been very badly wounded by a bomb splinter during the bombing by the British aircraft impressed everybody, not so much by his courage, which was remarkable, as by his attitude towards the bombing of his home; 'C'était terrible,' he said. 'Mais je sais bien que cétait necessaire. Il faut souffrir pour nous débarasser des Boches.' There was no word of recrimination against the British; and when we had to evacuate the position, and leave him behind because he was too ill to be moved, they were all sad indeed.*
>
> MAJOR GENERAL RICHARD GALE, GOC, 6TH AIRBORNE DIVISION

When the paratroopers passed through Bricqueville they were challenged by German sentries. A firefight ensued during which seven Germans were killed and another was wounded. The wounded German was put on the cart along with the Canadian wounded and the group moved on.

Shortly afterwards, along the road from Bavent, the leading platoon ambushed a German staff car killing four of the officer occupants. The party continued through the *Bois du Bavent* until they reached 3 Para Bde HQ at le Mesnil at 0330hrs in the morning of 8 June.

Robehomme was again reoccupied by the Germans. It would remain in enemy hands until 17 August when it was liberated in the start of Operation PADDLE.

Continue along *Rue du Robehomme*, after 180 yards (165m) you reach a crossroads. Continue straight on along *Rue de Sources* and after 425 yards (389m) there, on your left-hand side, there is a small lane. It is this junction, and at the junction with the *Chemin de la Vieille Cavée* some 170 yards (155m) along this lane, that the engineers laid their anti-tank mines across the road to deny the Germans access to Robehomme via the road.

Continue for a further 375 yards (343m), following the road around to the left, until you reach the junction with the D224 in Bricqueville. Turn right and drive for 0.75 miles (1.21km) until you reach the T junction with the D95.

K. Bavent

Turn right at the junction onto the D95 and then, after 180 yards (165m) take the next left onto the *Rue de Marais* (D224). Drive for 770 yards (704m) and on your left you will see Bavent Church. Continue along the road, now *Rue du Lavoir* past the church and park on the right near the pond. This area is called:

1) *Place Alexandre Lofi*. The area is named in honour of Second Lieutenant (aka *Enseigne de Vaisseau*, naval equivalent of Sub Lieutenant, army equivalent of Second Lieutenant) Alexandre Lofi. He was a French officer that commanded the seventy-one men of *No. 8 (French) Troop* of 1 BFM Cdo. Between 9 June and 13 July, while *Commandant* Phillipe Kieffer was being treated for his wounds, Second Lieutenant Lofi was appointed commander of 1 BFM Cdo.

On 17 August during Operation PADDLE, 1 BFMC, attached to 4 Cdo of 1 SS Bde, helped liberate Bavent and Robehomme. To the right, just before the pond there is a:

2) *Memorial to 1 SS Bde*. This memorial is dedicated to 3 Cdo, 4 Cdo, 6 Cdo and 45 RM Cdo of 1 SS Bde. This memorial was dedicated in 1984, on the 40th Anniversary of the Normandy landings, to the memory of 1 SS Bde by the grateful population of Bavent and Robehomme.

By mid-August the commandos had been on the front line continuously for over two months. It had been initially believed that the commandos would be withdrawn to prepare for further special operations once the bridgehead had been established. However, such was the need for well trained soldiers that the commandos, like the airborne troops, remained at the front fighting alongside the regular infantry.

Return to your vehicle and drive back along *Rue du Lavoir*. Park your vehicle in the area *Place de l'Eglise* which is on your right just before:

3) *Bavent Church and Churchyard*. On the church wall there is the now familiar green and white Commonwealth War Grave sign. In the churchyard there is the grave of thirty-five year old

Lieutenant David Haig-Thomas. His first regiment was the RASC, but he had joined the commandos and was attached to C Troop of 4 Cdo for the invasion of Normandy.

This was the only troop of 4 Cdo who wore the coveted airborne wings on their battledress. Lieutenant Haig-Thomas was assigned as liaison officer between the 6th Airborne Division and the commandos. He and his runner Private Ryder were the only two men of the troop to drop by parachute into Normandy. The remainder came in on landing craft on SWORD Beach.

Lieutenant Haig-Thomas was killed soon after landing, by a stick grenade, when ambushed by some Germans. He was a remarkable character having rowed three times for Cambridge University and also represented Great Britain in the 1932 Los Angeles Olympics. He was also a keen explorer, naturalist and wildlife photographer and had worked with the great British conservationist, artist and ornithologist, Peter Scott.

Retun to your vehicle and turn right onto *Rue du Marais* (D224) and then, after 50 yards (46m) take a left, opposite the church, down *Rue du Champs*. Some 320 yards (293m) on your left hand side is Bavent Cemetery. Inside there is a stone upon which there is a:

4) *Memorial Marker for the Ashes of Brigadier Derek Mills-Roberts*. The memorial marker, in a small area surrounded by a low small hedgerow, states that beneath this stone rest the ashes of Brigadier Derek Mills-Roberts CBE DSO and Bar MC Legion d'Honneur and Croix de Guerre with Palm.

Lieutenant Colonel Mills-Roberts was CO of 6 Cdo until 12 June. On this date he took over command of 1 SS Bde after Brigadier The Lord Lovat was wounded at Amfréville (see Ch. 6, B & C1). He was then also promoted to Brigadier. His commando memoirs were published in 1956 in a book called *Clash By Night*. He died, aged seventy-one years, on 1 October 1980.

L. Petiville

Continue to drive on *Rue des Champs*, along the single track for a further 450 yards (411m) until you reach the junction with *Route de Troarn* (D95) and then turn left and drive for 750 yards (685m) into Petiville. Alternatively, if the single track is not accessible, return, down the *Rue des Champs*, into Bavent, and turn left onto *Rue du Marais* (D224). Continue for 750 yards (686m) until you reach the T junction with the D95. Turn left and continue for 0.85 miles (1.37km) into Petiville.

At the T junction in Petiville turn right onto *Rue de l'Eglise* (D95), continue for 200 yards (183m) and pull into the parking area on your right. On the opposite side of the road, in front of Petiville Church, there is:

1) *No. 3 Commando Memorial.* This memorial is dedicated to the men of 3 Cdo, under the command of Lieutenant Colonel Peter Young DSO MC of 1 SS Bde, who liberated Petiville on 17 August 1944. This memorial was unveiled on 7 June 1994 on the 50th Anniversary of the Normandy landings.

M. Varaville

Return to your vehicle and continue along the *Rue de L'Eglise* (D95), past the church, and along *Route de Varaville* (D95) for just over 1.1 miles (1.77km) until you reach the junction with D513. On your right at this junction is a grey marble:

1) *Memorial to 1 Cdn Para and 9 Para.* This memorial was dedicated in June 1994, to the 750 men of 9 Para, under the command of Lieutenant Colonel Terence Otway DSO, who were to land near here with the task of neutralising the guns at the Merville Battery.

The memorial is also dedicated to 1 Cdn Para who were tasked with: protecting 9 Para as they advanced to the Merville Battery; helping destroy the bridge over the River Divette and attacking the German fortified strongpoint in Varaville.

There is acknowledgement that this was all accomplished by 1000hrs (recorded as 1030hrs in the war diaries) on 6 June and that during the course of this action 1 Cdn Para lost nineteen men killed in action, ten wounded and eighty-four were taken prisoner. The inscription also mentions that 9 Para had only seventy-five men left after their attack (see Ch. 3 & 4) and that this sacrifice for the return of freedom should never be forgotten. On the base of the memorial there is a bronze:

Petiville, 3 Cdo Memorial.

2) *Varaville Memorial Plaque.* This plaque was dedicated in June 1997 to the community of Varaville by veterans of 1 Cdn Para. It was presented in gratitude of the risks the citizens of Varaville, and the surrounding area, took to assist members of the battalion during the Normandy Campaign.

Turn Right onto the D513 and after just 200 yards (183m) turn left onto the lane, heading south-west-west, that after 90 yards (82m) leads to:

3) *Gatehouse for Château de Varaville.* This gatehouse was the scene of some fierce fighting for the Canadians. C Coy 1 Cdn Para had been assigned the task of destroying a nearby German signal exchange, destroying the bridge over the River Divette at Varaville along with sappers of No. 3 Troop of 3 Para Sqn RE and neutralizing enemy positions in Varaville which would include the area in and around the *Château de Varaville.*

Only about thirty men from C Coy were actually dropped on DZ V, the rest were dispersed over a wider area. While some were within the general area of the DZ, others were dropped a considerable distance away. The 2ic of C Coy, Captain John Hanson, and his stick were dropped 10 miles (16.09km) from the DZ. Another stick landed on the west side of the River Orne and less than 1 mile (1.61 km) from the SWORD Beach.

C Coy had dropped before the main force of 1 Cdn Para along with the pathfinders from 22 (Ind) Para Coy, and a detachment from both 9 Para and 3 Para Bde HQ. This was done to allow C Coy time to secure the DZ. As a result of the dispersed drop C Coy was not able to meet at its RV. Instead the separate groups of paratroopers made their way towards Varaville and the château.

In the meantime, two sticks from 22 (Ind) Para Coy, commanded by Lieutenant Robert 'Bobby' E. V. de

Varaville Memorial Plaque.

Château de Varaville gatehouse.

Latour, began setting up their navigational aids for the pilots carrying the main body of paratroopers from 9 Para and 1 Cdn Para. By 0040hrs at least one EUREKA was set up and a T set out on the ground using holophane lights and coding the letter V was also operational. The main drop commenced at 0050hrs, but would also be dispersed over a wide area.

Major Hugh MacLeod, CO of C Coy 1 Cdn Para, had landed near the north end of the DZ. Nearby his runner, Private Peter Bismutka, had also landed and the two men began to move towards their RV at the south-west side of the DZ. As they moved they were caught up in the bombing of the Merville Battery by the RAF. This had started at 0030hrs but some of the 100 Lancaster Bombers accidently dropped their 4,000lb (1814kg) bombs over or near the DZ.

Shaken, but fortunately sustaining no casualties from the unexpected bombing, Major MacLeod and his runner made it to the RV just after 0030hrs. Unfortunately, instead of the 100 or so men he had expected to meet at the RV only fifteen had made it. Among the group were Lieutenant Hugh Walker and Sergeant G. Davies. Instead of the heavily armed force of paratroopers equipped with machine-guns, mortars, explosives and anti-tank weapons, the group were equipped with only one PIAT, three sten guns, rifles and a pistol.

Nevertheless, Major MacLeod ordered Sergeant Davies to take his platoon up to the bridge over the River Divette in Varaville and set up defensive positions until the engineers arrived to blow the bridge. The rest of the men, under Major MacLeod, headed toward the gatehouse for the *Château de Varaville*. By securing the area around the château they would be protecting the DZ from any German attacks from Varaville.

The château was soon cleared and the men moved on to the

212

gatehouse. This building overlooked a German strongpoint which was made up of an earth and concrete trench with machine-gun posts positioned at regular intervals. Positioned nearby was a pillbox with a 75mm (2.95in) anti-tank gun. Major MacLeod linked up with more men from C Coy as they approached the gatehouse. One group entered and searched the gatehouse finding it empty. However, it was clear from all the bunks that the Germans were using it as a barracks and had only recently vacated their beds to take up their action stations. The remaining men, under Lieutenant Walker, set up defences around the building and in a shallow ditch near the gatehouse.

Upon reaching the second floor of the gatehouse Major MacLeod looked out to observe the German defensive positions around their strongpoint. But his men had already been spotted by the Germans and within seconds an artillery round hit the building. Fortunately no one was injured. Major MacLeod called for Corporal Winslow Oikle to bring his PIAT up to the second floor. Lieutenant Walker and four other men also went up.

Cpl Oikle fired his PIAT at the concrete pillbox, but the round fell short. As he hastily reloaded the cumbersome weapon, the Germans retaliated with another round from the 75mm (2.95in) gun. A high-explosive round tore through the wall of the room in which the Canadians were taking cover. The PIAT ammunition exploded and twenty-one year old Lieutenant Walker, twenty year old Corporal Oikle, nineteen year old

Memorial plaque to 1st Canadian Parachute Battalion at the *Château de Varaville* gatehouse.

Private John Jowett and Private Leslie Neufeld were killed instantly. Major MacLeod and Private Bismutka were fatally wounded and Private Thompson lost part of his hand.

Private William S. Ducker, the medic, despite being under heavy fire, was able to evacuate the wounded with the help of Private Sylvester. Twenty-five year old Major MacLeod died within minutes, in the lap of Captain John Hanson who then assumed command of the group. Private Thompson and Private Bismutka were taken to the RAP that had been set up in the château. Private Bismutka died the following day. Twenty-two year old Private Ducker was awarded the MM for his action on D-Day. He was later wounded and died on 19 June 1944.

Major MacLeod and Lieutenant Walker now rest in Ranville CWGC Cemetery (VA, B, 1 and VA, B, 2). Private Bismutka rests in Bretteville-sur-Laize CWGC Cemetery (VII, B, 2) and Private Ducker rests in Hermanville CWGC Cemetery (1, W, 17). The bodies of Corporal Oikle and Privates' Jowett and Neufeld were never

Private William Ducker tending a wounded German prisoner.

recovered or later identified and have no known grave. Their names are inscribed on the CWGC Bayeux Memorial (Panel 27, Column 2).

Further stragglers continued to arrive, bringing the total number of men at the gatehouse to over thirty. Although the group had lost the PIAT they had gained a machine-gun with the new arrivals. Later, Corporal Dan Hartigan also arrived with a 2inch (50.8mm) mortar.

Captain Hanson heard that Brigadier James Hill, CO 3 Para Bde, had arrived in Varaville after his miss-drop. He set off with his batman to meet the commander but was caught in a firefight. He was slightly wounded but his batman was killed. C Coy, with

214

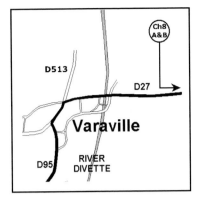

elements of brigade HQ and Royal Engineers, managed to take up defensive positions all around Varaville and also completely encircled the German strongpoint.

In the meantime Lieutenant McGowan and his platoon had landed some distance from the DZ, but on approaching Varaville they managed to ambush two German infantry sections that were attempting to enter the village. After suffering some casualties the German reinforcements surrendered. Lieutenant Samuel McGowan then moved his men to take up firing positions on the German strongpoint.

But the Canadians were not fighting the Germans alone. Their war diary records help from others:

> *During this time the local inhabitants were of great assistance, the women dressing wounds and the men offering assistance in any way. One Frenchman in particular distinguished himself. Upon being given a red beret and a rifle he killed three German snipers. This man subsequently guided the Brigade Commander and his party towards le Mesnil. Although I believe he was a casualty of the bombing attack that caught the party enroute to le Mesnil* (see Ch. 4, AFTERMATH).
>
> WAR DIARY, 1 CDN PARA, 6TH AIRBORNE DIVISION

Heavy sniping and mortar fire from the surrounding woods near Varaville continued to harass the Canadians as they continued their siege around the German strongpoint. At one point an enemy patrol, from outside the strongpoint, managed to re-enter the château, now a Canadian RAP, and captured all the wounded and medical staff. Despite a counter-attack by the Canadians the Germans managed to escape taking their prisoners with them.

At around 0830hrs a German, under a white flag, came out from the strongpoint to request evacuation of their wounded. Captain Hanson provided the Germans with a cart and soon some six or seven wounded, some walking, others in the cart, appeared on the lane between the château and the gatehouse. To everyone's surprise, a German machine-gunner opened fire on

215

his own men riddling the cart with bullets.

The siege continued amid sporadic mortaring, machine-gun and rifle fire. An hour or so later, Corporal Hartigan used a drainage ditch to crawl up, with his mortar, to within direct firing range of the German gun position. Using the trunk of a tree to stabilise the base of the mortar he held it near horizontal and fired off, in quick succession, four rounds into the emplacement. This he followed with several smoke bombs. Expecting a rapid response from the Germans, he quickly crawled back to the relative safety of a deeper ditch.

But the Germans had been worn down and sometime around 1030hrs a white flag appeared and forty-two German prisoners were taken. In addition four Canadians who had been captured by the Germans, having parachuted within the perimeter of the strongpoint, were released.

At 1500hrs leading elements of 6 Cdo arrived at Varaville. At 1730hrs C Coy 1 Cdn Para withdrew from Varaville and moved to their battalion HQ at le Mesnil. Some 15 yards (14m) in front, and to the left, of the gatehouse entrance there is:

4) *1 Cdn Para Memorial Plaque.* This bronze plaque is dedicated to the six men of 1 Cdn Para, mentioned in this chapter, who were killed in this gatehouse by the enemy shell fired from a German bunker that was within sight of the second floor window.

This plaque was unveiled on 6 June 2004, on the 60th anniversary of D-Day. The memorial also pays tribute to the citizens from Varaville for the assistance 1 Cdn Para received in defeating the German troops.

Return to your vehicle and along the lane to the junction with the D513. Continue straight across the junction and along *Avenue de la Libération* (D27). Some 200 yards (183m) on your left there is:

5) Varaville Churchyard. It was in the grounds of the church that C Coy 1 Cdn Para set up their Company HQ. During the early hours of the morning they were able to stop at least one group of Germans from advancing through the village.

Continue for a further approximately 300 yards (274m) and you will cross over a small bridge over the River Divette. Find a safe place to park and return to the bridge. This is:

6) Site of Varaville's Small Masonry Single Span Bridge. This

The River Divette Bridge in Varaville.

bridge has replaced the bridge destroyed by the engineers of No. 3 Troop, 3 Para Sqn RE, under the command of section leader Lieutenant Edward 'Ted' Baillie of No. 3 Troop and C Coy from 1 Cdn Para in the early hours of D-Day. On the west side of the bridge, just below the sign for the river, *La Divette*, there is a marble stone upon which is mounted a red:

7) *Memorial Plaque to 3 Para Sqn RE and 1 Cdn Para*. This memorial is dedicated to the engineers and Canadians for successfully destroying the bridge here over the River Divette.

The first engineer to arrive at the bridge had been section leader Lieutenant Ted Baillie. Soon after another section leader, Lieutenant Inman, from No. 3 Troop arrived. He was also accompanied by some other engineers and a supply of explosives. He left five sappers and 200lbs (183kg) of explosives before he continued, with his remaining men, on to Robehomme.

Captain Geoff Smith had made it to the bridge as did a sergeant and his platoon from 1 Cdn Para. While the Canadian paratroopers provided a defence for the engineers, No. 3 Troop successfully blew a 15ft (4.57m) gap in the bridge.

The area around the demolished bridges could not be held and covered due to the shortage of troops. Eventually the Germans were able to cross the River Dives and River Divette, after they had made some repairs or constructed temporary bridges.

Nevertheless, the primary objectives for the Royal Engineers

Memorial plaque to 3 Para Sqn and 1 Cdn Para by the bridge over the River Divette in Varaville.

from 3 Para Sqn and the paratroopers from 1 Cdn Para, were all completed. There is no question that these operations were successful in delaying the Germans from reinforcing and building up their forces in the area of operations of the 6th Airborne Division. Most importantly, during the crucial first twenty-four hours while the Allies established their bridgehead.

This concludes the tour of the bridges in the Dives valley that were to be destroyed by 3 Para Sqn RE. However, you may wish to use Varaville as the starting point for two extra stops that are listed in the next and final chapter.

CHAPTER EIGHT

Memorial Tour of the 6th Airborne Division Battlefield No. 4

Additional Places of Interest

Distance between stops by vehicle: 5.5 miles (8.85km)
Total walking distance at stops: 0.03 miles (0.05km)
Recommended time allowed for tour: 1 hour

A. River Dives Bridge Near Varaville

From the Bridge over the River Divette in Varaville, continue along the D27 for 2 miles (3.22km) until you reach the bridge over the River Dives.

Unlike Pegasus and Horsa Bridge there are no memorials at this site on the edge of *Commune de Périers en Auge*. Nevertheless, this is where glider No. 4 (662), chalk mark No. 94, with serial code PF723, and destined for Ranville Bridge over the River Orne, landed in the first hour of 6 June 1944.

The glider had been towed by a Halifax bomber, serial LL344-P, from 644 Sqn, 38 Group, RAF, piloted by Flying Officer G. Clapperton. There were also five more air crew. The two officers on board, from 2 Oxf Bucks, were Lieutenant Anthony 'Tony' Hooper and 2ic Captain Brian Priday. The total complement on this glider was twenty-eight troops (including five engineers) plus two glider pilots (for full roster of tug crew, glider crew and assault troops see Battleground Europe book *Pegasus Bridge & Horsa Bridge* Appendix F)

Their glider was landed safely by Staff Sergeant Lawrence and Staff Sergeant Shorter just 40 yards (36m) from the north-east corner of this bridge. The glider came to rest, facing the bridge, in a small ditch that ran parallel with the river and with its starboard side wing tip tilted down over the River Dives.

An error by the tug pilot had resulted in the glider being released too far to the east, over Cabourg. For the glider pilots, who were not immediately aware of the error, the two waterways and bridges over the River Dives and *le Grand Canal* that runs just 170 yards (155m) to the east must have looked very much like their objective as they made their descent. Despite the navigational error, the glider pilots managed to skilfully land their glider between the only two bridges in this area. Unfortunately their real objective was over 7 miles (11.27km) due west-west-south.

219

Glider No. 94 and River Dives Bridge.

Upon landing the troops, realising they were in the wrong place, disembarked and set up a defensive perimeter around the glider. Captain Brian Priday sent Lieutenant Hooper towards the nearby bridge. Concerned that the glider with its broad white D-Day stripes may become a target for any Germans in the area, Captain Priday moved the men away from the glider. He then joined Lieutenant Hooper at the bridge. No shots had been fired and on reaching the bridge there appeared to be no Germans guarding or attempting to defend it. However, an ominous sign that the enemy was nearby was a single German steel helmet left resting on the wall of the bridge.

Captain Priday returned to his men with the intention of working out their position. As he did, the Germans who had been at the bridge had by now recovered from their shock, regrouped, and began to open fire on the abandoned glider. Captain Priday and his men scrambled for cover, many finding a deep dry ditch. As the enemy fire subsided, Captain Priday held a brief Orders Group (O Group). He decided to send men out in different directions to secure their position and recce for any distinctive landmarks so that they could establish their whereabouts.

After questioning the glider pilots, who were full of remorse for their landing, Captain Priday was soon able to establish their location next to the River Dives. He also appreciated that the landing was through no fault of the glider pilots, as they would not have been able to glide their aircraft over to the River Orne bridge even if they had realised they were over the wrong area after being released from the tug.

Captain Priday then decided on his next course of action. First he was going to capture the bridge as this would create a distraction to the German forces in this area, helping to further confuse the enemy as to the real objectives for the 6th Airborne Division. Secondly, the quickest route to joining Major John Howard, and the rest of D & B Coy at the River Orne and Caen Canal bridges, started at the other side of this bridge.

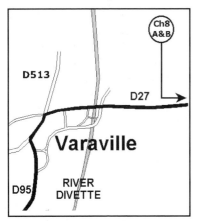

Lieutenant Hooper led a small party forward to the bridge, followed by Captain Priday. Soon fighting broke

The place where glider No. 94 landed next to the River Dives.

out, with grenades being thrown by both sides and machine-gun and small arms fire echoing in the night air and lighting up the area. The airborne troops continued their fight and soon gained control. Captain Priday's men then took up defensive positions at both ends of the bridge.

As Captain Priday prepared covering fire so that the remainder of his men could cross the bridge, Lieutenant Hooper and his party continued down the road in the direction of Varaville. Their aim was to take control of a nearby small wooded area. As Captain Priday tried to contact the remaining party on the east side of the bridge, one of Lieutenant Hooper's men returned to report that the wood was clear and that the platoon commander was waiting for him.

> Before we could move we heard voices coming out of the darkness and footsteps down the middle of the road. Very soon I knew why. He was being marched along with his hands in the air and a Boche escorted him. I was wondering what to do when Hooper edged over towards the spot where only a few minutes before he had left me. This gave me a view of the German against the skyline.
>
> CAPTAIN BRIAN PRIDAY, 2 OXF BUCKS

Together with Lance Sergeant Rayner, Captain Priday shouted *Jump Tony!* Only 10 yards (14.9m) away from his two comrades Lieutenant Hooper jumped into the roadside ditch. His escort was mown down by Sten gun fire. As the German's dead body hit the ground his reflexes pulled the trigger on his sub-machine-gun. One bullet hit Captain Priday's map case another went through Lance Sergeant Rayner's arm.

At this point, the enemy occupying the wood opened fire on the bridge. In the confusion, the Germans still manning a machine-gun near the bridge returned fire towards the woods. Captain Priday decided it was a good time for his men to move away from the bridge and ordered his men to make for fields beyond the hedgerow on the south west side of the bridge. As they dashed across the road Private Eric Everett was shot in the head and

Captain Brian Priday

222

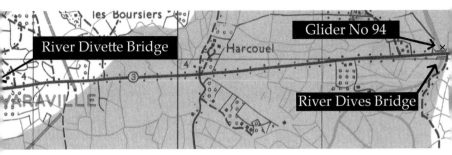

killed instantly.

Only about sixteen men made it to the field. To their surprise they found the whole field flooded. For the next two hours they waded, swam and used their toggle ropes to pull each other across the flooded plains. At one point they were joined by part of a stick of paratroopers from 7 Para who had been mistakenly dropped far from their designated drop zone. Eventually the group made dry land and were able to take shelter in the barn of a nearby farmhouse.

A second group, led by Sergeant Peter Barwick had also managed to get away from the bridge over the River Dives. The two groups met up on the high ground around Robehomme, before moving off to Ranville. At 0230hrs on the morning of 7 June Captain Priday and about twenty of his men were rejoined with Major John Howard. Their return was just in time to join 2 Oxf Bucks' attack in the bloody battle for Escoville (see Ch. 6, G2). During that day-long battle to try and take Escoville, 2 Oxf Buck sustained about sixty casualties. Lieutenant Hooper was one of those wounded and evacuated. For his action on that day he was awarded the Military Cross:

During the morning of 7 June 1944 D Coy seized and held a sector of Escoville. We were actively sniped from the start and subjected to a continuous bombardment by a large close support gun fired from an enemy self-propelled mounting. This self-propelled gun set fire to a building behind Hooper's Bren position. The fire isolated Hooper's force. He expertly controlled the evacuation of his position to one nearer HQ, leaving himself to the last, together with a few other men, he was cut-off by MG 42's and was wounded in both feet. His cool manner was admired by his men who have since reported the above details to me.

CITATION FOR MILITARY MEDAL,
LIEUTENANT ANTHONY CHARLES HOOPER, 2 OXF BUCKS

223

The death of twenty-two year old radio operator Private Eric Everett, at the River Dives Bridge, was confirmed by both Captain Priday and Lance Sergeant Rayner. However, there must have been some errors in the documentation reporting his death, as he was subsequently reported as killed on 7 June 1944 in CWGC records. He now rests in Ranville Commonwealth War Cemetery (IA, J, 13). After considering the following: the time that the glider landed; the subsequent battle for the River Dives Bridge; and that Private Everett was killed instantly; it is reasonable to assume that Private Everett was the first British soldier reported to die from enemy fire. Nevertheless, there is little doubt that Lieutenant Den Brotheridge was the first reported British fatal casualty of enemy fire in Normandy, even though he did not succumb to his wounds until some time after he was wounded.

B. Grangues Memorial

Continue along the D27 for 2.72 miles (4.38km). The *Château de Grangues* is on the right. Continue past the château for 300 yards (274m) and take the next left turning, at the calvary, down *Chemin de l'Eglise*. Continue for 0.65 miles (1.05km) you come to a 'T' junction. Grangues Churchyard is opposite. Park opposite the church, on your right, and cross the road to enter the churchyard. The memorial is on the right just through the gate.

This memorial is testament to just how far afield the men of the

Field over which Captain Priday and his men crossed to Robehomme.

6th Airborne Division were scattered on the night of 5/6 June, 1944. Dedicated in June, 1994, it was erected in memory of fifty-two men from the Army, Navy and Air Force who all died in a series of unfortunate circumstances.

Two Stirling bombers, EJ 116 and EF 295 of 620 Sqn RAF, were carrying between them men from 7 Para, 6 AARR, 591 Para Sqn RE, and HQ RE. A few pilots had been confused by the patches of low cloud and heavy anti-aircraft fire as they approached the Normandy coast, and had unfortunately mistaken the River Dives for the River Orne. EJ 116 was seriously damaged when hit by ack-ack and crashed about 400 yards (366m) from the *Château de Grangues* killing all of its six crew and nineteen paratroopers.

Aboard EF 295, among the heavily laden paras, were the Royal Engineers who were carrying, in addition to their other equipment, some bicycle innertubes wrapped around them like bandoliers. These were packed with explosives for use in clearing the anti-glider poles on the ground. As they neared what they thought was their DZ the paratroopers were hooked up and ready to jump.

> *Then there was a sound like pebbles being thrown against the fuselage and the sky seemed full of lines of orange tracer shells floating up, mostly towards us. Suddenly there was a blinding flash inside the cabin. One of the explosive sausages had been hit; it immediately burned fiercely and gave off a suffocating greenish smoke which filled the cabin. At the same time both the port engines were hit and caught fire.*
>
> LIEUTENANT 'JOHNNIE' SHINNER, HQ ROYAL ENGINEERS

The explosive fire in the aircraft cabin was around the No. 5 man in the stick. The four paratroopers in front of him were able to jump through the exit hole. The rest were trapped between the fire and the cockpit. An escape hatch was ripped off to let out some of the suffocating smoke, but it was too late to jump as the aircraft was now losing height rapidly.

> *It is difficult to judge time in such circumstances – the mind races and minutes seem like hours; probably about two minutes passed before the inevitable crash. On impact the tail, in which were the tail gunner and wireless operator, was torn off and landed in a small copse. The main body then ploughed on for more than 100 metres [109 yards] losing engines and outer wing sections on the way, before coming to rest in a small*

meadow. Miraculously, the tail gunner and wireless operator survived, though both were badly injured. The four aircrew at the nose were killed and were engulfed in the fierce fire that broke out. Four parachutists were killed and nine survived with varying degrees of injury. When we came to rest I found myself hung head down by my static line, which had become entangled with my left leg and the ceiling. Fortunately another survivor came my way, cut me loose with his fighting knife and we staggered the few steps to the point where the fuselage had broken off.

LIEUTENANT JOHNNIE SHINNER, HQ ROYAL ENGINEERS

The aircraft had crashed about 500 yards (457m) from the *Château de Grangues* which was being used as a German company HQ. Immediately Germans were on the scene rounding up the survivors. They were then put in a stable under armed guard. Lieutenant Shinner, however, was tied up and taken away in a car for interrogation.

By the time of the next lift, at 0320hrs, more pilots had made the same error. This time it was the tug pilots towing the gliders. One glider, carrying part of 6th Airborne Division HQ, including GSO 3 (Int) Captain John Max, crashed in the grounds of the château. Three were killed on impact. A second glider also crashed in a near vertical descent into some nearby trees. All aboard were killed, among them a Royal Navy telegraphist.

But the carnage was not to stop there. Later that morning a seventeen year old Red Cross worker, *Mlle* Therese Anne, was taken to a trench where the bodies of the eight prisoners were laid out. She was not allowed to take their ID and only told that there had been an attempted break-out by the prisoners through the night. A year later, when the British grave registration and concentration units had the grim task of exhuming and reinterring the bodies of the servicemen killed and buried all over the battlefields of France, they were able to identify these eight men. Autopsies revealed that seven had been shot through the heart and one through the head. Unfortunately, the perpetrators of this crime were never discovered.

Fifty years later the two survivors of this incident, Lieutenant Johnnie Shinner RE, and A.E. Pryce, who was the rear gunner in EF 295, attended the unveiling of the Grangues Memorial in memory of the fifty-two men who never returned.

This concludes your tours around the battlefields of 6th Airborne Division.

C. Other CWGC Cemeteries, Communal Cemeteries and Churchyards

The five tours described in this work cover only a fraction of the total number of cemeteries and churchyards where men rest, from the 6th Airborne Division, who were killed or died from wounds.

In total the 821 men killed in this battle are now buried in one of the following forty-one cemeteries and churchyards in France: Abbeville Communal Cemetery extension, Banneville-la-Campagne, Bavent Churchyard, Bayeux War Cemetery, Bénouville Churchyard, Beny-sur-Mer Canadian War Cemetery, Beuzeville Communal Cemetery, Branville Churchyard, Bretteville-sur-Laize Canadian War Cemetery, Bréville Communal Cemetery, Brucourt Churchyard, Calais Canadian War Cemetery, Cambes-en-Plaine War Cemetery, Escoville Churchyard, Fatouville-Grestain Churchyard, Fecamp *(le Val aux Clercs)* Cemetery, Hermanville War Cemetery, Hérouvillette New Communal Cemetery, Honfleur Communal Cemetery, Hottot-les-Bagues War Cemetery, Houlgate Communal Cemetery, La Delivrande War Cemetery Douvres, Périers-en-Auge Churchyard, Pont-Audemer Communal Cemetery, Pont L'Évêque Communal Cemetery, Putot-en-Auge Churchyard, Ranville War Cemetery, Ryes War Cemetery Bazenville, St Desir War Cemetery, St Germain-Village Churchyard, Sté Marie

Cemetery Le Havre, St Vaast-en-Auge Churchyard, Tilly-sur-Seulles War Cemetery, Touffréville Communal Cemetery, Tourgéville Military Cemetery, Troarn Communal Cemetery, Trouville Communal Cemetery, Vatteville-la-Rue Churchyard, Vauville Churchyard, Verneuil-sur-Avre Communal Cemetery and Villeneuve-St-Georges Old Communal Cemetery.

It should not be forgotten that many also died as a result of horrific wounds sustained whilst in battle. Those who died of their wounds after they had been evacuated back to the UK are now buried in one of the following thirty-three cemeteries or crematoria: Beaconsfield Cemetery, Buckinghamshire; Belfast City Cemetery, Northern Ireland; Birmingham Handsworth Cemetery, Warwickshire; Biscot Churchyard, Luton, Bedfordshire; Bootle Cemetery, Lancashire; Brookwood Military Cemetery, Woking, Surrey; Cadder Cemetery, Lanark; Checkendon Churchyard, Oxfordshire; Coddington All Saints Churchyard, London; Coryton Churchyard, Devon; Deptford Brockley Cemetery, Lewisham; Enfield Lavender Hill Cemetery, Middlesex; Grangemouth Grandsable Cemetery, Stirling; High Wycombe Cemetery, Buckinghamshire; Longside Cemetery, Aberdeen; Manchester Southern Cemetery, Lancashire; Manor Park Cemetery, East Ham, Essex; Middlesbrough Linthorpe Cemetery, Yorkshire; Mountain Ash Cemetery, Glamorgan, Wales; Northwood Cemetery, Ruislip-Northwood, Middlesex; Oscott College Cemetery, Birmingham, Warwickshire; Oxford Botley Cemetery, Berkshire; Oxford Rose Hill Cemetery, Oxfordshire; Plymouth City Crematorium, Devon; Southgate Cemetery, Middlesex; Southhampton Hollybrook Cemetery, Hampshire; Streatham Park Cemetery, Mitcham, Surrey; St Nicholas at Wade Cemetery, Kent; Twickenham Cemetery and Teddington Cemetery, Middlesex; Walthamstow St Mary Cemetery, Essex; Watchfield Military Cemetery, Berkshire; Wellingborough Cemetery, Northhamptonshire; Whitstable Cemetery, Kent.

APPENDIX A

CHAPTER NOTES AND SOURCES

Chapter One

1. Montgomery, Volume II *Normandy to the Baltic, Invasion*, Corgi Books (1974), p. 231.
2. Report by Dwight D. Eisenhower to Combined Chiefs of Staff (1946), (referred to hereafter as Eisenhower Report) pp. 16, 11, 12 & 15 respectively.
3. Airborne Forces compiled by Lt Col TBH Otway DSO, Imperial War Museum (1990), p. 94. (Referred to hereafter as Otway, Airborne Forces).
4. Gale, *With the 6th Airborne in Normandy*, Sampson Low, Marston & Co. Ltd. (1948), pp. 10-11.
5. ibid., p. 33.
6. Compiled in part from: Facsimile of Major Lacoste's Top Secret intelligence assessment report of 8 May 1944, and a report on the 6th Airborne Division Operations in Normandy June 1944, (compiled for battlefield studies by the Airborne Assault Normandy Trust - referred to hereafter as 'AANT, Battlefield Study').
7. Compiled in part from AANT, Battlefield Study.
8. Saunders, *The Green Beret*, Michael Joseph Ltd. (1949), pp. 261-263.
9. Gale, *With the 6th Airborne in Normandy*, Sampson Low, Marston & Co. Ltd. (1948), p. 50.
10. Harclerode, *'Go To It' The Illustrated History of the 6th Airborne Division*, Bloomsbury (1990) p. 77.
11. Report On The Operations Carried Out by 6 Airborne Division In Normandy 5 June – 3 Sept 44.
12. Anon., *Part II, The Air Plan*, Staff College Camberley Course Documents (1947).
13. Crookenden, *Dropzone Normandy*, Ian Allen Ltd. (1976). p. 201.
14. Weeks, *Airborne Equipment: A History of its Development*, David & Charles Ltd. (1976). pp. 127, 55, 57 & 58.

Chapter Two

1. Maguire, *Dieppe August 19th 1942*, Jonathan Cape (1963), pp. 183 & 184.
2. Wilmot, *The Struggle for Europe*, Collins (1952). p. 186.
3. ibid., pp. 186 & 187.
4. ibid., p. 199.
5. Eisenhower, *Crusade in Europe*, William Heinemann Ltd (1948). pp. 262-27.

Chapter Three

1. Intelligence assessment for Neptune-Bigot dated 8 May 1944 & 9 Para War Diary.
2. Willes, *Out of the Clouds: 1 Cdn Para Bn*, Port Perry Printing Ltd. (1995), pp. 51, 52.
3. Otway DSO, *Airborne Forces*, Imperial War Museum (1990). p. 180.

Chapter Four

1. Golley, *The Big Drop*, Jane's Publishing Company Ltd. (1982), p. 106.
2. Adelin, *Get in! Get in!*, Private Publication (1994), p. 13.
3. Golley, *The Big Drop*, Jane's Publishing Company Ltd. (1982). p. 114.
4. Johnson & Dunphie, *Brightly Shone the Dawn*, Leo Cooper (1980), pp. 53, 54.
5. Plaice, Ellis, 'Silent Guns', *The London Illustrated News Red Berets '44* (1994), pp. 38-39.
6. Adelin, *Get in! Get in!*, Private publication (1994), p. 13.
7. *op cit.* Otway DSO, p.180.
8. Crookenden. *Dropzone Normandy*. Ian Allen Ltd. 1976. p. 217.
9. Saunders, *The Green Beret*, New English Library (1971). p. 264.

APPENDIX B

RECOMMENDED READING & BIBLIOGRAPHY

Recommended Reading

Since the first edition of this work was completed in 1999, there has been quite a number of additional works published relating to the 6th Airborne Division in Normandy. In particular, the growth of the internet and world wide web has allowed many documents, articles and photographs to become much more easily available for the battlefield enthusiast and historians alike. Some of those publications are mentioned in the following bibliography; however, a few sources do deserve special mention as they will provide the reader of this work with much extra interesting information about this subject.

Many of the National Archive documents listed below, and more, are available for viewing on the website: **www.pegasusarchive.org/normandy/main.htm** Built and maintained by Mark Hickman, this is undoubtedly one of the most valuable sources regarding information on the 6th Airborne Division that has been made freely available on the web. There is also much additional information as well as many articles, links and photographs available to view.

For information directly from those higher ranking officers who were in Normandy the following are particularly recommended: *Dropzone Normandy* by Napier Crookenden. This covers all the airborne landings in Normandy, and *With The 6th Airborne Division In Normandy* by R.N. Gale, is an account by the commanding officer of the division.

With regards further eyewitness accounts of veterans who served in Normandy; Neil Barber, in 2002, had published his work *The Day The Devils Dropped In: The 9th Parachute Battalion in Normandy – D-Day to D+6*. In this book the author has edited many eyewitness accounts together covering the events early in June 1944 and it will provide the reader with much extra interesting detail of this period (available from **www.pen-and-sword.co.uk**).

For those wishing to know more individual detail about the officers and NCOs who led the 6th Airborne Division, Carl Rijmen (aka Rymen) published his work, *Gale's Eyes*, in 2009. After many years of research he has compiled a list of nearly every officer and NCO who served in the 6th Airborne Division. Although this work is not generally available, a copy of the work, and cost, can be obtained by emailing: **pegasuscr2002@yahoo.com**

In addition to much correspondence, many interviews and tours around the battlefields with veterans during the last two decades, this work has also been compiled with use of the following documents, publications and articles:

Official Sources

'6 Ab Div Outline Plan Map', Scale 1:25,000, printed by 42 Survey Engineer Group, source AANT.

AANT Battlefield Study, '6th Airborne Division Operations in Normandy 1944', extracts from PRO docs.

Anon, *By Air To Battle: The Official Account of the British Airborne Division*, HMSO (1945).

Anon, 'Report On Operations In Normandy 5 June – 3 Sep 44', compiled fr PRO docs, reference unknown.

Lacoste, Major, 'Top Secret intelligence assessment report of 8 May 1944', source and reference unknown.

Report by Dwight D. Eisenhower to Combined Chiefs of Staff, HMSO (1946).

National Archives (formerly Public Record Office)

WO 171/425: 6 Ab Div HQ
WO 171/2950: 1 Cdn Para
WO 171/1241: 8 Para Bn
WO 171/595: 5 Para Bde HQ
WO 171/1245: 12 Para
WO 171/1249 22 (Ind) Para Coy
WO 171/1383: 1 RUR
WO 171/1279: 12 Devons
WO 171/1018: 2 Airldg Lt AA Bty
WO 171/960: 4 Airldg A Tk Bty
WO 171/1510: 3 Para Sqn RE
WO 171/1605: 249 Fd Coy RE
WO 171/429: 6 Ab Div Sigs
WO 171/1235: No. 2 Wing Glider Pilot Regt
WO 171/2453: 398 Ab Comp Coy RASC
WO 177/793: 195 Airlanding Fd Amb
WO 171/433: 6 Ab Div Ord Fld Pk
WO 171/436: 6 Ab Div Pro Coy
WO 218/65: 3 Commando
WO 218/68: 6 Commando
ADM 202/99: 4 SS Bde
WO 171/1004: 191 Fd Regt RA

WO 171/593: 3 Para Bde HQ
WO 171/1240: 8 Para Bn
WO 171/1242: 9 Para Bn
WO 171/1239: 7 Para
WO 171/1246: 13 Para
WO 171/591: 6 Airldg Bde
WO 171/1357: 2 Oxf Bucks
WO 171/435: 6 AARR
WO 171/959: 3 Airldg A Tk Bty
WO 171/1019: 53 (WY) Airldg Lt Regt
WO 171/1652: 591 Para Sqn RE
WO 171/1622: 286 Fd Pk Coy RE
WO 171/1234: No. 1 Wing Glider Pilot R
WO 171/2371: 63 Ab Div Comp Coy RAS
WO 171/2525: 716 Ab Lt Comp Coy RAS
WO 222/613: 224 Para Fd Amb
WO 171/434: 6 Ab Div Ord Fld Pk
WO 218/59: 1 SS Bde HQ
WO 218/66: 4 Commando
ADM 202/82: 45 (Royal Marine) Cdo
WO 171/1266: 5 Black Watch
WO 171/845: 13/18 Hussars

Publications

Titles in bold are written by, or diaries of, veterans of the campaign
Adelin, Louis, *Get in! Get in!*, Private Publication (1994).
Anderson, Dudley, *Three Cheers For The Next Man To Die*, Robert Hale (1983
Arthur, Max, *Men of The Red Beret*, Hutchinson (1992).
Bailey, Roderick, *Forgotten Voices of D-Day*, Edbury Press (2009).
Barber, Neil (Ed), *Fighting With The Commandos: Stan Scott No. 3 Cdo*, Pen Sword Books Ltd. (2008).
Barber, Neil, *The Day The Devils Dropped In*, Pen & Sword Books Ltd. (2002).

Barley, Eric & Fohlen, Yves, *Para Memories: 12 (Yorkshire) Para Bn*, Parapress Ltd. (1996).

Bellis, Malcolm A, *Regiments of The British Army 1939-45 (Artillery)*, Military Press International (1995).

Bernage, Georges, *Red Devils in Normandy*, Heimdal (2002).

Bouchery, Jean, *The Canadian Soldier*, Historie & Collections (2003).

Bowman, Martin W., *Remembering D-Day*, Harper Collins Pub. (2004).

Chant, Christopher, *Order of Battle: Operation Overlord*, vol. I, Ravelin Ltd. (1994).

Chatterton, George, *The Wings of Pegasus*, Macdonald (1962).

Collier, Richard, *Ten Thousand Eyes*, Collins (1958).

Crookenden, Napier, *Dropzone Normandy*, Ian Allen Ltd. (1976).

Davies, Howard P., *British Parachute Forces 1940-45*, Arms & Armour Press (1974).

Delaforce, Patrick, *Monty's Highlanders: 51st Highland Division*, Tom Donovan Publishing Ltd. (1997).

Delve, Ken, *D-DAY The Air Battle*, The Crowood Press (2004).

Doherty, Richard, *Normandy 1944*, Spellmount (2004).

Dover, Major Victor, *The Sky Generals*, Cassell Ltd. (1981).

Dunning, James, *The Fighting Fourth No. 4 Commando At War*, Sutton (2003).

Durnford-Slater, Brigadier John, *Commando*, William Kimber & Co. Ltd. (1953).

Edwards, Denis, *The Devil's Own Luck*, Pen & Sword Books Ltd. (1999).

Edwards, Commander Kenneth, *Operation Neptune*, Collins (1946).

Eisenhower, Gen Dwight D., *Crusade in Europe*, William Heinemann Ltd. (1948).

Ellis, Major L.F., *Victory in The West*, vol. I, HMSO (1962).

Flint, Keith, *Airborne Armour*, Helion & Co. (2004).

Ford, Ken, *D-Day 1944 (3) Sword Beach & British Airborne Landings*, Osprey Publishing (2002).

Gale, R. N., *A Call To Arms*, Hutchinson (1968).

Gale, R.N., *With The 6th Airborne Division in Normandy*, Sampson, Low & Marston (1948).

Golley, John, *The Big Drop*, Janes (1982).

Gregory, Barry & John Batchelor, *Airborne Warfare 1918-1945*, Phoebus Publishing Co. (1979)

Harclerode, Peter, *Go To It!*, Bloomsbury (1990).

Harclerode, Peter, *Para*, Arms & Armour Press (1992).

Hargreaves, Richard, *The Germans In Normandy*, Pen & Sword Books Ltd. (2006).

Hartigan, Dan, *A Rising of Courage: Canada's Paratroops in Normandy*, Drop Zone Publishers (2000).

Hastings, Max, *Overlord*, Michael Joseph Ltd. (1984).

Hogg, Ian V. (Intro.), *German Order Of Battle 1944*, Arms & Armour Press (1975).

Holt, Major & Mrs, *Normandy D-Day Landing Beaches*, Pen & Sword Books Ltd. (1999 & 2006).

Horn, Lt Col, Bernd & Michel Wyczynski, *Tip Of The Spear: 1 Cdn Para*, The Dundurn Group (2002).

Howard, John & Bates, P., *The Pegasus Journals*, Pen & Sword Books Ltd. (2006

Howarth, David, *Dawn Of D-Day*, Chivers Press (1959).

Isby, David C. (Ed.), *Fighting The Invasion: The German Army At D-Day*, Greenhill Books (2000).

Leeming, Raymond, *And Maybe A Man: With The Royal Signals Of 6 Ab Div*, Parapress Ltd. (1995).

Jefferson, Alan, *Assault On The Guns Of Merville*, John Murray Pub. Ltd. (198?

Johnson, Garry & Christopher Dunphie, *Brightly Shone The Dawn*, Frederick War (1980).

Linnell, Captain T. Geoffrey, *48 Royal Marine Commando*, Private Publication (1946).

Lynch, Tim, *Silent Skies*, Pen & Sword Books Ltd. (2008).

Maguire, Eric, *Dieppe August 19th 1942*, Jonathan Cape (1963).

McNish, Robin, *Iron Division*, Ian Allen Ltd. (1978).

Middlebrook & Everitt, *The Bomber Command War Diaries: 1939-1945*, Viking (198

Mills-Roberts, Brigadier Derek, *Clash By Night*, William Kimber & Co. Ltd. (1956).

Montgomery, *Normandy to the Baltic, Invasion*, vol. II, Hutchinson & Co. Ltd. (19

Neillands, Robin, *The Raiders: The Army Commandos*, Weidenfeld & Nicolson Ltd (1989).

Nolan, Brian, *Airborne: The Heroic Story of 1 Cdn Para*, Lester Publishing Ltd. (1995).

Norton, G.G., *The Red Devils*, Leo Cooper (1971).

NVA, Members of Dorset 84 Branch, *Memories Of World War II*, Private Publication (2002).

NVA, Members of South East 23 Branch, *Memories Of Normandy 1944*, Private Publication (2005).

Orr, David & Truesdale, David, *The Rifles Are There: 1 & 2 Bn The Royal Ulster Rif Pen & Sword (2005).

Otway, T., *Airborne Forces*, Imperial War Museum (1990).

Pine-Coffin, P & B. Maddox, *The Tale Of Two Bridges*, Private Publication (200

Poett, N., *Pure Poett*, Leo Cooper (1991).

Ramsey, Winston G. (ed.), *Normandy After The Battle*, vol, I, After The Battle (1977).

Rijmen, Carl, *Gale's Eyes: 6 Ab Div Who Was Who in Normandy*, Private Publicatic (2009).

Robins, Bernard & Fay, *Remembered With Honour: 8 Para*, Private Publication (20

Salmond, J. B., *The History of the 51st Highland Div 1939-1945*, William Blackwoo and Sons Ltd. (1953).

Saunders, Hillary St George, *The Green Beret*, Michael Joseph Ltd. (1949).

Saunders, Hillary St George, *The Red Beret*, Michael Joseph Ltd. (1950).

Scarfe, Norman, *Assault Division*, Collins (1947).

Shannon, K. & Wright, S., *One Night in June*, Airlife Publishing Ltd. (1994).

Shave, J., *'Go To It' The Story of the 3 Para Sqn Royal Engineers*, The Airborne Engineers Association (2003).

Shaw, F. & Shaw, J., *We Remember D-Day*, Private Publication (1983).

Shilleto, Carl, *Fallen Heroes of Normandy 1944: The Commonwealth War Cemeteries & Sword Books Ltd. (2012).

234

Shilleto, Carl, *Pegasus Bridge Merville Battery*, Pen & Sword Books Ltd. (1999).

Shilleto, Carl, *The D-Day Beaches of Normandy*, Leger (1999).

Shilleto, Carl and Mike Tolhurst, *The Traveller's Guide to D-Day and The Battle For Normandy*, Interlink Pub. (2000).

Smith, Claude, *The History of The Glider Pilot Regiment*, Leo Cooper (1992)

Thompson, Major General Julian, *Ready For Anything*, Weidenfeld & Nicolson Ltd. (1989).

Todd, Richard, *Caught in the Act*, Hutchinson (1987).

Tucker, Ron, *A Teenager's War*, Spellmount (1994).

Tugwell, Maurice, *Airborne to Battle*, William Kimber, (1971).

Van Der Bijl, Nick, *Commandos In Exile: The Story of 10 (Inter-Allied) Cdo 1942-1945*, Pen & Sword (2008).

Vaughan, John, *All Spirits*, Merlin Books Ltd, (1988).

Weeks, John, *Airborne Equipment. A History of its Development*, David & Charles Ltd. (1976).

Weeks, John, *Assault From The Sky*, Westbridge Books (1978).

Wheldon, Sir Huw, *Red Berets into Normandy*, Jarrold & Sons Ltd. (1982).

Willes, John A., *Out of The Clouds; 1 Cdn Para Bn*, Port Perry Printing Ltd. (1981 & 1995).

Wilmot, Chester, *Struggle For Europe*, Collins (1952).

Wilson, Chris & Col John Nowers, *D-Day June 1944 and The Engineers*, Royal Engineers Museum (1994).

Wynn, Humphrey & Susan Young, *Prelude To Overlord*, Airlife (1983).

Young, Brigadier Peter, *Storm From The Sea*, Greenhill Books (2002).

Zetterling, Niklas, *Normandy 1944: German Military Effectiveness*, J.J. Fedorowicz Pub Inc. (2000).

Articles & Papers

Anon., '6th Airborne Division Roll of Honour 1944-45', pp. 1-44, source unknown (no date).

Anon., 'The Register Of The Graves (6 AB Div)', pp. 1-25, Source unknown - prob. CWGC - (no date).

Anon., 'Part II, The Air Plan', Staff College Camberley Course Documents (1947).

Anon., 'The Airborne Light Tank Squadron, 6 AARR', *The Royal Hussars Journal*, pp. 161-165, no date.

Buck, Captain T.G., 'Ham & Jam Battlefield Tour 1996', *The Bucks Bugle*, pp. 1-36, (1996).

Collins, C.L., 'Flying Tanks', *Pegasus Journal*, pp. 93-94, no date.

Lowman, Brigadier F.H., 'The 6th Ab Div Engineers on D-Day 1944', *Corps History*, Vol IX, pp. 339-343, (no date).

Plaice, Ellis, various articles, *Red Berets '44, The London Illustrated News'*, pp. 3-65, (1994).

Rymen, Carl, 'The Herouvillette Murders', *After The Battle*, No. 145, pp. 14-27, (2009).

Useful Websites

Archives & Research (British, Canadian & French Forces)
www.nationalarchives.gov.uk
www.cwgc.org
www.pegasusarchive.org/normandy/frames
www.1940.co.uk/history/article/merville/merville.htm
www.6commando.com
www.6juin1944.com/en_index.html
www.bayonetstrength.150m.com/British/Airborne/british_parachute_battalion
%201944%20to%201945.htm
www.britisharmedforces.org
www.britisharmedforces.org/pages/nat_jim_wallwork.htm
www.britisharmedforces.org/pages/nat_richard_todd.htm
www.combinedops.com/Combined_Ops_index.htm
www.gliderpilotregiment.org.uk
www.gotoitgunners.co.uk
www.normandy1944.info
www.normandie44lamemoire.com/versionanglaise/indexus.html
www.paradata.org.uk/events/normandy-operation-overlord
www.prinsesirenebrigade.nl/
www.raf38group.org
www.theairbornesoldier.com
www.trueloyals.com
www.ww2battlefields.info/

Archives & Research (German Forces)
www.atlantikwall.co.uk
www.axishistory.com

British Library
http://portico.bl.uk/

Archive Film
www.britishpathe.com/results.php?search=Normandy+1944&o=0

Pegasus Journal
www.army.mod.uk/infantry/regiments/5904.aspx

Normandy Veterans Association
www.nvafriends.nl/index.php?cid=36

Museums (France)
www.batterie-merville.com/index_uk.html and www.the-snafu-special.com
www.junobeach.org/e/4/can-tac-par-e.htm
www.musee-4commando.org/1st_bfmc_120.htm

www.memorial-pegasus.org/mmp/musee_debarquement/index.php

Museums (UK)
www.airborneassault.org.uk
www.ddaymuseum.co.uk
www.d-daytanks.org.uk/regiments/6th-airborne.html
www.flying-museum.org.uk
www.iwm.org.uk
www.remuseum.org.uk/campaign/rem_campaign_6adiv.htm

The Parachute Regimental Association
www.army.mod.uk/infantry/regiments/5905.aspx

Commando Veterans Association
www.commandoveterans.org/site

The Royal British Legion
www.poppy.org.uk

Airborne Charities and Projects
www.abfc.org.uk
www.airborneforcesmemorial.org.uk
www.army.mod.uk/infantry/regiments/4795.aspx
www.assaultgliderproject.co.uk
www.airborneforcesmemorial.org.uk
www.fallenheroesphotos.org
www.sopara.org.uk

Living History Groups
www.1canpara.com/
www.1canpara-hq.org
www.6th-airborne.org
www.7thpara.netfirms.com

Research Services
www.ww2cemeteries.co.uk/research.htm
www.findasoldier.co.uk

Forums
www.ww2talk.com
http://forum.axishistory.com

Battlefield Tours
www.ddayhistorian.com
www.guidedbattlefieldtours.co.uk
www.leger.co.uk
www.normandybattletours.com

APPENDIX C

ORDER OF BATTLE

6th Airborne Division, Normandy Landings, 6 June, 1944

Divisional Headquarters

GOC	..	..	..	Maj Gen Richard Gale
ADC	..	..	..	Captain Tom Haughton
AA & QMG	..	..	..	Lt Col Shamus Hickie
ADMS	..	..	..	Lt Col M. MacEwan
GSO 1 (Air)	..	..	..	Lt Col W. Bradish
GSO 1 (Ops)	..	..	..	Lt Col Bobby Bray
GSO 2 (Ops)	..	..	..	Major David Baird
GSO 2 (Int)	..	..	..	Major Gerry Lacoste
GSO 3 (Ops)	..	..	..	Captain M. Spurling
GSO 3 (Int)	..	..	..	Captain J. Max
GSO 3 (Air)	..	..	..	Captain Nick Pratt

3rd Parachute Brigade

Commander	..	..	..	Brig James Hill
1 Cdn Para Bn	..	..	..	Lt Col George Bradbrooke
8 Para Bn		..	..	Lt Col Alastair Pearson
9 Para Bn	..	..	..	Lt Col Terence Otway

5th Parachute Brigade

Commander	..	..	..	Brig Nigel Poett
7 Para Bn	..	..	..	Lt Col Geoffrey Pine-Coffin
12 Para Bn	..	..	..	Lt Col Johnny Johnson
13 Para Bn	..	..	..	Lt Col Peter Luard

22nd (Independent) Parachute Company (Pathfinders)

Commander	..	..	..	Major Francis Lennox-Boyd

6th Airlanding Brigade

Commander	..	..	..	Brig Hon Hugh Kindersley
Deputy	..	..	..	Colonel Reggie Parker
1 RUR	..	..	..	Lt Col R. Carson
2 Oxf Bucks	..	..	..	Lt Col Michael Roberts
12 Devons	..	..	..	Lt Col Dick Stevens

Royal Armoured Corps

6 AARR	..	..	..	Lt Col Godfrey Stewart

Royal Artillery

CRA	..	..	..	Lt Col Jack Norris
2 Airldg Lt AA Bty	..	..	..	Major W. Rowat
2 Forward Observer Unit	..	..	Major Harry Rice
3 Airldg A Tk Bty	..	..	..	Major W. Cranmer
4 Airldg A Tk Bty	..	..	..	Major T. Dixon
53 (WY) Airldg Lt Regt..	..	..	Lt Col Tony Teacher
210 Airldg Lt Bty	..	..	..	Major Hon C. Russell
211 Airldg Lt Bty	..	..	..	Major Tim Craigie
212 Airldg Lt Regt	..	..	..	Major Matt Gubbins

Royal Engineers

CRE	..	..	..	Lt Col Frank Lowman
3 Para Sqn RE	..	..	..	Major Tim Roseveare
591 Para Sqn RE	..	..	..	Major P. Wood

249 Fd Coy RE	..	..	..	Major A. Rutherford
286 Fd Pk Coy RE	..	..	..	Major Jack Waters

Royal Signals

6 Ab Div Sigs	..	..	..	Lt Col D. Smallman-Tew

Army Air Corps

No.1 Wing Glider Pilot Regt	..	..		Lt Col I. Murray
No.2 Wing Glider Pilot Regt	..	..		Lt Col P. Griffiths

Royal Army Service Corps

CRASC	..	..	..	Lt Col J. Watson
63 Ab Div Comp Coy	..	..		Major A. Bille-Top
398 Ab Comp Coy	..	..	..	Major M. Phipps
716 Ab Lt Comp Coy	..	..		Major A. Jones.

Royal Army Medical Corps

195 Airlanding Fd Amb	..	..		Lt Col Bill Anderson
224 Para Fd Amb	..	..		Lt Col D. H. Thompson
225 Para Fd Amb	..	..		Lt Col Bruce Harvey

Royal Army Ordnance Corps

6 Ab Div Ord Fd Pk	..		..	Major W.L. Taylor

Royal Electrical and Mechanical Engineers

CREME	..	..	..	Lt Col R. Powditch
6 Airborne Div Wkshop	..	..		Major E. Bonniwell
9 Airldg LAD	..	..	..	———————
10 Airldg LAD	..	..	..	———————
12 Airldg LAD	..	..	..	———————

Royal Corps of Military Police

6 Ab Div Pro Coy, Commander				Captain Irwin
245 HQ Pro Coy	..	..	..	———————

Royal Army Intelligence Corps

317 Fd Security Sec	..	..	..	Captain F.G. Macmillan

Under Command of 6th Airborne Division during Campaign

1 Special Service Brigade

Commander	..	..	..	Brig The Lord Lovat
3 Commando	..	..	..	Lt Col Peter Young
4 Commando*	..	..	..	Lt Col Robert Dawson
6 Commando	..	..	..	Lt Col Derek Mills-Roberts
45 (Royal Marine) Cdo	..	..		Lt Col Charles Ries
1 *BMFC*, No 1 & No 8 Tp, 10 (IA) Cdo*	..			*Comdt* Philippe Keiffer

* Under Command of 3rd Infantry Division

4 Special Service Brigade

Commander	..	..	..	Brig B.W. Leicester
41 (Royal Marine) Cdo	..	..		Lt Col E. Palmer
46 (Royal Marine) Cdo	..	..		Lt Col C.R. Hardy
47 (Royal Marine) Cdo	..	..		Lt Col C.F. Phillips
48 (Royal Marine) Cdo	..	..		Lt Col J.C. Moulton

Princess Irene Brigade	..	..	*Lt Kol Artille* A. C. de Ruyter van Steveninck
1 Belgian Piron Brigade	..	..	*Colonel* Jean Piron

APPENDIX D

NORMANDY BATTLEFIELD TOURS QUICK REFERENCE AND SATELLITE
NAVIGATION DATA FOR 6TH AIRBORNE DIVISION SECTOR

The satellite navigation coordinates (Google Earth) are listed below for all main
locations. Some of the memorials, exhibits or headstones are not listed
individually as these can be found in close proximity to the location and
because some memorial seat bench plaques and exhibits are periodically
relocated, but remain in the same general area. All coordinates are given in
Degrees, Minutes and Seconds. Additional information and photographs of the
memorials, exhibits and locations can be viewed at www.earth.google.com (NB.
you may need to activate the appropriate layer).

CHAPTER FIVE

A. Sallenelles

1) *Memorial Plaque to No. 4 Special Service Bde*
lat: 49,15,33.00N *long*: 00,13,52.44W
2) *Memorial Plaque to Edouard Gérard*
lat: 49,15,49.95N *long*: 00,13,42.95W
3) *1 Belgian Bde and Colonel Jean Piron Memorial*
lat: 49,15,53.11N *long*: 00,13,36.61W
4) *German Naval Radar Station*
lat: 49,16,10.01N *long*: 00,13,15.51W

B. Merville-Franceville-Plage

1) *The Merville Battery Observation Post*
lat: 49,17,03.08N *long*: 00,13,07.44W
2) *No. 45 Royal Marine Commando Memorial*
lat: 49,16,42.52N *long*: 00,12,13.19W
3) *Memorial to Allied Forces & Merville-Franceville Civilians*
lat: 49,16,42.58N *long*: 00,12,13.25W
4) *Merville-Franceville Village Memorial*
lat: 49,16,42.62N *long*: 00,12,13.34W
5) *Belgian Piron Brigade Memorial*
lat: 49,16,42.69N *long*: 00,12,13.42W

C. Merville Churchyard

1) *Commonwealth War Graves Commission Plaque*
lat: 49,16,23.95N *long*: 00,11,56.24W
2) *Unkown First World War Soldier's Headstone*
3) *Sgt A.K. Eley and RAF Aircrew Headstone*
4) *Memorial Plaque to Sgt J.J Vaulkhard*
5) *Andre Alexandre's Headstone*
6) *Jacoues Auradou's Headstone*
7) *Les Anciens Combattants Prisonniers de Guerre Plaques*
8) *Les Rescapes Du Marquis Des Glières Plaque*

D. The Merville Battery Museum

1) *9 Para Memorial*
lat: 49,16,13.03N *long*: 00,11,46.39W
2) *OVERLORD l'Assault Marker No 1*
lat: 49,16,12.28N *long*: 00,11,46.08W

3) *Major Charles Strafford Memorial*
4) *Sergeant Roy William Wright Memorial Plaque (1)*
5) *Lieutenant Barney Ross Memorial Plaque*
6) *Lieutenant Colonel Terence Otway Memorial Plaque*
7) *Major William 'Bill' Mills Memorial Plaque (1)*
8) *Sergeant Sidney Frank Capon Memorial Plaque*
9) *Major William 'Bill' Mills Memorial Plaque (2)*
10) *Sergeant Roy Wright Memorial Plaque (2)*
11) *No. 1 Casemate (type H611)*
lat: 49,16,11.27N *long*: 00,11,48.44W
12) *No. 3 Commando Memorial Plaque*
lat: 49,16,11.05N *long*: 00,11,48.25W
13) *Combatants of all Nationalities Memorial*

14) *No. 2 360° Open Gun Platform*
lat: 49,16,09.90N *long*: 00,11,50.43W
15) *No. 2 Casemate (type H612)*
lat: 49,16,10.92N *long*: 00,11,51.65W
16) *John Gooday Memorial Plaque*
17) *No. 3 Casemate (type H612)*
lat: 49,16,10.62N *long*: 00,11,53.88W
18) *Memorial to No. 3 Commando*

19) *No. 3 360° Open Gun Platform*
lat: 49,16,09.85N *long*: 00,11,53.16W
20) *Private Ronald Sydney Jepp Memorial Plaque*
21) *No. 4 Casemate (type H669)*
lat: 49,16,09.12N *long*: 00,11,55.05W

22) *No. 4 360° Open Gun Platform.*
lat: 49,16,08.09N *long*: 00,11,54.44W
23) *Louis of 224 Para Fd Amb Memorial Plaque*
24) *No. 3 and No. 4 Casemate Ammunition Magazine*
lat: 49,16,08.66N *long*: 00,11,52.90W
25) *Guard Bunker*
lat: 49,16,07.30N *long*: 00,11,52.20W
26) *6th Airborne Division Memorial Plaque*
27) *Canteen, Guard Room and Anti-Aircraft Gun Position*
lat: 49,16,07.91N *long*: 00,11,51.07W
28) *Command Post*
lat: 49,16,07.92N *long*: 00,11,49.82W
29) *5.5in (139.7mm) Medium Gun*
lat: 49,16,08.86N *long*: 00,11,49.14W
30) *No. 1 and No. 2 Casemate Ammunition Magazine*
lat: 49,16,08.76N *long*: 00,11,49.12W
31) *Private Frank Delsignore Memorial Plaque*
32) *Anti-Aircraft Position*
lat: 49,16,10.06N *long*: 00,11,47.74W
33) *Bronze Bust of Lieutenant Colonel Terence Otway*
lat: 49,16,10.35N *long*: 00,11,47.42W
34) *Lieutenant Colonel Terence Otway Memorial Plaque*
lat: 49,16,10.41N *long*: 00,11,47.17W
35) *Frederick Scott Walker Memorial Plaque*
lat: 49,16,10.57N *long*: 00,11,46.97W

36) *Douglas C47 Transport Plane*
lat: 49,16,12.81N *long*: 00,11,49.41W

E. Gonneville-en-Auge (aka Gonneville-sur-merville)
1) *Carrefour du 9ème Bataillon*
lat: 49,15,51.22N *long*: 00,11,14.62W
2) *Memorial to 9 Para*
lat: 49,15,51.16N *long*: 00,11,14.94W

CHAPTER SIX

A. The Calvary Cross and Haras de Retz
1) *Calvary RV*
lat: 49,15,44.13N *long*: 00,11,52.16W
2) *Château Haras de Retz*
lat: 49,15,36.83N *long*: 00,11,55.71W

B. Bréville (-les-Monts)
1) *Carrefour 6th Airborne Division*
lat: 49,14,24.76N *long*: 00,13,34.42W
2) *Memorial to the 6th Airborne Division*
lat: 49,14,24.93N *long*: 00,13,34.49W
3) *Overlord l'Assault Marker*
lat: 49,14,25.10N *long*: 00,13,34.43W
4) *Bréville Churchyard*
lat: 49,14,26.13N *long*: 00,13,35.06W
5) *Rue du Général Gale*
lat: 49,14,26.54N *long*: 00,13,31.95W
6) *Civilian and Military Victim's Memorial Plaque*
lat: 49,14,28.08N *long*: 00,13,34.75W

C. Amfréville
1) *No. 6 Commando Memorial*
lat: 49,14,43.31N *long*: 00,14,00.28W
2) *Commando Commemorative Plaque*
lat: 49,14,43.00N *long*: 00,13,59.49W
3) *OVERLORD l'Assault Marker*
lat: 49,14,44.38N *long*: 00,14,00.35W
4) *Memorial Cross & Plaques to No. 1 SS Brigade*
lat: 49,14,50.54N *long*: 00,14,06.78W
5) *Amfréville Church*
lat: 49,14,51.02N *long*: 00,14,03.79W
6) *Place du Commandant Kieffer*
lat: 49,14,54.25N *long*: 00,14,04.62W
7) *No. 3 Commando Memorial*
lat: 49,14,55.77N *long*: 00,14,08.67W
8) *Rue du 4ème Commando*
lat: 49,15,12.03N *long*: 00,13,48.68W
9) *Place Colonel Robert Dawson*
lat: 49,15,14.63N *long*: 00,14,01.49W
10) *No. 4 Commando Memorial*
lat: 49,15,14.72N *long*: 00,14,01.94W

D. Château St Côme & Bois des Mont

1) *Château St Côme*
lat: 49,14,08.46N *long*: 00,13,12.45W
2) *Princess Irene Brigade Memorial.*
lat: 49,14,05.33N *long*: 00,13,23.11W
3) *9th Parachute Battalion Memorial*
lat: 49,14,04.81N *long*: 00,13,22.88W
4) *51st Highland Division Memorial*
lat: 49,14,04.25N *long*: 00,13,23.64W
5) *Bois des Monts*
lat: 49,14,01.61N *long*: 00,13,25.07W
6) *Captain Wilkinson's Stone Cross Headstone*
lat: 49,14,00.64N *long*: 00,13,23.52W
7) *Memorial Plaques to Sgt 'Sid' Capon*
8) *Tool Shed and Wood Store (Dressing Station)*
lat: 49,14,00.47N *long*: 00,13,23.00W

E. le Mesnil

lat: 49,13,36.05N *long*: 00,12,58.57W
1) *Brigadier James Hill DSO MC Square*
lat: 49,13,34.53N *long*: 00,12,59.34W
2) *3 Para Bde Memorial Plaque*
lat: 49,13,34.47N *long*: 00,12,59.32W
3) *1st Canadian Parachute Battalion Memorial*
lat: 49,13,34.79N *long*: 00,12,59.52W
4) *Potérie de Bavent*
lat: 49,13,32.77N *long*: 00,13,09.12W
5) *le Ferme de Mesnil*
lat: 49,13,33.36N *long*: 00,13,11.73W
6) *224 Para Fd Amb RAMC Memorial Plaque*
lat: 49,13,37.30N *long*: 00,13,15.03W

F. Hérouvillette

1) *'The Pegasus Trail' Orientation Table (3)*
lat: 49,13,20.74N *long*: 00,14,11.84W
2) *Memorial Plaque to 2 Oxf Bucks*
lat: 49,13,10.32N *long*: 00,14,29.29W
3) *Hérouvillette Communal Cemetery*
lat: 49,13,10.41N *long*: 00,14,29.33W

G. Escoville

1) *Place Six Juin 1944*
lat: 49,12,39.70N *long*: 00,14,35.16W
2) *Escoville Memorial to the British Liberators*
lat: 49,12,40.42N *long*: 00,14,36.90W
3) *Escoville Church & Churchyard*
lat: 49,12,39.71N *long*: 00,14,36.30W

H. Longueval

1) *1st Battalion Royal Ulster Rifles Memorial*
lat: 49,13,00.43N *long*: 00,17,10.38W

CHAPTER SEVEN

A. DZ/LZ N (South)
1) *Rue des Airbornes*
lat: 49,13,51.35N *long*: 00,15,13.97W

B. Bois de Bavent
1) *Chemin du 8ème Para Britannique*
lat: 49,13,01.50N *long*: 00,13,02.29W
2) *8 Para Firm Base*
lat: 49,12,11.34N *long*: 00,12,54.04W

C. Manoir du Bois
lat: 49,12,08.96N *long*: 00,12,30.79W
1) *8th Parachute Battalion Memorial*
lat: 49,12,04.02N *long*: 00,12,41.42W
2) *Memorial Plaque to Sergeant Fred Collett*
lat: 49,12,04.02N *long*: 00,12,41.42W
3) *Memorial Plaque to Brigadier Alastair Pearson*
lat: 49,12,03.91N *long*: 00,12,41.27W

D. Memorial to Pte Thomas W. Billington & Pte Arthur Platt
lat: 49,11,43.35N *long*: 00,13,24.30W

E. Touffréville
1) *8 Para RV*
lat: 49,11,30.14N *long*: 00,13,37.83W
2) *Rue du 8ème Para Bn*
lat: 49,11,26.59N *long*: 00,13,31.46W
3) *Place Caporal E. D. O'Sullivan*
lat: 49,11,19.21N *long*: 00,13,27.71W
4) *Trouffréville Churchyard*
lat: 49,11,18.33N *long*: 00,13,27.94W

F. Sannerville
1) *3rd British Infantry Division Memorial*
lat: 49,10,59.29N *long*: 00,13,15.06W
2) *Group Captain Charles Appleton Memorial Plaque*
lat: 49,10,59.23N *long*: 00,13,14.48W

G. le Maizeret
1) *No. 41, 46, 47 & 48 Royal Marine Commando Memorial*
lat: 49,11,21.03N *long*: 00,12,28.60W

H. Troarn (and St Samson)
1) *Troarn 1944 Railway Level Crossing*
lat: 49,10,57.36N *long*: 00,11,15.52W
2) *Troarn Communal Cemetery*
lat: 49,10,47.07N *long*: 00,11,09.95W
3) *Troarn Eastern Crossroads*
lat: 49,10,46.72N *long*: 00,11,10.99W
4) *Place Paul Quellec*
lat: 49,10,55.44N *long*: 00,10,56.07W

5) *Troarn War Memorial*
lat: 49,10,55.79N *long*: 00,10,56.28W
6) *Memorial Plaque to 3 Para Sqn RE*
lat: 49,10,55.91N *long*: 00,10,56.19W
7) *Voie Major J.C.A. Roseveare*
lat: 49,10,56.59N *long*: 00,10,52.94W
8) *Site of Troarn's 110ft (33.53m) Masonry Arch Bridge*
lat: 49,11,03.45N *long*: 00,09,51.29W
9) *Memorial to Major J.C.A. Roseveare*
lat: 49,11,03.07N *long*: 00,09,52.03W

I. Bures sur Dives
1) *Rue du Capitaine Juckes*
lat: 49,11,50.05N *long*: 00,10,34.06W
2) *Bures War Memorial*
lat: 49,11,56.89N *long*: 00,10,25.24W
3) *Site of Bures 80ft (24.38m) Steel Lattice Girder Bridge*
lat: 49,12,02.04N *long*: 00,10,06.14W
4) *Capitaine Juckes Memorial*
lat: 49,12,02.43N *long*: 00,10,06.72W
5) *Site of Bures 80ft (24.38m) Steel Lattice Girder Railway Bridge*
lat: 49,12,14.30N *long*: 00,09,56.90W

J. Robehomme
1) *Site of Robehomme 80ft (24.38m) Steel Lattice Girder Bridge*
lat: 49,13,33.09N *long*: 00,08,26.67W
2) *Memorial Plaque to 3 Para Sqn RE and 1 Cdn Para*
lat: 49,13,32.93N *long*: 00,08,27.32W
3) *Site of le Hom (aka le Hoin & le Hain) Objective*
lat: 49,14,05.01N *long*: 00,08,43.04W
4) *Robehomme Church*
lat: 49,13,52.42N *long*: 00,09,17.43W
5) *Robehomme Memorial Plaque*
lat: 49,13,51.52N *long*: 00,09,14.74W
6) *1 Cdn Para Memorial Plaque*
lat: 49,13,51.57N *long*: 00,09,14.70W

K. Bavent
1) *Place Alexandre Lofi*
lat: 49,13,48.37N *long*: 00,11,23.43W
2) *Memorial to No 1 SS Bde*
lat: 49,13,48.46N *long*: 00,11,21.96W
3) *Bavent Church and Churchyard*
lat: 49,13,46.51N *long*: 00,11,09.16W
4) *Memorial Marker for the Ashes of Brig Derek Mills-Roberts*
lat: 49,13,56.72N *long*: 00,11,02.43W

L. Petiville
1) *No. 3 Commando Memorial*
lat: 49,14,30.95N *long*: 00,10,31.93W

M. Varaville
1) *Memorial to 1 Cdn Para and 9 Para*
lat: 49,15,06.21N *long*: 00,09,44.07W

2) *Varaville Memorial Plaque*
lat: 49,15,06.21N *long*: 00,09,44.07W
3) *Gatehouse for Château de Varaville*
lat: 49,15,10.82N *long*: 00,09,45.86W
4) *1 Cdn Para Memorial Plaque*
lat: 49,15,10.70N *long*: 00,09,44.86W
5) *Varaville Churchyard*
lat: 49,15,14.12N *long*: 00,09,29.40W
6) *Site of Varaville's Small Masonry Single Span Bridge*
lat: 49,15,15.11N *long*: 00,09,16.62W
7) *Memorial Plaque to 3 Para Sqn RE and 1 Cdn Para*
lat: 49,15,14.90N *long*: 00,09,16.76W

CHAPTER EIGHT

A. River Dives Bridge Near Varaville
lat: 49,15,26.69N *long*: 00,06,39.22W

B. Grangues Memorial
lat: 49,15,56.66N *long*: 00,03,26.42W

C. Other CWGC Cemeteries
1) *Banneville-la-Campagne*
lat: 49,10,34.73N *long*: 00,13,47.13W
2) *Bayeux War Cemetery*
lat: 49,16,26.74N *long*: 00,42,50.42W
3) *Bayeax War Memorial*
lat: 49,16,27.68N *long*: 00,42,49.03W
4) *Beny-sur-Mer Canadian War Cemetery*
lat: 49,18,08.57N *long*: 00,27,02.00W
5) *Bretteville-sur-Laize Canadian War Cemetery*
lat: 49,03,37.90N *long*: 00,17,30.71W
7) *Cambes-en-Plaine War Cemetery*
lat: 49,14,11.63N *long*: 00,23,09.57W
8) *Hermanville War Cemetery*
lat: 49,17,10.69N *long*: 00,18,31.76W
9) *Hottot-les-Bagues War Cemetery*
lat: 49,09,37.16N *long*: 00,37,34.71W
10) *La Délivrande War Cemetery, Douvres*
lat: 49,17,24.88N *long*: 00,22,39.33W
11) *Ranville War Cemetery*
lat: 49,13,52.04N *long*: 00,15,28.15W
12) *Ryes War Cemetery, Bazenville*
lat: 49,17,59.38N *long*: 00,36,03.83W
13) *St Désir War Cemetery*
lat: 49,08,18.55N *long*: 00,09,47.19W
14) *Tilly-sur-Seulles War Cemetery*
lat: 49,10,25.69N *long*: 00,38,16.98W

APPENDIX E

FALLEN HEROES PROJECT, CWGC, AANT, MEMORIAL PEGASUS AND MERVILLE BATTERY

Fallen Heroes of Normandy Project

A Photographic Remembrance: an appeal for photographs or information about the servicemen (of all nationalities) who now rest in the Commonwealth cemeteries or French churchyards of Normandy. Formally launched in 2009, the aim of this not-for-profit project is to compile a detailed record of photographs and information of those whose graves are maintained by the CWGC in Normandy.

Information about the individuals and any photographs of the original cross markers or cemeteries, churchyards and areas as they were in the 1940s are also sought.

All information and or photographs received will be acknowledged by email and on the completed database. The project details and completed content to date, are available online at **www.fallenheroesphotos.org**

Please email any information and scanned photographs (preferably a jpeg file with a resolution of 300 dpi) to **fallenheroes@btinternet.com**

Or post photographs or information to (please note that only copies should be sent as we are unable to return any material donated):

Carl Shilleto, Military Historian,
c/o The Regimental Museum,
3 Tower Street,
York
YO1 9SB UK

The Commonwealth War Graves Commission

Established in May 1917 by Royal Charter, the Commonwealth War Graves Commission is dedicated to marking and maintaining the graves of all those who were killed in the two World Wars, from the forces of the Commonwealth. The cost of this work is shared between Australia, Britain, Canada, India, New Zealand and South Africa in proportion to the number of graves each country has. There are 23,260 burial grounds in 149 countries with a total of 1,694,988 names commemorated. From the Second World War 347,410 graves have been identified, while a further 23,479 remain unidentified. In addition 231,893 people have no known grave and are commemorated on memorials. The Head Office is at: 2 Marlow Road, Maidenhead, Berkshire, SL6 7DX. Tel: 01628 634 221. There is also an internet web site: **www.cwgc.org**. A short guide of all the Common-wealth Cemeteries in Normandy can be downloaded from the above website.

The Airborne Assault Normandy Trust

As mentioned in the introduction, the AANT was established to help preserve the history and memory of the 6th Airborne Division in Normandy.

Donations, made payable to **The Airborne Assault Normandy Trust**, which will be acknowledged, can be forwarded to: Airborne Assault Normandy, Browning Barracks, Aldershot, Hampshire GU11 2BU.

Memorial Pegasus Museum (Musée Mémorial Pegasus)

Inaugurated on 4 June 2000 by HRH The Prince of Wales, the Memorial Pegasus is dedicated to the men of the 6th Airborne Division and their role during the Battle of Normandy.

The museum was built, with the help and assistance of the Airborne Assault Normandy Trust, by the D-Day Commemoration Committee. The collection, on display in the museum and memorial garden, is both historically unique and important, situated as it is, on the battlefield itself.

If any veterans of the 6th Airborne Division, their families or friends, are able to donate any items relating to the battles in Normandy, such donations will be gratefully received, acknowledged, catalogued and preserved for posterity within the museum collection.

For further information and details of how to donate any personal items, please contact:

Curator, Mark Worthington, Memorial Pegasus, Avenue du Major Howard 14860 Ranville, France. Tel: 0033 231781944, Fax: 0033 231781942, email: info@memorial-pegasus.org

Merville Battery Museum (la Batterie de Merville)

Opened in 1982, with the help of the Airborne Assault Normandy Trust, the Merville Battery Museum is dedicated to preserving the history of the 9th Parachute Battalion. In recent years the area has been excavated to reveal more of the German fortifications and defence structures. In addition, all four casemates are now open to the public and the exhibition has been extended to cover other aspects of history of Merville and the German battery.

If any veterans of the 9th Parachute Battalion, their families or friends, are able to donate any items relating to the battles around Merville, such donations will be gratefully received, acknowledged, catalogued and preserved for posterity within the museum collection.

For further information and details of how to donate any personal items, please contact:

Pascaline Dagorn, Musée de la Batterie de Merville, Place du 9eme Bataillon, 14810 Merville-Franceville, France. Tel:0033 231914753, Fax: 0033 231246036, email: museebatterie@wanadoo.fr

INDEX

Locators in italics refer to references in maps NB. Index does not include prelims or appendices